Mastering
OS/2 REXX

Mastering
OS/2 REXX

Gabriel F. Gargiulo

A Wiley–QED Publication

John Wiley & Sons, Inc.

New York • Chichester • Brisbane • Toronto • Singapore

ISBN 0-471-51901-4

Printed in the United States of America

10 9 8 7 6 5 4 3 2 1

**To my sons,
Marc and Michael**

CONTENTS

PREFACE

REXX, the mainframe procedure language, has made its grand entrance on the personal computer, and is now available to all who own a personal computer and OS/2. REXX is modern, different, and robust. IBM has positioned REXX to serve as a common development language in its MVS, VM, and OS/2 programming environments. Learning REXX opens the door to mastery of OS/2 and to today's mainframe systems as well.

I have long derived pleasure from the study and use of spoken languages and, with the coming of REXX, of computer languages as well. I wrote this book to help you obtain "native fluency" in REXX. Join me in exploring this fascinating language on your OS/2 system.

No book is possible through the efforts of just one person. I would like to extend special thanks to Richard C. "Rit" Forcier for his suggestions and review of the manuscript. Bret Curran and Brian Curran also reviewed the manuscript and suggested several changes which I incorporated into the text. This book would not have been a success without their help. I thank Beth A. Roberts and Edwin Kerr of QED for their patience and support throughout the long process of authoring this book.

My associates and I are available to teach REXX on OS/2 as well as under mainframe MVS and VM. My courses are based on my books and carry extensive references to them thus making the books a valuable classroom tool. All courses are available for purchase or rental. I can be reached at (203) 646-9531.

Your suggestions and comments about the book are welcome and should be mailed to me in care of QED.

Gabe Gargiulo

INTRODUCTION

REXX is IBM's new programming language for batch files. Batch files are procedure files that contain operating system commands (OS/2 commands in our case) and programming language statements, such as IF, that control the execution of the system commands.

Your old DOS and OS/2 batch files that were not written in REXX will still work under OS/2, but you will probably want to write all your new batch files in REXX. You'll very likely find REXX much easier to use and many times more powerful. If you know how to write DOS batch files you'll be able to switch to REXX rapidly. You'll appreciate the fact that REXX is clear, concise, structured, complete, and a pleasure to use.

REXX has been used for over a decade on the mainframe, where it is nudging out archaic languages such as CLIST on MVS/TSO and EXEC2 on VM/CMS. Mainframe programmers are used to using REXX under Netview, a program product used by operations and support personnel, and under QMF, a subset of the DB2 Database Management System.

REXX is very much the same REXX no matter where it is found. The differences lie in the commands that it passes to the operating system where it is found. On OS/2 you pass OS/2 commands; on MVS you pass TSO commands; on VM/CMS you pass CMS commands. I cover TSO commands, how you pass them to TSO, and how you produce useful programs on TSO in my book *REXX in the TSO Environment* Gabriel F. Gargiulo, QED, 1993).

REXX is IBM's answer to the tower of Babel that it created with MVS, VM, and the personal computer's OS/2 all speaking wildly different languages. You won't have to learn another language to work with TSO, CMS, Netview, or QMF. That will make you much more valuable to your employer.

This book is about the REXX language as it is found on IBM's OS/2 operating system. You will learn REXX as it is currently implemented and used under OS/2. This book is not a rehashing of the IBM manuals, nor is it a watered-down version of REXX in some other operating system.

You can immediately become more productive on OS/2 with this book, because you will learn how to put commonly done tasks into a short program and run the program, instead of always typing in a series of commands.

The emphasis is on how things work, with a minimum of time spent on the theoretical aspects of the language. You will learn quickly with this book, because you can try out the examples and practice with the computer problems on your system. In doing the computer problems you will build up a library of extremely useful and pertinent examples of all the aspects of the REXX language that you and others will find invaluable when creating REXX programs.

This book makes heavy use of OS/2 commands, such as DIR and TYPE. It does not teach OS/2 commands. If you need more detailed information than the text provides about OS/2 commands, you can refer to Appendix C, which is a reference on the OS/2 commands used in this book, or you can refer to any one of the fine books on the market. I suggest the following: *OS/2 2.0 Workplace Shell: The User's Guide and Tutorial*, Maria E. Tyne (QED 1992) and *Using OS/2 2.0*, Barry Nance (QUE 1992).

This book does not go into all the finer points and highly technical details of REXX. My background as an instructor has prepared me to simplify complicated things to aid in understanding. The mind-boggling advanced options are best left in the vendor's manuals, to which I refer you: *Procedures Language 2/REXX Reference* S10G-6268-00 (IBM 1992), *Procedures Language 2/REXX User's Guide* S10G-6269-00 (IBM 1992).

In *REXX in the OS/2 Environment* you'll learn how to do the following with REXX:

1. Pass commands to OS/2.
2. Interact with the keyboard and monitor.
3. Manipulate strings of data.
4. Create new functions and/or subroutines.
5. Write programs that repeat with REXX's loop control structure.
6. Intercept and use information displayed by OS/2 commands.
7. Read and write records in files.
8. Manipulate data using arrays of variables.
9. Use REXX's internal data queue.
10. Use the Presentation Manager in REXX programs.
11. Create and use dialogue boxes that simplify the entering of responses to your program's questions.
12. Create REXX functions that can be copied and shared by other OS/2 users.

Who should read this book? This book is designed for programmers, endusers, database administrators, production support personnel, operations personnel, support personnel, and anyone who needs more than just batch files and the basic system supplied by IBM. Anyone who wants or needs the ability to create programs for personal use with a minimum of effort and overhead should read this book.

Structure of the Book

The book is presented in separate chapters and five appendixes. Study each chapter, and do the workshops on the computer. In many workshops I show you the results you should expect. Appendix A contains the solutions to all the workshops. Save your answers to the workshops, and you'll own a complete library of every imaginable type of REXX program you'll ever need. Appendix B describes the OS/2 commands used in the book. Appendixes C, D, and E contain a complete reference on all the REXX verbs, functions, and variables used in the OS/2, TSO, and VM/CMS environments.

Chapter 1

WHAT YOU CAN DO WITH REXX

This chapter will present REXX's capabilitics.

Topics

1.1 EXECUTING OS/2 COMMANDS

REXX's main purpose is to pass commands to OS/2 (see Figure 1.1). You can put one or more OS/2 commands into a REXX program and execute them by just typing in the name of the REXX program. Using REXX's built-in logic and control structures, you can make passing commands an easy and error-free task.

REXX is a complete programming language in itself and doesn't need OS/2 in order to be useful; you may create a REXX program that contains no OS/2 commands. Using just the features of REXX, you can perform tasks that might have been programmed in a language like C or BASIC.

1.2 AUTOMATING REPETITIVE TASKS

Sometimes you find yourself keying in a series of OS/2 commands over and over again, often with unintended errors (see Figure 1.2). You can place these commands within a REXX program (see Figure 1.3), and then REXX can pass those commands to OS/2. This eliminates any errors associated with rekeying. Take my advice: put the commands in a REXX program, execute the program, and you can be sure that the commands are right.

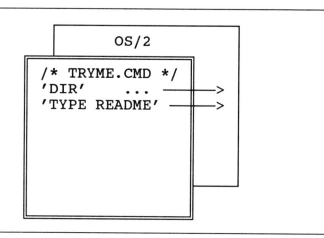

Figure 1.1. Passing commands to OS/2.

```
C:

CD \WPERF

WP
```

Figure 1.2. OS/2 commands you might execute frequently.

```
/*TRYME2.CMD (Figure 1.3)*/

'C:'

'CD \WPERF'

'WP'
```

Figure 1.3. Frequently executed OS/2 commands placed in a REXX program.

1.3 INTERACTING WITH THE PRESENTATION MANAGER

The OS/2 Presentation Manager allows you to execute your program inside of a neatly formatted screen (see Figure 1.4) in which you can type and view data, debug your program, and display Dialogue Boxes (see Figure 1.5.)

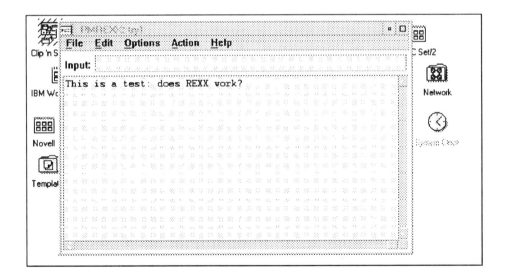

Figure 1.4. A Presentation Manager execution screen.

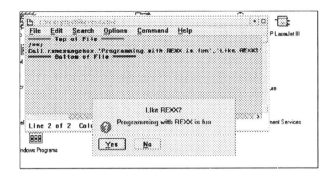

Figure 1.5. A dialogue box that you can display with the Presentation Manager.

1.4 CREATING NEW COMMANDS

With REXX you can create programs that behave as if they were new OS/2 commands. For example, suppose you are always doing a DIR *.CMD command to view the names of your REXX programs and OS/2 batch files. You can put the commands into a REXX program named PROGDIR.CMD and execute those commands very easily by just typing in PROGDIR.

Your new commands written in REXX, as well as the old OS/2 commands, can all be executed while you are in an OS/2 window or in OS/2 Full Screen (see Figure 1.6).

```
[C:\REXXPRGS]dir l*.cmd

The volume label in drive C is OS2.
The Volume Serial Number is 2200:6414
Directory of C:\rexxprgs

LOOP       CMD       49   7-30-93  10:03a
LIKEREXX CMD       89   8-13-93   3:16p
        2 file(s)           138 bytes used
                        765952 bytes free

[C:\REXXPRGS]
```

Figure 1.6. Executing an OS/2 command and a REXX program from within an OS/2 window.

1.5 USING REXX FOR PERSONAL PROGRAMMING TASKS

REXX is so easy you may want to use it for those short (or long) programs that help you out in your everyday affairs (see Figure 1.7.) You can do simple or complex programming tasks with REXX. If you want to program a complete payroll system with REXX, please go ahead and do it. You'll enjoy the ease and clarity of REXX.

Percent Calculator

Please type in starting amount
50
Please type in percent (expressed as whole number, for example 10 for 10%)
20
20% of 50 is 10

Figure 1.7. Using a REXX program to simplify everyday calculations.

Chapter 2

WHERE DOES REXX FIT IN ON OS/2?

This chapter is about the very practical aspects of REXX programs as they are found on OS/2. I will tell you the difference between a REXX program and an OS/2 Batch File and how OS/2 knows the difference.

Topics

2.1   What Is a REXX Program?
2.2   Differences Between Batch Files and REXX
2.3   On-Line Help
2.4   Questions/Problems

2.1 WHAT IS A REXX PROGRAM?

A REXX program (also called an *exec*) is a disk file that is on your personal computer and is accessible to your OS/2 system. The file contains records or lines. Each record may contain one or more OS/2 commands and/or REXX instructions. The records are written in ordinary ASCII format, what is commonly called a text file or a DOS file. Please note that most word processors can create this type of file but only if explicitly requested. Chapter 3 will show you how to create REXX programs with the OS/2 Extended Editor.

A REXX program file name has the extension ".CMD." Batch Files under OS/2 may have the extension ".CMD," too, or more commonly ".BAT." If you happen to have two programs, one with an extension of .CMD and another with an extension of .BAT, OS/2 will find and execute the one with the extension of .CMD and ignore the other. To summarize:

• REXX programs must have an extension of .CMD.
• OS/2 Batch Files may have an extension of either .CMD or .BAT.

• A program with an extension of .CMD takes precedence over one with .BAT.

REXX programs may be placed in any directory, from the Root directory down to the lowest level subdirectory. You will see later in this book that I recommend placing your REXX programs in a subdirectory named REXXPRGS.

Your REXX program must contain a REXX comment on its first line. A REXX comment consists of the forward slash, an asterisk, some optional comments, another asterisk, and another forward slash. The comment tells OS/2 that it is looking at a REXX program, not an OS/2 Batch File. An example of a REXX comment is: /*MYFIRST.CMD, a REXX program */.

You must execute your REXX program while on an OS/2 Window, in OS/2 Full Screen or from the program icon in an open file directory. You cannot run your program from a DOS Window. In order to use the Presentation Manager you must be in an OS/2 Window or in OS/2 Full Screen. I'll show you exactly how to execute your program in the next chapter.

Here is a summary of what really matters to OS/2:

• It must be able to find the program
  — in the default directory, or
  — through the OS/2 PATH command in the file CONFIG.SYS,
  — from the complete drive and directory specified when executing.
• The program has the extension ".CMD".
• The program contains a REXX comment /* */ on the first line.
• You execute the program in an OS/2 Window, OS/2 Full Screen, or from a program icon.

Figure 2.1 shows some REXX program names. You really can't tell just by looking at the names whether these are REXX programs or OS/2 Batch Files.

WORDPROC.CMD

PERCENT.CMD

PROGRAM1.CMD

P1.CMD

Figure 2.1. Some potential names of REXX programs.

A REXX program executes interactively in an OS/2 Window, under the OS/2 Presentation Manager, or under OS/2 Full Screen. It will not execute in a DOS Window or when DOS has been booted. You can watch it execute, wait for it to finish, or cancel it if you wish. You may also open or use other OS/2 windows or features and do something else, such as word processing, while your REXX program is running. OS/2 is a multitasking operating system and will continue to run your REXX program at the same time as your word processing.

2.2 DIFFERENCES BETWEEN BATCH FILES AND REXX

If you have used DOS or OS/2 for any length of time, you have probably used OS/2 Batch Files, a sample of which is shown in Figure 2.2. OS/2 Batch Files can do many of the same things REXX can but not so easily and clearly. Batch Files and REXX are as different as night and day (see Figure 2.3 for an example of REXX). If you want to know more about the differences, you can refer to Chapter 20, which is about converting from Batch Files to REXX.

OS/2 Batch Files are limited in their capabilities and often remain somewhat obscure. Until REXX came on the scene, there was no alternative. The choice was between OS/2 Batch Files or just typing in the commands yourself one at a time. If you want to learn Batch File programming well, I recommend an excellent little book, *MS-DOS Batch Files, Second Edition,* by Kris Jamsa (Microsoft Press, 1991).

```
REM PRNTGAME.BAT (Figure 2.2)
REM Writes game directory to a file & prints
it
@Echo off
C:
CD \
CD \MYGAMES
DIR > GAMES.LST
COPY GAMES.LST LPT1:
ECHO Game directory print submitted
```

Figure 2.2. An example of an OS/2 Batch File. The REXX version is in Figure 2.3.

```
/* Prntgame.cmd (Figure 2.3)
   Writes game directory to a file & prints it
*/
'@Echo off'
'C:'
'CD \'
'CD \MYGAMES'
'DIR > GAMES.LST'
'COPY GAMES.LST LPT1:'
Say 'Game directory print submitted'
```

Figure 2.3. An example of an REXX program. The OS/2 Batch File version is in Figure 2.2.

THE MAJOR DIFFERENCES BETWEEN BATCH FILES AND REXX

Command line parameters. Batch Files can accept up to nine words or parameters (%1 – %9) that you type in when you execute the Batch File. They can handle more than nine by means of a very strange command SHIFT that has no parallel in any known programming language on earth, the solar system, or this galaxy. REXX can accept an unlimited number of command line parameters.

Literals. Batch Files have no way of designating a literal. REXX, by contrast, has an excellent way of showing a literal: quotation marks or apostrophes.

Variables. Batch Files don't really have variables. They have Named Parameters, which actually reflect the value given to them by means of an OS/2 SET command. You are really setting OS/2 environment variables, and this will affect all programs that run subsequently. These variables are not true variables because they cannot be modified at will inside your batch program. They are placed in your program with a percent sign (%) before and after — for example, %PROGDIR%.

REXX variables can be created, set, and used at will inside of your program, and they do not affect OS/2 environment variables.

OS/2 commands. Batch Files contain OS/2 commands written in the exact way they would be typed in at the OS/2 prompt.

REXX requires you to put apostrophes or quotation marks around OS/2 commands. If you don't, REXX will try to interpret your OS/2 commands, and they won't work.

String manipulation. Batch Files have nothing to distinguish them when it comes to string manipulation. REXX is the queen of string manipulation. Its PARSE instruction and a multitude of functions make it easy to do anything you want with character data.

Mathematics. Batch Files have no mathematical capabilities.

REXX can do enough arithmetic to please almost anyone. Those who really like trigonometric functions and fractional exponents will probably forgive REXX for not having them when they see that REXX can do arithmetic to *any* precision.

Control structures. Batch Files have a rather strange IF, a simple GOTO, and a loop verb FOR that raises many eyebrows.

Control structures and REXX grew up together. REXX fulfills every programmer's dreams about control structures. REXX has all the desired attributes of IF, including the flexibility to request strict character-by-character comparisons, as well as a more natural, human-like kind of comparison.

Rat's nest programs are possible in REXX, but REXX's designer took steps to penalize anyone who would abuse structured programming concepts.

Clarity. Batch Files are often clear in their meaning simply because they can't do very much at all. REXX is very clear. It is very much English-like while it embodies most worthwhile programming capabilities.

Usefulness. Once you acquire the skill to write Batch Files, you find that it is akin to knowing how to repair an Edsel. Batch Files are like nothing else in the entire spectrum of programming languages.

REXX is becoming a kind of Esperanto, or universal language, in the programming world. It looks a lot like BASIC, PLI (especially), and C (a little — *nothing* else really looks like C!). I have used REXX in IBM's VM/CMS programming system, in OS/2, and in PC-DOS with Personal REXX created by Mansfield Software, and have found that it is the same in each environment. REXX is your key to other IBM programming environments. Here in tabular form are the major characteristics of Batch Files and REXX:

Batch Files	REXX
Old	New
Bad for data strings	Good string handling
Few control structures	Excellent control structures
Useless for math	Good for math
No functions	Many good functions
Unique	Common

2.3 ONLINE HELP

You can consult OS/2's online help for REXX for information about all the REXX verbs or instructions and functions. Here's how to go about doing it.

On the OS/2 desktop, open the Information Icon by double clicking on it (Figure 2.4).

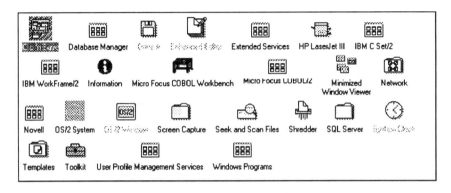

Figure 2.4. Selecting the Information Icon.

Double click on REXX Information (Figure 2.5).

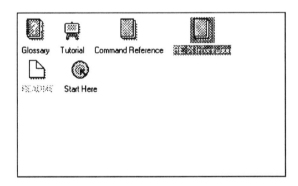

Figure 2.5. Selecting REXX Information.

Choose a topic and double click on it (Figure 2.6).

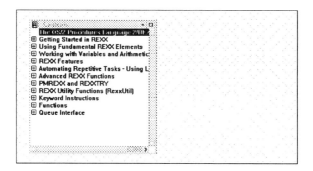

Figure 2.6. Choosing a Help topic.

You'll be able to read the description of the topic and print it if you wish.

2.4. QUESTIONS/PROBLEMS

1. What is another name for a REXX program?

2. REXX programs must be written in _____ format.

3. REXX programs must have the extension _____.

4. A REXX program must be executed in a _____.

5. What is the minimum shortest example of the item required at the beginning of each REXX program?

6. Which has true programming variables, REXX or Batch Files?

Chapter 3

HOW TO CREATE AND EXECUTE A REXX PROGRAM

This chapter will show you exactly how you can create and execute a REXX program on your OS/2 system.

Topics

3.1 CREATING AND EXECUTING, STEP BY STEP

This section assumes a very basic knowledge of how to use your computer and keyboard and how to manipulate OS/2 icons with a mouse. If you need further information about those subjects, I refer you to a book on OS/2 that I recently purchased, *OS/2 Workplace Shell* by Maria E. Tyne (QED 1993).

If you already know how to create a shadow of the Enhanced Editor and of an OS/2 Window, put them onto your desktop and open both icons in order to use them, you may want to skip this entire section. If not, read on. I am not going to omit any part of the process, so it may seem redundant. I assure you it won't seem tedious after you use it several times. If you are still with me, I will now guide you step by step through the process of creating a

15

REXX program and running it. Later in this chapter I discuss the Enhanced Editor and other ways of creating a program, as well as some details about how you can run your program. If you have never created a REXX program on OS/2, please use the method shown in this section.

There are two parts in this section. The first guides you through the steps that you need to perform *just once.* The second part tells you what to do the second and subsequent times you turn on your OS/2 system and want to create and use REXX programs.

PART 1: STEPS TO BE PERFORMED JUST ONCE

1. (Figure 3.1) Start from the OS/2 Desktop.

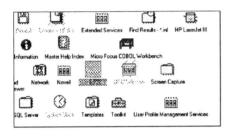

Figure 3.1. The OS/2 Desktop.

2. (Figure 3.1) Opening the OS/2 System Window. From the OS/2 Desktop, select OS/2 System, by moving the mouse arrow over the OS/2 System Icon, and by pressing the left mouse button twice in rapid succession. This is known as Double Clicking. The OS/2 System Window appears (Figure 3.2).

Figure 3.2. The OS/2 System Window.

3. (Figure 3.2) Opening the Command Prompts window. While in the OS/2 System window, double click on the Command Prompts icon. The Command Prompts window appears (Figure 3.3).

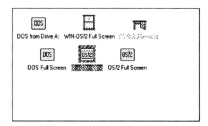

Figure 3.3. The Command Prompts window.

4. (Figure 3.3) Creating a shadow of the OS/2 Window for your desktop. While in the Command Prompts window, position the mouse arrow on the OS/2 Window icon, and press the *right* mouse button once. A pop-up menu appears (Figure 3.4).

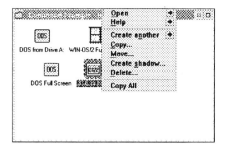

Figure 3.4. A pop-up menu.

5. (Figure 3.4) On the pop-up menu that appears click on Create Shadow. The Command Prompts Create Shadow Notebook appears (Figure 3.5).

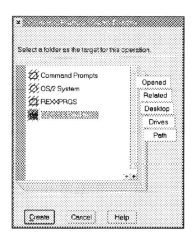

Figure 3.5. The Create Shadow Notebook.

6. (Figure 3.5) Telling OS/2 where to put the shadow. On the Create Shadow Notebook click on OS/2 2.1 Desktop. The words OS/2 2.1 Desktop are highlighted (Figure 3.6).

Figure 3.6. The Create Shadow Notebook.

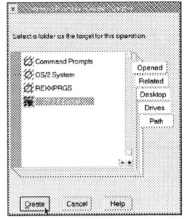

7. (Figure 3.6) Actually creating the shadow. On the Create Shadow Notebook click on CREATE. This will put a shadow of the OS/2 Window icon on your desktop, where it will be easier to find the next time you need it. (A shadow is recognized by its gray lettering.) The Command Prompts Window appears (Figure 3.7).

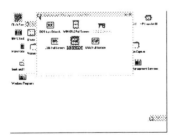

Figure 3.7. The Command Prompts Window.

8. (Figure 3.7) Closing the Command Prompts Window. Double click on the small icon in the upper left of the Command Prompts Window. The window is closed and the OS/2 System window appears (Figure 3.8).

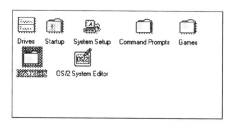

Figure 3.8. The OS/2 System Window.

9. (Figure 3.8) Getting into the Productivity Window. Double click on the Productivity icon in the OS/2 System window. The Productivity Window appears (Figure 3.9).

Figure 3.9. The Productivity window.

10. (Figure 3.9) Creating a shadow of the Enhanced Editor. Click on the Enhanced Editor icon in the Productivity window with the *right* mouse button. A pop-up menu appears (Figure 3.10).

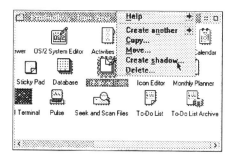

Figure 3.10. A pop-up menu.

11. (Figure 3.10) Click on Create Shadow in the pop-up menu of the Enhanced Editor. The Create Shadow Notebook appears (Figure 3.11).

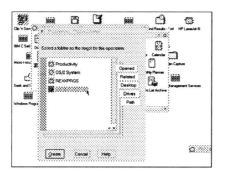

Figure 3.11. The Create Shadow Notebook.

12. (Figure 3.11) Selecting the desktop as the destination for the Enhanced Editor shadow. Click on OS/2 2.1 Desktop. The words OS/2 Desktop are highlighted (Figure 3.12.)

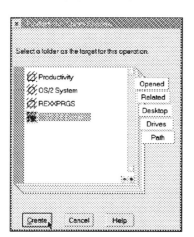

Figure 3.12. The Create Shadow notebook.

13. (Figure 3.12) Creating a shadow of the Enhanced Editor. Click on Create in the Settings Notebook of the Enhanced Editor. The Productivity window appears (Figure 3.13).

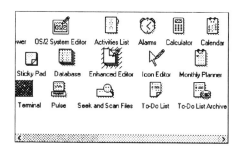

Figure 3.13. The Productivity Window.

14. (Figure 3.13) Closing the Productivity window. Double click on the icon in the upper left. The OS/2 System Window appears (Figure 3.14).

Figure 3.14. The OS/2 System Window.

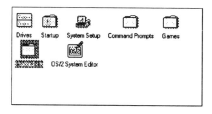

15. (Figure 3.14) Closing the OS/2 System Window. Double click on the icon in the upper left. The OS/2 Desktop appears (Figure 3.15).

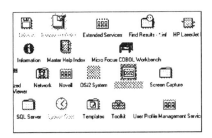

Figure 3.15. The OS/2 Desktop.

16. (Figure 3.15) Opening an OS/2 Window. Double click on the OS/2 Window icon on the Desktop. An OS/2 Window appears (Figure 3.16).

Figure 3.16. An OS/2 Window.

17. (Figure 3.16) Creating a directory named REXXPRGS to contain your REXX programs. Please feel free to use another name for your directory if you wish. I will, however, assume that you have created one named REXXPRGS and continue to use REXXPRGS throughout this book. Type in C: and press ENTER. This assures that your hard disk is the default disk drive. Type in CD\ and press ENTER. This assures that your current directory is the root directory C:. Type in MD REXXPRGS and press ENTER. This creates a directory named REXXPRGS. Type in CD \REXXPRGS and press ENTER. This makes REXXPRGS your default directory for this OS/2 Window.

Figure 3.17. An OS/2 Window.

18. (Figure 3.17) Closing the OS/2 Window. Double click on the icon in the upper left. The OS/2 Desktop appears (Figure 3.18). You should not need to perform these 18 steps again.

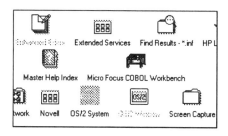

Figure 3.18. The OS/2 Desktop.

PART 2: STEPS TO BE PERFORMED EVERY TIME YOU WANT TO WRITE AND EXECUTE REXX PROGRAMS

1. (Figure 3.19) Start from the OS/2 Desktop.

Figure 3.19. The OS/2 Desktop.

2. (Figure 3.19) Opening the Enhanced Editor. Double click on the Enhanced Editor icon. The Enhanced Editor Window appears (Figure 3.20).

Figure 3.20 The Enhanced Editor Window.

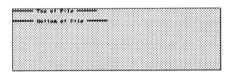

3. (Figure 3.20) Typing in the program. Position the cursor to the spot between = = = **top of file** = = = and = = = **bottom of file** = = = in this figure. Type in the program (Figure 3.21). If you need more information about using the Enhanced Editor please refer to the next section.

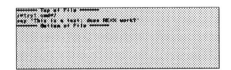

Figure 3.21. Your program that you have typed in.

4. (Figure 3.21) Opening the FILE action menu. Click on FILE. The FILE action menu appears (Figure 3.22).

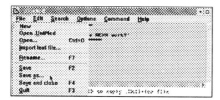

Figure 3.22. The FILE action menu.

5. (Figure 3.22) Saving the program with the correct name. Click on SAVE AS on the FILE action menu. The SAVE AS menu appears (Figure 3.23).

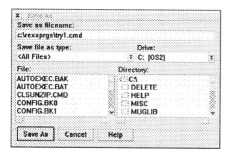

Figure 3.23. The SAVE AS menu.

6. (Figure 3.23) Specifying the program name that you will save. Assuming that you want to save your program with the name of TRY1.CMD, type in C:\REXXPRGS\TRY1.CMD. I recommend you always include the disk drive and directory in the name. Click on SAVE AS. The SAVE AS menu disappears (Figure 3.24).

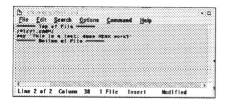

Figure 3.24. The Enhanced Editor Window covering up the OS/2 Window icon.

7. (Figure 3.24) Uncovering the OS/2 Window icon. Place the mouse cursor on the left border of the Enhanced Editor window, click, and hold the button down. Drag the border to the right until the OS/2 window icon is uncovered. Release the mouse button (Figure 3.25). *Note:* Your OS/2 Window icon will probably not be found in the same place as on my desktop.

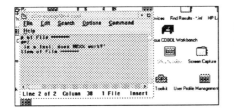

Figure 3.25. The OS/2 Window icon reappearing.

8. (Figure 3.25) Opening an OS/2 Window. Double click on the OS/2 Window icon. An OS/2 Window opens up (Figure 3.26).

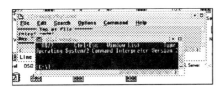

Figure 3.26. An OS/2 Window.

9. (Figure 3.26) Moving the OS/2 Window to a more convenient place. Click on the top border of the OS/2 Window and drag it down so it uncovers the Enhanced Editor window. Release the mouse button. Click on the bottom border of the OS/2 Window and drag it down until the OS/2 Window is a convenient size (Figure 3.27). Feel free to arrange your windows any way you want.

Figure 3.27. A suggested arrangement of the windows.

10. (Figure 3.27) You now have a convenient workplace, with the Enhanced Editor window at the top and the OS/2 Window at the bottom. To go from one to the other you have only to move the mouse cursor to the desired window and click once.

Figure 3.28. Executing your program in an OS/2 Window.

11. (Figure 3.28) Executing your program. Type C:, press ENTER, type CD \REXXPRGS, press ENTER, then type the program name. You must be in an OS/2 Window or Full Screen. You cannot execute your program from a DOS Window. The program executes. To cancel it if you need to, press CTRL and C at the same time.

Figure 3.29. Your program has executed and its displayed output appears.

12. (Figure 3.29) The results of your program now appear. You can scroll up and down in the OS/2 Window to see the results.

3.2 USING THE OS/2 ENHANCED EDITOR

I prefer to create my REXX programs using OS/2's Enhanced Editor, a very powerful and easy to use text editor. The Enhanced Editor is not a word processor, so it has just the features you need for creating ASCII or DOS Text files that do not contain printer formatting commands.

The OS/2 Enhanced Editor recognizes that you are creating a REXX program and assists you in creating REXX control structures such as DO and SELECT. It automatically creates ENDs for the DOs and OTHERWISEs for the SELECTs, so you won't forget them.

This Editor is a What You See Is What You Get Editor. Typing in lines of your program is easy and so is correcting mistakes. It uses the common set of pull-down and pop-up menus so common today in the Windows and OS/2 environments, so you won't have to learn another set of strange function keys.

You will most likely use the editor inside of one window and test or run your programs inside of another window. You will be able to move the windows around for your convenience and generally have both windows showing at the same time, making it a pleasure to create and use your programs.

Although the Enhanced Editor has an excellent HELP facility, I feel I should tell you the basics. Since I have already told you how to open an Enhanced Editor Window and an OS/2 Window (Section 3.1) I won't repeat that here. I will tell you how to edit and change a program that you have already created, how to save it and replace it, and how to move text around.

Editing and changing an existing program

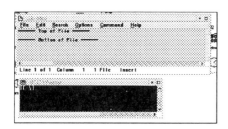

Figure 3.30. Enhanced Editor.

1. (Figure 3.30). While in the Enhanced Editor (with an empty Editor file named .UNTITLED), click on the word FILE in the upper left. An action menu appears (Figure 3.31).

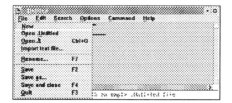

Figure 3.31. Action menu.

2. (Figure 3.31). Click on OPEN. This displays a list of files that you have already used in the Enhanced Editor (Figure 3.32).

Figure 3.32. Open menu showing a list of files.

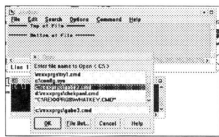

3. (Figure 3.32). Select one of the files displayed by clicking on it with the mouse cursor, or you may type in a name in the blank area. Click on OK. This imports the program into the editor (Figure 3.33).

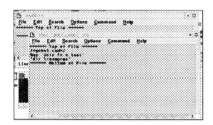

Figure 3.33. The program has been imported into the Editor.

4. (Figure 3.33). The program is displayed by the editor.

Saving your program

If you have already given a name to your program, you can just press F2 to save it. If you haven't already given it a name (it says .UNTITLED at the top), you can click on FILE, then on SAVE AS, then type in the name complete with drive and directory.

Moving text around

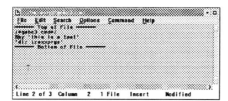

Figure 3.34. Moving text around.

(Figure 3.34). The easiest way I have found to move text around is to first highlight it by clicking at the beginning of the text and holding down the mouse button while you drag the mouse cursor to the end of the text, then releasing the mouse button. The highlighted text appears in reverse video (Figure 3.35).

Figure 3.35. The text that will be moved has been highlighted.

(Figure 3.35). Press SHIFT and DELETE at the same time. This cuts out the highlighted text (Figure 3.36).

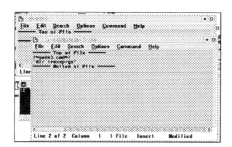

Figure 3.36. The text has been deleted.

(Figure 3.36). Move the mouse cursor to the desired location. Press SHIFT and INSERT. This will place the cut text in the new location (Figure 3.37).

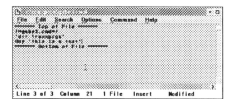

Figure 3.37. The text has been moved.

3.3 USING A WORD PROCESSOR

If you know how to use a word processor you might prefer to create your program with it instead of the Enhanced Editor. The most important thing to remember is that you must direct your word processor to create an ASCII file, a plain DOS Text file. Another caution: Some word processors do not release the file until you exit from the word processor. If you try to run your program and you receive the message that the program is unreadable, you may need to exit from your word processor.

3.4 CREATING DIRECTLY FROM THE KEYBOARD

If you are going to create a very short program, you may key it in directly from the keyboard. You will not, however, have any chance to make corrections if you do it this way, unless you go into the Enhanced Editor. I suggest you use a directory named REXXPRGS to contain all your REXX programs. Open an OS/2 Window or OS/2 Full Screen. If you do not already have a directory named REXXPRGS, type:
```
C:
CD \
MD REXXPRGS
```

After creating your REXXPRGS directory, if needed, type the following command. It will enable you to type in your program right from the keyboard.
```
COPY CON:   C:\REXXPRGS\MYPROG.CMD
```
You may substitute any other suitable name for the program. Press ENTER. Start typing in the program. Press ENTER at the end of each line of the program. When you finish, press CTRL and Z. Then press ENTER. Now you can execute your program.

3.5 DIRECTORIES AND PATHS

WHERE TO PUT YOUR PROGRAM

A REXX program may be placed in any directory or directory within a directory (subdirectory). I suggest you use one named REXXPRGS, the name used as an example throughout the book.   If you haven't already created one, do this in an OS/2 Window or OS/2 Full Screen:

```
C:
CD \
MD  REXXPRGS
```

TELLING OS/2 HOW TO FIND YOUR PROGRAM

You will have to tell OS/2 about the directory containing your REXX programs so it can find your programs. The same rules apply to the search for OS/2 programs (.CMD extension) as for other programs (.EXE extension) and DOS batch files (.BAT or .CMD extension). OS/2 does not use the AUTOEXEC.BAT file that tells DOS the path to follow to find programs, but uses the CONFIG.SYS file instead. You may modify the CONFIG.SYS file to include your REXX directory in OS/2's search path, or if you would rather not make any changes to OS/2's most critical file, you may wait until you are in an OS/2 Window or OS/2 Full Screen and then tell OS2 about your program directory. Here are three ways of telling OS/2 about your program directory. Please choose one.

1. Make a copy of the CONFIG.SYS file with the COPY command. You will use this copy to recover if your changes prevent you from booting OS/2. Using the Enhanced Editor, add C:\REXXPRGS; to the extreme right of the SET PATH command in the CONFIG.SYS file. If you are unsure of how to do this, please don't. If your CONFIG.SYS file is not right, you may not be able to boot OS/2. If you do this correctly, OS/2 will always be able to find your REXX programs after you reboot. I will assume that you have *not* done this throughout the remainder of the book.

2. Before executing your program in an OS/2 Window or OS/2 Full Screen, change to the directory containing your REXX programs, then type in the program name (MYPROG in this example):

```
C:
CD \
CD \REXXPRGS
MYPROG
```

Throughout this book I'll be assuming that this is what you are doing. It's simpler and safer than the other ways and makes it easier for you to execute other REXX programs or user-written functions or subroutines from within your programs.

Later, if you want to execute another program in the same OS/2 Window or Full Screen, you will need to type in only the program name, not the first three lines shown.

3. In an OS/2 Window or OS/2 Full Screen specify the drive and directory along with the program name when you execute the program:

```
C:\REXXPRGS\MYPROG
```

This way will work even if you have already chosen option 1 or 2 above.

3.6 EXECUTING IN AN OS/2 WINDOW AND OS/2 FULL SCREEN

You will probably execute most of your programs in an OS/2 Window, because it is very convenient. If you have done what I recommended in the first part of this chapter, you will have an OS/2 Window icon on your desktop. If so, you just need to double click on the icon, and you'll have an OS/2 Window to execute your programs in. For the remainder of the book, I'll assume that you are executing in an OS/2 Window. Just a reminder: You cannot execute your program in a DOS Window. Only OS/2 knows REXX.

There is no particular advantage to executing your program in OS/2 Full Screen over any other method, but here's how to do it. On the OS/2 Desktop, click on the OS/2 System icon. Then click on the Command Prompts icon. Then click on OS/2 Full Screen. Then continue with Step 12 in Section 3.1.

3.7 EXECUTING FROM THE DIRECTORY CONTAINING YOUR PROGRAMS

Here is another very convenient way to execute your program. You need to open a window containing the directory REXXPRGS. It is then very easy to execute your program: You just double click on the icon labelled with the name of the program you wish to execute. OS/2 will automatically open an OS/2 Window to execute your program. Here are the steps to follow.

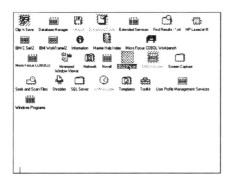

Figure 3.38. The OS/2 Desktop.

1. (Figure 3.38) Starting with the OS/2 Desktop, double click on OS/2 System. The OS/2 System Window appears (Figure 3.39).

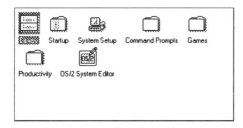

Figure 3.39. The OS/2 System Window showing the DRIVES icon.

2. (Figure 3.39) Double click on the DRIVES icon in the OS/2 System Window. The DRIVES Window opens, showing the available drives (Figure 3.40).

Figure 3.40. DRIVES icons.

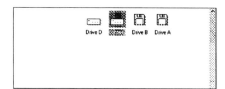

3. (Figure 3.40) Double click on the Drive C icon in the DRIVES Window. A window opens showing directory icons (Figure 3.41).

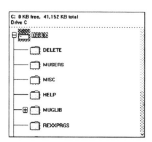

Figure 3.41. Directory icons.

4. (Figure 3.41) Double click on the directory containing your REXX programs. A window opens for your programs (Figure 3.42).

Figure 3.42. Icons for the files in your program directory.

5. (Figure 3.42) Double click on the icon for the program you wish to execute. After it finishes, you'll have to close all the windows you have opened by double clicking on each window's icon in the upper left.

3.8 EXECUTING WITH THE PRESENTATION MANAGER (PMREXX)

The Presentation Manager opens a window to execute your program in and display its output. The window also gives you a convenient line on which to type any input that your program requests. In addition, you can conveniently start interactive debugging from this window. Finally, you can scroll and save the output that your program displays.

To use the Presentation Manager, get into an OS/2 Window or OS/2 Full Screen. Then type PMREXX before the name of your program when you execute it (as shown in Figure 3.43).

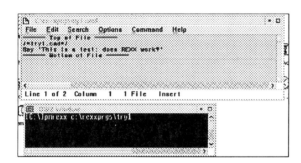

Figure 3.43. Executing a REXX program named TRY1 with the Presentation Manager.

The program's output is displayed in the window. If the program requests input, type it in the line labeled INPUT: (Figure 3.44).

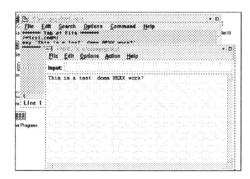

Figure 3.44. The Presentation Manager window displayed when it executes the program TRY1.

When you wish to close the Presentation Manager window, double click on the icon in the upper left (Figure 3.45).

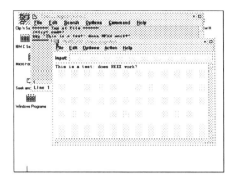

Figure 3.45. Closing the Presentation Manager Window.

Here is how to tell, in a program, if the program is being executed in the Presentation Manager.

```
/*testpm.cmd (Section 3.8)*/
if address() = 'PMREXX'
then say 'Presentation Manager is present'
else say  'Presentation Manager not present'
```

ADRESS() is a function that tells your program if it is executing under OS/2 without the Presentation Manager (gives a reply of CMD) or with the Presentation Manager present (gives a reply of PMREXX).

3.9 INTERRUPTING THE PROGRAM

To cancel your program while it is executing press CTRL and C, then ENTER, or CTRL and BREAK, then ENTER. Under the Presentation Manager you can cancel your program by clicking on the icon in the upper left and then closing the window. REXX signals an error and stops your program. If you have a halt trap (see Chapter 9), you can gain control inside of the program when you interrupt the program. Then you can exit the program or resume execution.

If you don't have a halt trap, OS/2 will simply cancel your program. It will not ask "Terminate batch file?" the way DOS does. This means you cannot resume execution without starting the execution all over again.

3.10 ADVANCED OS/2 OPTIONS

When executing your program from an OS/2 Window or an OS/2 Full Screen there are several advanced features you can request: piping, redirection of data, tokenizing (a form of compiling), and OS/2 command display suppression. These features of OS/2 are requested on the same line that you execute your program on in an OS/2 Window or in OS/2 Full Screen.

PIPING

Piping is requested by using the broken vertical bar (¦). It is placed between the name of the command you are executing and the name of an OS/2 pipe. OS/2 passes the output of the your command directly to the pipe without displaying it on the screen. The pipe will display your program's output after processing it.

Here is how you would execute a program (shown in Figure 3.47) that displays 50 lines of output and passes the output into the OS/2 pipe filter program MORE: SHOW50 ¦ MORE. Figure 3.46 shows the resulting display. Press ENTER to see the next page of output.

```
──────────────────────────────────────────────────────────────1
 2
 3
 4
 5
 6
 7
 8
 9
10
11
12
13
14
15
16
17
18
19
20
21
22
23
-- More --
```

Figure 3.46. Result of executing the command SHOW50 ¦ MORE.

```
/*SHOW50.CMD (Figure 3.47)*/
DO I = 1 to 50
  Say I
END
```

Figure 3.47. The program SHOW50.

There are three pipe filter programs supplied with OS/2: FIND, MORE, and SORT. Your REXX program can send its output to any one of these three pipes, and the pipe will perform its action on your program's output. MORE displays a page's worth of lines and then waits for you to press ENTER in order to show you another page. FIND searches for specific character strings. SORT rearranges data in alphabetical order.

Please note that piping has absolutely nothing to do with REXX character string concatenation or with the OR operator used with IF, although all three use the same symbol, the vertical broken bar (¦). Figure 3.48 shows character string concatenation in a REXX program. Figure 3.49 shows the logical operator OR used with an IF.

```
/*STRCONC.CMD (Figure 3.48)*/
Say "This will show concatenation" ¦¦,
    "of two data strings"
```

Figure 3.48. Data concatenation with ¦¦.

```
/*LOGOR.CMD (Figure 3.49)*/
A = 1
B = 2
C = 3
IF A = 1 ¦  B = 9
Then say "One or the other is true"
```

Figure 3.49. Logical OR with ¦.

REDIRECTING INPUT

Normally your program will receive input from the keyboard when it does a PULL, a PARSE PULL (Chapter 7), or a CALL LINEIN (Chapter 18). This is used for dialogue with the user, asking questions, and receiving answers.

The input redirection symbol (<) will cause your program to accept its input from a file instead of from the keyboard. The program will not stop to ask you to type in something because it will read from the file. Figure 3.50 shows the program NAMEPLSE getting its input from the file NAME.DAT and displaying a name that it found in the file. Figure 3.51 shows the input file.

```
NAMEPLSE < NAME.DAT
Please type in your name
Thank you, Marie
```

Figure 3.50. The program NAMEPLSE getting its input from a file and displaying the name that it found in the file.

```
Marie
Marc
Mike
```

Figure 3.51. The file NAME.DAT that the program NAMEPLSE gets its input from.

Each time the program does a PULL, PARSE PULL, or CALL LINEIN it will read one more line from the data file. If it runs out of lines of data (more PULLS than lines), it will read a null, or zero characters, from the file and will not go to the keyboard looking for its input.

REDIRECTING OUTPUT

The output redirection symbol (>) will cause your program to put its output into a file rather than on the screen. You can later TYPE the file name or view it with the Enhanced Editor to see what is in it. Figure 3.52 shows the program SAYHI putting its output into a file. Figure 3.53 shows the program SAYHI, and Figure 3.54 shows the resulting file OUTFILE.DAT after the program SAYHI runs.

```
SAYHI > OUTFILE.DAT
```

Figure 3.52 The program SAYHI sending its output into a file rather than to the screen. It is being executed in an OS/2 Window or Full Screen.

```
/*SAYHI.CMD (Figure 3.53)*/
Say 'Hi'
```

Figure 3.53. The program SAYHI.

```
Hi
```

Figure 3.54. The file OUTFILE.DAT after the program SAYHI runs.

SUPRESSING COMMAND DISPLAY

Normally all OS/2 commands that are found in your program will be displayed as they execute. One way to stop them from being displayed is by using the /Q switch when you execute your program. Figure 3.55 shows the program MYFILES (which simply does an OS/2 DIR command) being executed with the /Q switch, and Figure 3.56 shows the resulting display. For comparison I will show you the same program being run without the /Q switch and the resulting display in Figure 3.57.

Figure 3.55. Executing the program MYFILES with the /Q switch to suppress display of OS/2 commands.

C:\REXXPRGS\MYFILES

Figure 3.56. Executing the program MYFILES without the /Q switch.

Figure 3.57. The display produced by the program MYFILES being executed without the /Q switch.

There is of course another way to suppress command display: '@ECHO OFF' at the beginning of your program. This way is equally valid. See Chapter 5.

TOKENIZING

Since REXX is an interpreted language, OS/2 has to read your program and interpret it every time you execute it. This takes a slight amount of time, which might become significant in a large application. You can cut down the time it takes to execute your program by tokenizing it. Tokenizing does not change your original program file but creates another file that you cannot access.

Tokenize your program by "executing" it with the //T switch. This will tokenize it but not execute it. To execute it you'll have to do it again, without the //T switch. Figure 3.59 shows how you would tokenize the program BUS. Figure 3.60 shows how you would run the program after that (no different from the normal way of running a program).

```
C:
CD \
CD \REXXPRGS
BUS //T
```

Figure 3.59. Tokenizing the program BUS.

```
C:
CD \
CD \REXXPRGS
BUS
```

Figure 3.60. Executing the tokenized program BUS.

3.11 QUESTIONS/PROBLEMS

1. Perform the initial setup described in Section 3.1, Part 1 of this chapter.

2. Perform the steps described in Section 3.1, Part 2 of this chapter.

3. Create a REXX program named TRY1.CMD using the Enhanced Editor. Place the following statements in the program. A comment containing the name of the program and the REXX statement: Say 'This is a test: does REXX work?'

4. Execute the program in an OS/2 Window.

5. Execute the program in OS/2 Full Screen.

6. Execute the program using the Presentation Manager.

7. If you use a word processor to create your program, what must you be careful about?

Chapter 4

REXX SYNTAX: THE RULES OF THE LANGUAGE

In this chapter I would like to acquaint you with the syntax of REXX, its grammatical components. You need to know something about REXX's syntax in order to write good programs, but I have found that you don't need to know everything. That is why I have simplified the syntax of REXX to save you time in learning it.

Topics

4.1 A Sample Program
4.2 The Components of REXX
4.3 The Literal
4.4 The Variable
4.5 Concatenation: Stringing Data Together
4.6 Questions/Problems

4.1 A SAMPLE PROGRAM

Take a look at the sample REXX program in Figure 4.1. This program doesn't do any meaningful processing, but it will help us get started with REXX.

The numbers in the vertical column to the left of the program are not actually part of the program. I will use these numbers here just for referencing the lines of the program but won't use them again after that. The Enhanced Editor will tell you which line number you are looking at, so you can relate to the line numbers shown by REXX when you get a syntax error while running your REXX program.

45

```
1          /*SAMPLE.CMD (Figure 4.1)*/
2          A = 1
3          B = 2
4          C = A + B
5          Say 'THE ANSWER IS '   C
6          CALL SUBR1
7
8          SAY 'HELLO';SAY 'GOODBYE'
9          SAY 'HELLO';
10         SAY,
11         'HELLO'
12         EXIT
13          SUBR1:
14           'DIR C:\REXXPRGS\*.CMD'
15           RETURN
```

Figure 4.1. A sample REXX program.

Line 1 is a comment that tells us the name of the REXX program. It is more than a comment, however, because it tells OS/2 that this is a REXX program, not a Batch File. Please start your REXX programs with a comment like that. Specifically, line 1 must start with /* in positions 1 and 2. You may say anything you want in the comment, but I recommend you include at least the program's name. You may end the comment on the same line or on another line with a */.

You may place comments anywhere in your program, but generally you should place them in such a way that they don't impede readability. This means on a line by themselves or off to the right of an instruction.

Line 2 is the simplest of REXX statements. It is an assignment statement that puts a 1 into the variable A. The assignment statement has no verb. You can recognize an assignment because it starts with a variable at the beginning of a line, has an equal sign ($=$), and a literal, variable, expression, or function that is put into the first variable.

Line 3 is another assignment.

Line 4 asks REXX to place the sum of the variable A and the variable B into the variable C.

Line 5 displays 'THE ANSWER IS 3' on the monitor screen. Notice that there are three things on this line: the verb SAY, the literal 'THE ANSWER IS,' and the variable C. REXX displays the literal exactly as written and changes the variable C into its value, 3.

Please notice that REXX verbs are not surrounded with apostrophes or quotes.

A literal should be enclosed in apostrophes (') or quotation marks (").

You may use upper and lower case as convenient, except when literals are being compared, because upper and lower case are significant.

Line 6 executes the subroutine SUBR1. Control goes into the subroutine. When the subroutine is finished, the program continues with line 7.

Line 7 is completely blank. You may use blank lines wherever you wish to improve readability.

Line 8 — If you want to put more than one instruction on a line, you will have to use the semicolon to separate them. I don't generally recommend this. Instead, I suggest you put one statement on a line, which makes a program easier to read.

Line 9 — If nothing follows it on the same line, the semicolon is not needed. I suggest you not use it when there is nothing else on the line, since it adds nothing to readability.

Lines 10 and 11 — Most of the time a REXX instruction or verb will fit quite well on one line of your program, but sometimes you may need two or more lines. When this happens simply put a comma at the end of the first line. This tells REXX to take this line together with the next. For example, normally SAY and 'HELLO' should be on the same line, but if you wanted to use two lines for this one instruction, you would put a comma at the end of the first line.

Line 12 ends the program. The word EXIT will always end your REXX program and send control back to the OS/2 Window, to OS/2 Full Screen, the Program directory or wherever you were when you executed the program. You need an EXIT whenever you have subroutines or condition traps at the end of your program to prevent your program from falling into them accidentally. You can, however, omit the EXIT if it will be the last statement on the last line.

If you desire, you can end the program with a *return code*. For example, EXIT 10 ends the program with the return code 10. All this does is pass the number 10 to OS/2 or the program that called it, usually another REXX program. The program that called your program can examine the return code in the special variable RC and take some action based on it if it wishes. This is totally optional, and I wouldn't do it unless the calling program expected a return code.

Notice that EXIT is not enclosed in apostrophes or quotes. That is because it is a REXX instruction or verb. If it had been enclosed in apostrophes or quotes, REXX would not have recognized it, and would have passed it to OS/2. OS/2 would have recognized it and understood it as a command to close the OS/2 Window or the OS/2 Full Screen that it is executed in.

Line 13 is the start of the subroutine, which is defined by the label SUBR1:. Labels are used for transfers of control, with CALL for subroutines (round trip) and SIGNAL for a direct transfer of control (one way).

Line 14 is an OS/2 command. OS/2, not REXX, will execute this command. REXX's only job here is to pass the command to OS/2 for execution. This command will list all the files in your REXXPRGS directory. Please note that the command is enclosed in apostrophes ('). Quotation marks (") work as well. You must use one or the other to prevent REXX from trying to interpret the OS/2 command and giving you a syntax error. OS/2 will not give you a syntax error, unless there is something wrong with the OS/2 command. There is a list of the OS/2 commands you are likely to need in Appendix B.

Line 15 is the end of the subroutine. RETURN sends control back where it came from: to the instruction right after the CALL.

In general, there are no column rules for REXX. Start your program in any column and continue in any column you choose. Words should be separated by one or more spaces.

4.2 THE COMPONENTS OF REXX

I have broken REXX down, somewhat arbitrarily, into eight components: keywords, the assignment statement, the literal, the variable, the command, the label, the function, and the comment. I will explain each one in turn:

Keyword. Like most languages, REXX has verbs with a specific meaning. Each verb is a keyword and is found first in the sentence. There are not many different REXX verbs. Here they are, summarized. You will find a complete description of each of them in Appendix C.

• ADDRESS passes commands to a specific environment or command processor.

• ARG receives information passed from the command line or function/subroutine invocation.

• CALL invokes a subroutine and turns on or off an error trap that continues executing.

• DO begins a loop.

• DROP undefines a variable.

• ELSE introduces "false" outcome with IF.

• END terminates DO loop, SELECT.

• EXIT ends the program.

• EXPOSE allows sharing of a subroutine's variables.

• IF is conditional execution.

• INTERPRET processes data as if it were an instruction.

• ITERATE goes to the beginning of a loop.

• LEAVE exits from a loop.

• NOP does nothing.

• NUMERIC controls precision, indefiniteness in comparisons, and exponential notation.

• OTHERWISE is the default alternative in the SELECT.

• PARSE is for string manipulation.

• PROCEDURE protects variables in a function/subroutine.

• PULL removes data from the stack.

• PUSH puts data into the stack, LIFO.

• QUEUE puts data into the stack, FIFO.

• RETURN in a function/subroutine, sends control back to the instruction after the one that invoked the function/subroutine.

- SAY displays a line on the terminal.

- SELECT introduces the CASE structure.

- SIGNAL turns on or off a condition trap — unconditional transfer of control.

- THEN introduces "true" outcome with IF.

- TRACE controls tracing and interactive debugging.

Assignment. This feature is recognized by its second component, the equal sign. The first component is a variable and may not be in quotes. The variable is made equal to whatever is to the right of the equal sign. Examples:

```
/*asgex01.cmd (Section 4.2)*/
A = 5
Say A
TOTAL = 5 + 1
Say Total
NAME = "BETH"
Say NAME
```

Literal. The literal is itself. It stands for nothing else. Literals are normally enclosed in quotes or apostrophes. I recommend you always enclose literals in quotes or apostrophes, although REXX can interpret a literal as such if you forget the quotes or apostrophes. REXX will first look to see if the string of characters is a variable. If it is, then REXX uses the contents of the variable. If it isn't, then REXX takes the character string as a literal, but will convert it to upper case. I recommend you not make use of this feature (but it is handy when you forget the quotes or apostrophes). Examples:

```
/* Litex01.cmd (Section 4.2)*/
Say "HELLO"
Say 'GOODBYE'
Say 12345
Say "12345"
Say HELLO
Say '313233'X   /*(hex string)*/
```

Variable. The variable holds information, which may change during the execution of the program. Examples:

```
/* varex01.cmd (Section 4.2) */
A = 1
B = 2
NAME = 'Kelly'
RECORD_COUNTER = 12
RECORD.I = 'This is the record'
```

Command. A command is something that is understood by the operating system that REXX is found in, OS/2, but not by REXX. REXX passes it to OS/2 for OS/2 to process. More on this later in Chapter 12. Examples:

```
/*Cmdex01.cmd (Section 4.2)*/
'DIR'
'CD \REXXPRGS'
'ERASE JUNK*.TMP'
```

Label. A label is used to name a subroutine, a user-written function, or an error trap, or it is the target of a transfer of control instruction. A label must be the first thing on the line and end with a colon. The label may also be alone on the line. Examples:

```
/*Labex01.cmd (Section 4.2)*/
Signal Compute
Say 'After Signal Verb'
COMPUTE: Say 1 + 1
Call SUBROUTINE1
EXIT
SUBROUTINE1:
Say 'I am in the subroutine'
RETURN
```

Function. A function is a built-in capability of REXX that performs arithmetic or a character string operations on data that is passed to it. There is a complete list and description in Appendix D. Examples:

```
/*Funex01.cmd (Section 4.2)*/
SAY LENGTH("ABCD")
SAY LEFT("ABCD",3)
```

Comment. A comment consists of a slash asterisk (/*), some text of your choosing, and an asterisk slash (*/). REXX ignores anything you say in your comment. A comment may start and end on the same line, or it may end on another line. REXX comments may be nested, so /* /* must be followed by */ */. Your REXX program must begin with a comment in columns 1 and 2 on the first line. Examples:

```
/*My REXX program */
/*an example of a comment: /* comment */ */
/* when one line is not enough for all you
have to say, use several */
```

4.3 THE LITERAL

THE NULL STRING

Figure 4.2 illustrates a null string. You may have a null string or a literal containing no characters. You signify the null string by two consecutive quotes or apostrophes.

```
Say ''
```

Figure 4.2. The null string.

APOSTROPHES IN LITERALS

What do you do if a literal needs an apostrophe, as in the name O'Connor? You may bound the literal in quotation marks, as in "O'Connor," or you may double the apostrophes, as in 'O''Connor.' See Figure 4.3.

```
/*Apoex01.cmd (Figure 4.3)*/
Say "O'Connor"
Say 'O''Connor'
```

Figure 4.3. Apostrophes in literals.

EXPONENTIAL NOTATION

If there is an E in a number, the number is assumed to be in scientific notation. This shouldn't be a problem unless you have many addresses like 23E63 Street. See Figure 4.4.

Exponential notation uses a number, an E, an optional plus or minus sign, and another number that tells to what power of 10 the first number is raised.


```
/*Expex01.cmd (Figure 4.4)*/
SAY    1E+2 + 1E+2
```

Figure 4.4. Exponential notation.

NUMERIC LITERALS

See Figure 4.5. If you wish, you may make it perfectly clear that a numeric literal is going to be used in arithmetic or in numeric comparisons by putting a plus sign or a minus sign in front of it. If you do that, REXX will never treat it as a mere character string.

Numeric literals are unusual in REXX in that they may have quotes or apostrophes, unlike in COBOL. This means that the "1" in Figure 4.5 is legal in REXX.

```
/*numex01.cmd (Figure 4.5)*/
 A =  1
 A = +1
 B = -1
 SAY A + B

 SAY "1" + "2"

 SAY    +1E+2 /* 100 */
 SAY 1 + 1E+2 /* 101 */
 SAY 1E+2     /* 1E2 not taken as number */
```

Figure 4.5. Examples of legal numeric literals.

CONTINUING LITERALS

Although a literal may be up to 251 characters in length, you may not want to create a line that long. Instead, I suggest you concatenate two literals to produce a longer one, as in Figure 4.6.

```
/*litex02.cmd (Figure 4.6)*/
LONG_VAR = "LONG STRING TO END OF LINE" ||,
           "REST OF STRING ON NEXT LINE"
Say LONG_VAR
```

Figure 4.6. Concatenating a long literal.

Figure 4.7 shows another way to create a long literal occupying more than one line, which works under some versions of REXX, but not under OS/2.

```
/*litex03.cmd (Figure 4.7)*/
/* won't work on OS/2*/
LONG_VAR = "FIRST LINE, NO QUOTES AT END
NEXT LINE, NO QUOTES AT BEGINNING"
Say long_var
```

Figure 4.7. Creating a long literal another way.

THE HEX STRING

If you put the letter X after a literal in quotes or apostrophes, REXX believes you have given it a hex string. This means that you have put the hexadecimal representation of character strings in the quotes. Valid hexadecimal representations may use the digits 0 through 9 and the letters A through F (see Figure 4.8).

```
/*Hexex01.cmd (Figure 4.8)*/
   SAY '31323334'X       /* ---> 1234 */
```

Figure 4.8. Displaying a hex string.

A PITFALL

Any time you put an X after a quoted string, REXX takes it as a hex string (see Figure 4.9).

```
/*hex02.cmd (Figure 4.9)*/
/*not to do*/

X = 5 + 6

SAY "THE ANSWER IS "X
/*syntax error: attempts hex interpretation*/
```

Figure 4.9. An example of a pitfall in using literal strings.

STYLE WITH LITERALS

Your use of literals has a strong effect on the neatness and readability of your program. I would like to make the following suggestions regarding style:

- Always use quotation marks or apostrophes around literals.

```
SAY "HELLO"
SAY 'HELLO'
```

- Don't use quotation marks or apostrophes around numbers. Avoid:

```
SAY "1" + "2"
```

- Use apostrophes with OS/2 commands because some OS/2 commands use quotation marks; this will avoid conflict.

```
'FIND "Marie F." MEMOPRES.DOC'
'START "SAMPLE PROGRAM WINDOW" /B MYPROG.EXE'
```

- By means of careful spacing, make it easier to determine what is actually contained inside the quotes or apostrophes.

```
SEARCH_STRING = 'Marie F.'
'FIND '    SEARCH_STRING    'MEMOPRES.DOC'
```

- Don't let a literal spill over onto a second line by omitting an ending quote or apostrophe on the first line. Don't do this:

```
SAY "THIS HAS BEEN A VERY
NICE DAY DONT YOU THINK?"
```

- Use a continuation comma when you need a second line for your literal.

```
SAY "THIS HAS BEEN A VERY ",
"NICE DAY DONT YOU THINK?"
```

- Or use a concatenation symbol when you need a second line for your literal.

```
GREETING = "THIS HAS BEEN A VERY "  ||,
"NICE DAY DONT YOU THINK?"
```

4.4 THE VARIABLE

VALID VARIABLE NAMES

Naming variables in REXX presents few problems (see Figure 4.10). Variable names must begin with a letter and may be as long as 250 characters. The underscore character may be used for readability. The period is not used for readability but to separate the parts of compound variables (see Figure 4.11). Please don't use any other special character in a variable name. REXX makes for more readable programs because its variable names may be upper case, lower case, or mixed.

I strongly suggest that you avoid REXX keywords. EXIT = "HI" will work but will also give you a very unreadable program.

Valid Variable Names	Invalid Variable Names	
A	1	(literal number)
a	1abcdef	(begin w numb)
Aa	a-a	(hyphen N.G)
a_A		
A123		
Salary_increase		

Figure 4.10. Examples of variable names.

<u>Compound variable names</u>

```
number.1
branch.dept.unit
A.1
RECD.I
```

Figure 4.11. Examples of compound variable names.

UNDEFINED VARIABLES

A variable that was never given a value is taken as a literal but converted to upper case (see Figure 4.12).

```
/*varex02.cmd (Figure 4.12) */
SAY Hello /*DISPLAYS "HELLO"*/
```

Figure 4.12. Displaying an undefined variable.

GIVING A VALUE TO A VARIABLE

Variables are given a value by means of the following:

• Assignment (the variable on the left of the equal sign is given a value). Example:

```
/*Assignment example*/
A = 5
```

• The REXX PARSE (see Chapter 7). Examples:

```
/*parex01.cmd (Section 4.4)*/
PARSE UPPER ARG NAME ADDRESS
Say 'Please type in your name'
PARSE UPPER PULL REPLY
Say 'Please type in your phone'
PULL REPLY
FULL_NAME = 'JOHN JONES'
PARSE VAR FULL_NAME FIRST_NAME LAST_NAME
```

- Reading files (see Chapter 18). Example:
```
/*Fioex01.cmd (Section 4.4)*/
RECORD = Linein('C:\REXXPRGS\TEST.DAT')
Say RECORD
```

- Controlled DO loops (the variable on the left of the equal sign is given a value). Example:

```
/*Lopex01.cmd (Section 4.4)*/
DO I = 1 TO 10
  Say I
END
```

- Some functions. Example:

```
/*funex02.cmd (Section 4.4) */
 function_to_load = "SYSQUERYCLASSLIST"
 call rxfuncadd    function_to_load,'rexxutil',,
      function_to_load
 CALL SYSQUERYCLASSLIST 'LINE.'
   SAY 'THE CLASSES REGISTERED ARE:'
   DO I = 1 TO LINE.0
     SAY LINE.I
   END
```

FINDING OUT THE VALUE OF A VARIABLE

REXX retrieves the value that is in a variable by means of the following:

- The SAY
```
/* Sayex01.cmd (Section 4.4)*/
GREETING = 'BONJOUR'
SAY GREETING
```

• Assignment (REXX finds out the value(s) contained in the variable(s) on the right of the equal sign and uses the values in the assignment). Example:

```
/*Asgex02.cmd (Section 4.4)*/
A = 5
Say A
```

• The REXX PARSE (see Chapter 9). Examples:

```
/* PARex02.cmd (Section 4.4)*/
Say 'Please type in yes or no'
PARSE UPPER PULL REPLY
Say REPLY 'was your answer'
FULL_NAME = 'Ima Nutt'
PARSE VAR FULL_NAME FIRST_NAME LAST_NAME
SAY FIRST_NAME
SAY LAST_NAME
```

• Controlled DO loops. Example:

```
/*DOex01.cmd (Section 4.4)*/
LIMIT = 10
DO I = 1 TO LIMIT
  Say I
END
```

• Any instruction containing a variable. The variable must not be found inside of quotation marks or apostrophes. Examples:

```
/*varex03.cmd (Section 4.4)*/
SAY GREETING
Extension = "CMD"
'DIR  *.'Extension
EXIT RETURN_CODE
```

STYLE WITH VARIABLES

The way you use variables can greatly influence the readability of your program. Here are some suggestions:

• Use meaningful names: ACCOUNT_NUMBER rather than NUM.

- Use meaningfully different names where different data items are involved: INPUT_ACCOUNT_NUMBER and HOLD_ACCOUNT_NUMBER rather than ACCT_NUM, ACCTNUMBER, and ACCOUNT.

- Never use the same variable name for two different purposes.

- Use upper and lower case if you like that style.

First_name
Account_number

- Describe all variables at the beginning of your program.

/* ACCOUNT_NUMBER is the client's account number */

- Do not use REXX keywords or reserved variables. Don't do:

```
/*BadEx01.cmd (Section 4.4)*/
EXIT = "QUIT"
SAY = "HELLO"
RESULT = 5 + 4
RC = 4 + 5
SIGL = 14 + 1
```

- Prefix "throwaway" variables with TEMP.
```
/*varex04.cmd (Section 4.4)*/
TEMP_LENGTH = LENGTH("ABCDEFG")
MIDDLE        = TEMP_LENGTH % 2
MIDDLE        = ABS(MIDDLE)
SAY "TWO CHARACTERS STARTING AT MIDDLE ARE:"
SAY SUBSTR("ABCDE",MIDDLE, 2)
```

4.5 CONCATENATION: STRINGING DATA TOGETHER

CONCATENATING WITHOUT SPACES

If two dissimilar items happen to be next to each other, they will be concatenated without spaces. For example, if you execute the instruction SAY "A"5, you will see A5 displayed, and the A and the 5 will be displayed without any spaces. REXX can see that they are two different items because of the quotation marks. Other special characters will also produce this result. Figure 4.13 shows an example of this.

A more positive way to join two items is with the concatenation operator "¦ ¦" (see Figure 4.14). The symbol for concatenation is two of the broken vertical strokes found on the keyboard. Please note that on some systems, particularly the IBM mainframes, you must use the solid vertical bar or the "[" symbol. Try these out on your system and highlight the one that works for you.

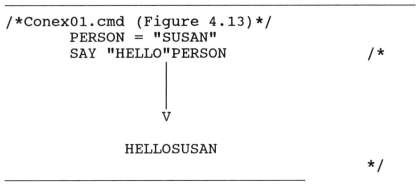

Figure 4.13. An example of concatenating with no space by juxtaposition.

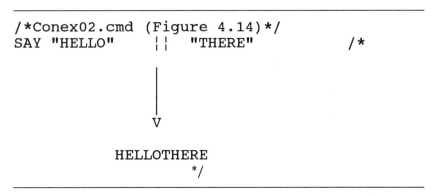

Figure 4.14. An example of concatenating with no space using the concatenation operator.

CONCATENATING WITH ONE SPACE

If you put two items next to each other with one or more spaces between them, one space will remain (see Figure 4.15). Remember this rule: One or more spaces become one space.

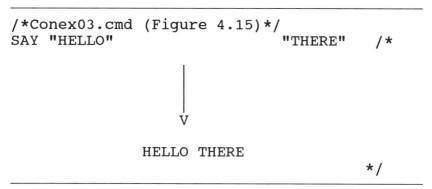

```
/*Conex03.cmd (Figure 4.15)*/
SAY "HELLO"                    "THERE"    /*



                    |
                    V

          HELLO  THERE

                                    */
```

Figure 4.15. An example of concatenating with a space.

4.6 QUESTIONS/PROBLEMS

1. What must a REXX program always start with?

2. What word or instruction in REXX means to display on the monitor?

3. What does this program do?

```
/*ch04p03.cmd*/
X = 10
Y = 20
Z = Y - X
SAY "THE ANSWER IS " Z
```

4. Do these have correct syntax?

   A. SAY "HELLO";SAY "GOODBYE"

   B. SAY "HELLO";

```
SAY;

"GOODBYE"
```

C.   COMPUTE;   C = 3 + 4

5. True or false: A label is the target of an instruction that transfers control to it.

6. True or false: The instruction EXIT must always be the very last line in the program.

7. Will REXX try to execute this line?

BARK "HELLO"

8. Write a program to execute the OS/2 commands:

PATH
DIR *.CMD /P

Include the comment:

This is a sample program

9. What does this program do?

```
/*ch04p09.cmd*/
SAY Greeting
```

10. What does this program do?

```
/*ch04p10.cmd*/
GREETING = "HELLO"
SAY GREETING
```

11. Can you tell what this does? Try it out if you don't know.

```
/*ch04p11.cmd*/
GREETING = "HAPPY HALLOWEEN"
SAY GREETING
DROP GREETING
SAY GREETING
```

12. What does this display on the screen?
```
/*ch04p12.CMD*/
SAY '323334'X
```

13. Write a program that displays these lines exactly as shown:

3 + 1 is 4

3 + 1 is 4'

O'brien

14. Which variable names are invalid and why?

A. 1_time only
B. PrOgRaMmEr_nAmE
C. prog_name"
D. input-data
E. Say

15. What does this program print out?

```
/*ch04p15.cmd*/
MESSAGE = MESSAGE
SAY MESSAGE
EXIT
```

16. In a program, assign the number 10 to a variable. Assign the number 20 to another variable. In one instruction display the total of the two.

17. First assign the variable DRIVE the value of your hard disk drive letter. Then execute the OS/2 command DIR followed by a disk drive letter:

DIR   disk drive letter

18. When this prints out, will there be a space between Sam and Antha?

SAY "SAM"   ¦ ¦   "ANTHA"

19. When this prints out, how many spaces will there be between Kelly and Beth?

SAY "KELLY"   "BETH"

Chapter 5

THE BASICS: SOME SIMPLE REXX VERBS

This chapter will get you started writing REXX. It is about the most common REXX verbs and a few OS/2 commands. You can try out all the sample programs shown on your system. There is a lot more to REXX, but this will start things in motion.

Topics

5.1   SAY: DISPLAY ON SCREEN

SAY is REXX's way of displaying data on the screen. Anything to the right of SAY is shown on your monitor. Please note that SAY is a REXX verb and that REXX verbs are not put inside of apostrophes or quotation marks. Here are some of the things you may display with SAY:

```
/*SAYIT.CMD(Section
5.1)*/
```
Literals: `SAY "Hello"`

Variables: `LAST_NAME = "Dupont"`

```
SAY LAST_NAME
```
Both literals and variables: `SAY "Hello" LAST_NAME`

Functions: `SAY LENGTH("ABCDEF")`

Expressions: `SAY 1 + 1`

```
SAY 'Hello' ¦¦ LAST_NAME
```

5.2   ASSIGNMENT

Assignment is making a variable equal to some value. Assignment takes the place of variable definitions or declarations. There is no variable definition or declaration in REXX. The first time a variable is used is when it is given a value. You may give it a value consisting of any one of the following:

```
/*ASGT.CMD    (Section
5.2)*/
```
Literals: `Greeting =  "Hello there"`

```
Say Greeting
```
Variables: `LAST_NAME = "Smith"`

```
Say LAST_NAME
```
Both literals and variables: `Sentence = "Hi" LAST_NAME`

```
Say Sentence
```
Functions: `Its_len =  LENGTH("ABC")`

```
Say Its_len
```
Expressions: `Sum = 1 + 1`

```
Say Sum
Sentence = 'Hi' ¦¦,
LAST_NAME
Say Sentence
```

5.3   PULL: ACCEPTING INPUT FROM THE KEYBOARD

PULL is the verb REXX uses to capture whatever you type in at the keyboard. Before doing a PULL, you must use SAY to display a message on the monitor asking for some specific input. Then PULL stops the program until you type in something. When you press ENTER your line of input is PULLed into the program, and the program resumes.

```
/*PULLEXMP.CMD (Section 5.3)*/
Say 'Please type in your name'
PULL name
Say 'Thank you,' name
```

5.4 ARG: ACCEPTING DATA SPECIFIED AT EXECUTION

ARG is what you use when you wish to capture the word or words typed in
to the right of the program's name when it is executed. For example, examine
the program in Figure 5.1, named TRYARG.

```
/*TRYARG.CMD (Section 5.4)*/
ARG MESSAGE
Say 'The words typed in next to the program',
    'name were:' MESSAGE
```

Figure 5.1. Example of the use of ARG in a REXX program.

Suppose you execute the program shown in Figure 5.1 program this way:

```
C:\REXXPRGS\TRYARG     REXX under OS/2
```

The program would capture the words "REXX under OS/2" in the variable
MESSAGE and display them on the monitor. Please try out this program.
Please notice that anything you type in is converted to upper case. More
about this in the chapter on PARSE (Chapter 7).

5.5   EXIT: ENDING THE PROGRAM

EXIT ends your REXX program (see Figure 5.3) . If EXIT is the last word
in your program, you don't need it, since execution will stop when control
reaches the physical end of the program. The only REXX verb that will not
end the program when it is at the physical end of the program is RETURN,
which goes back from a subroutine to the point where the subroutine was first
called. Note, however, that if your program encounters a RETURN and you
did not CALL a subroutine, the RETURN ends your program just as EXIT
does.

Use EXIT just before your subroutines and/or error traps. Subroutines are discussed in Chapter 9, and error traps are explained in Chapter 14.

One thing to be careful about: Please don't put the REXX EXIT in quotes or apostrophes (Figure 5.2). If you do, REXX will not recognize it but will pass it to OS/2, which will recognize it and close your OS/2 Window or OS/2 Full Screen. If you wish to close the Window or Full Screen, then by all means use "EXIT" or 'EXIT'. Figure 5.3 is an example of a program that uses REXX EXIT to stop the program.

```
/*OS2EXIT.CMD (Figure 5.2)*/
Say 'This is a sample REXX program'
'EXIT'
Say 'This statement will not be executed'
Say 'because the Window was closed'
```

Figure 5.2. Example of how OS/2 EXIT stops the program and closes the OS/2 Window or Full Screen session.

```
/*EXITEXMP.CMD (Figure 5.3)*/
Say 'This is a sample REXX program'
EXIT
Say 'This statement will not be executed'
```

Figure 5.3. Example of how REXX EXIT stops the program.

5.6 '@ECHO OFF'

This is not a REXX verb, but you will use it very often in your REXX programs. It stops OS/2 from displaying any OS/2 commands that you execute in your program. OS/2 commands are not part of REXX, and so they are placed inside apostrophes or quotation marks. OS/2 displays them as they execute, unless you put the statement '@ECHO OFF' at the beginning of your REXX program, right after the initial comment.

OS/2 will not display REXX verbs (such as IF, SAY, DO) as they execute. In the following example OS/2 will not display any of the statements as they execute. It will carry out the DIR OS/2 command, which does a directory listing and displays the listing on the monitor.

```
/*USEECHO.CMD (Section 5.6)*/
'@ECHO OFF'
Directory_to_show = 'c:\rexxprgs\'
'DIR ' directory_to_show
```

Another way to stop OS/2 commands from being displayed is to prefix them with @, as in the following example:

```
/*USE@.CMD (Section 5.6)*/
Directory_to_show = 'c:\rexxprgs\'
'@DIR ' directory_to_show
```

5.7   QUESTIONS/PROBLEMS

1. Write a program that accepts an extension like .BAT, .CMD, .DAT from the command line when the program is executed. Use the extension in an OS/2 DIR command: DIR *.*extension*.

2. Write a program that asks for an extension like .BAT, .CMD, .DAT, then reads it in when it is typed in. Use the extension in an OS/2 DIR command: DIR *.*extension*.

3.   Redo the first problem in this chapter, but suppress the display of the OS/2 command DIR.

4. Add the REXX verb EXIT to the end of your solution to the first problem in this chapter. What is the effect?

5. Add the OS/2 command EXIT to the end of your solution to the first problem in this chapter. What is the effect?

Chapter 6

IF-THE CONDITIONAL

In this chapter I will acquaint you with REXX's conditional verb IF and show you the unique REXX verb NOP that does nothing. I will also show you what operators you have to use if you are making more than one comparison in the same IF. I will explain how the inexact comparison works. Finally, I will explain REXX's unique "strictly equal" comparison.

Topics

6.1   IF SYNTAX

The syntax of the REXX IF is very straightforward (see Figure 6.1). IF introduces a condition. It contains a question: Is one thing equal to another, greater than it, less than it, or some other comparison? The full list of comparisons you can make appears in Figures 6.2 and 6.3.

```
IF comparison
THEN one-instruction

IF comparison
THEN one-instruction
ELSE one-instruction

IF comparison THEN instruction;ELSE instr.
```

Figure 6.1. Possible forms of the IF.

The following are important points to remember about conditionals with IF:

- IF is followed by a comparison. A comparison is one of the following:
    - Variable operator variable
    - Variable operator literal
    - Literal operator variable
    - Expression operator variable
    - Expression operator literal
  or some other combination of variables, literals, and expressions.

- You may not omit variables as in COBOL. This is legal in COBOL, not REXX:
    IF A = 1 or 2 ....

- Operators are shown in Figures 6.2 and 6.3. English words such as EQUAL, AND, and OR are not allowed.

- THEN is required.

- THEN is followed by *one* instruction or by a DO END sequence (see Figure 6.6).
  — The instruction may be a REXX verb or an OS/2 command

- NOP may be used as a "do nothing" instruction.

- ELSE is not required. It too is followed by *one* instruction or by a DO END sequence (see Figure 6.6).

- IF THEN ELSE should be on separate lines.

- Case is significant in comparisons. "Sue" is not equal to "SUE".

=	Equal. If numeric, when compared algebraically. (1.0 is equal to 001.000.) If not numeric, when padded with leading or trailing spaces. ("Sue" is equal to " Sue ".) Case is significant: "SUE" is not equal to "sue".
<>	Not equal, the negation of "=". Algebraic comparison and padding are performed.
><	Not equal, the negation of "=". Algebraic comparison and padding are performed.
\=	Not equal, the negation of "=". Algebraic comparison and padding are performed.
¬=	Not equal, the negation of "=". (The symbol "¬" may not be found on all keyboards.) Algebraic comparison and padding are performed.
^=	Not equal, the negation of "=". (The symbol "^" may not be found on all keyboards.) Algebraic comparison and padding are performed.
>	Greater than. Algebraic comparison and padding are performed.
<	Less than. Algebraic comparison and padding are performed.
>=	Greater than or equal to. Algebraic comparison and padding are performed.
¬<	Not less than. (The symbol "¬" may not be found on all keyboards.) Algebraic comparison and padding are performed.
\<	Not less than. Algebraic comparison and padding are performed.
<=	Less than or equal to. Algebraic comparison and padding are performed.
¬>	Not greater than. (The symbol "¬" may not be found on all keyboards.) Algebraic comparison and padding are performed.

Figure 6.2. Comparison operators. Part 1.

\>   Not greater than. Algebraic comparison and padding are performed.

==   Strictly equal on a character-by-character basis. No algebraic comparison or padding is done.

¬==   Strictly not equal, the negation of "==". (The symbol "¬" may not be found on all keyboards.) No algebraic comparison or padding is done.

\==   Strictly not equal, the negation of "==". No algebraic comparison or padding is done.

>>   Strictly greater than. No algebraic comparison or padding is done.

>>=   Strictly greater than or equal to. No algebraic comparison or padding is done.

<<   Strictly less than. No algebraic comparison or padding is done.

<<=   Strictly less than or equal to. No algebraic comparison or padding is done.

¬>>   Strictly not greater than. (The symbol "¬" may not be found on all keyboards.) No algebraic comparison or padding is done.

¬<<   Strictly not less than. (The symbol "¬" may not be found on all keyboards.) No algebraic comparison or padding is done.

&   And. The conditions on both sides of this operator must be true.

¦   Or. One or both of the conditions on either side of this operator must be true.

&&   Exclusive Or. Only one, but not both, of the conditions on either side of this operator must be true.

Figure 6.3. Comparison operators. Part 2.

6.2 HOW EQUAL IS EQUAL?

REXX doesn't always do things the same way other languages do. You may have noticed in Figures 6.2 and 6.3 that REXX has two "equal" operators, "=" and "==". Let's see how they are different:

- With numbers, "=" means numerically equivalent; for example, .01 and 000.010 are numerically equivalent. This will work only if both things being compared are valid numbers.

- With character strings, "=" considers leading and trailing spaces as equivalent. "   Apples   " is equal to "Apples".

- The strictly equal operator, "==", means "equal in all respects." So .01 and 000.010 wouldn't be equal, and "   Apples   " and "Apples" wouldn't be equal.

Figure 6.4 contains several examples of IF in REXX. I invite you to try them out on your system and experiment with them.

6.3 USING NOP

Sometimes you don't want to do anything at all when a condition is true but want to do something when a condition is false. In that case, you can use the verb NOP. NOP does nothing — it is a place holder. Figure 6.5 shows several examples of NOP.

Using NOP after ELSE is not useful except in a nested IF to ensure that every IF has its own ELSE.

6.4 MORE THAN ONE INSTRUCTION

Often you need to execute more than one instruction after the THEN or the ELSE. In that case you may use the DO END sequence (see Figure 6.6). All the instructions between the DO and the END are performed one after another. Every DO must have its END. It is very important to indent properly so that the DOs match with their ENDs and the program is thus readable.

```
/*ifex01.cmd (Figure 6.5)*/

IF "HI" = "hi"              /* case is significant */
THEN SAY "YES"             /*IT SAYS NO*/
ELSE SAY "NO"

A = 1                       /*MAKE A EQUAL 1*/
IF A = 1
THEN SAY "YES"             /*IT SAYS YES*/
ELSE SAY "NO"

IF A = 2
THEN SAY "YES"
ELSE SAY "NO"              /*IT SAYS NO*/


IF A = 2 THEN SAY "YES";ELSE SAY "NO" /*IT SAYS NO*/


IF A < 3
THEN SAY "LESS THAN 3"    /*LESS THAN 3*/


NAME = "JOHN"
OTHER_NAME = "    JOHN         "
IF NAME == OTHER_NAME
THEN SAY "STRICTLY EQUAL"
ELSE SAY "NOT STRICTLY EQUAL"   /*NOT STRICTLY*/


IF 1.0000000 = 00000001.00
THEN SAY "EQUAL"                    /*EQUAL*/
IF 1.0000000 == 00000001.00
THEN SAY "STRICTLY EQUAL"      /*NO!  */
ELSE SAY "NOT STRICTLY EQUAL"   /*NOT STRICTLY*/
```

Figure 6.4. Examples of IF.

```
/*ifex02.cmd (Figure 6.5)*/
A = 1                                    /*MAKE A EQUAL 1*/

IF A = 2
THEN NOP
ELSE SAY "NO"                            /*IT SAYS NO*/


IF A = 2 THEN NOP;ELSE SAY "NO" /*IT SAYS NO*/


IF A < 3
THEN SAY "LESS THAN 3"                   /*LESS THAN 3*/
ELSE NOP

IF TIME() < "16:00:00"
THEN NOP
ELSE SAY "TIME TO GO HOME "
```

Figure 6.5. Examples of NOP.

```
/*ifex03.cmd (Figure 6.6)*/
A = 5
B = 5
IF A = B
THEN
    DO
       SAY "A is equal to B"
       A = B - 1
       SAY "but now it isn't"
    END
ELSE
    DO
       SAY "A is not equal to B"
       SAY "how could that be?"
    END
```

Figure 6.6. An example of an IF with a DO END sequence.

6.5 FUZZ: THE INEXACT COMPARISON

FUZZ tells REXX to ignore one or more digits in a comparison; REXX will ignore the least significant (see Figure 6.7). The plus sign (+) in the examples ensures that REXX will do a numeric, not a character, comparison.

```
/*fuz01.cmd (Figure 6.7)  */
 /* Normally:*/

 IF +987654321 = +987654320
 THEN SAY "EQUAL"
 ELSE SAY "NOT EQUAL "     /* NOT EQUAL */

 /*but         */

 NUMERIC FUZZ 1             /*ignore one digit */
 IF +987654321 = +987654320
 THEN SAY "EQUAL"           /* are equal */
 ELSE SAY "NOT EQUAL "

 /*also        */

 NUMERIC FUZZ 2             /*ignore two digits*/
 IF +987654321 = +987654300
 THEN SAY "EQUAL"           /* are equal */
 ELSE SAY "NOT EQUAL "
```

Figure 6.7. The action of FUZZ.

FUZZ is affected by arithmetic precision, which is the number of digits REXX is using in arithmetic operations. This defaults to 9 but can be changed by the NUMERIC DIGITS instruction. If you have too few significant digits in your comparison, the FUZZ will do nothing. Assuming the default of nine significant digits, then NUMERIC FUZZ 1 says, "Out of the nine significant digits, ignore one low-order digit."

In Figure 6.7, the default precision is 9. In the first comparison the two numbers are unequal, as they would be everywhere else on earth. In the second comparison they are equal because NUMERIC FUZZ 1 told REXX to ignore the low-order digit. In the third comparison NUMERIC FUZZ 2 told REXX to ignore the two low-order digits, and REXX found the numbers equal.

Let's follow that logic a bit and see how it works. In Figure 6.8 the comparison is not equal because there are only four actual digits, not nine. So FUZZ can't work.

```
/*fuz02.cmd (Figure 6.8)*/
/* no Fuzzing here */
 NUMERIC FUZZ 1

 IF +5432 = +5430
 THEN SAY "EQUAL"
 ELSE SAY "NOT EQUAL"
/*not equal because there aren't 9 actual
digits*/
```

Figure 6.8. An example of FUZZ not giving equality.

Figure 6.9, on the other hand, has five actual digits in the comparison; that is what we told REXX with NUMERIC DIGITS 5. Since we told REXX there were five and there actually are five, FUZZ works.

```
/*fuz03.cmd (Figure 6.9)*/
/* Fuzzing */
NUMERIC DIGITS 5
NUMERIC FUZZ 1
IF +65432 = +65430    /*is equal*/
THEN SAY "EQUAL"
ELSE SAY "NOT EQUAL"
/* equal because there are 5 actual digits */
```

Figure 6.9. An example of FUZZ giving equality.

Almost finished. Figure 6.10 is like Figure 6.9, except that we lied to REXX: there are only four actual digits (leading zeros don't count). We said there were five, but there are only four, so FUZZ doesn't work.

```
/*fuz04.cmd (Figure 6.10) */
/* No fuzzing */
NUMERIC DIGITS 5

NUMERIC FUZZ 1

IF +05432 = +05430   /*not equal */
THEN SAY "EQUAL"
ELSE SAY "NOT EQUAL"
/* not equal because there aren't  5 actual
digits (leading zeros don't count)*/
```

Figure 6.10. An example of FUZZ not giving equality.

Finally, in Figure 6.11 we take back our lie, telling REXX there are four significant digits. There are four actual digits, so FUZZ works.

```
/*fuz05.cmd (Figure 6.11)*/
/* Fuzzing */
NUMERIC DIGITS 4
NUMERIC FUZZ 1
IF +05432 = +05430     /* equal */
THEN SAY "EQUAL"
ELSE SAY "NOT EQUAL"
/* equal because there are 4 actual digits */
```

Figure 6.11. An example of FUZZ giving equality.

6.6 BOOLEAN OPERATORS

Boolean operators allow you to do more than one comparison. Figure 6.12 shows the symbols that REXX uses for AND, OR, and Exclusive OR. Please note that you must use these operators, not the English words AND or OR. The symbol for OR is the broken vertical stroke (¦) that is found on standard PC keyboards. On some systems you must use the vertical stroke or the left bracket ([) symbol instead. Try these out on your system and highlight the one that works for you.

    &   AND

    ¦   OR: either one, or both

    &&   Exclusive OR: one is true,
                  not both.

Figure 6.12. Boolean operators.

In Figure 6.13 you will see several examples of Boolean operators in action. Notice how difficult it may be to find a good use for the Exclusive OR.

```
/*bol01.cmd (Figure 6.13)*/
IF TODAY = "MONDAY"        ¦    TODAY = "TUESDAY"
THEN SAY "HI HO! HI HO! OFF TO WORK I GO"

IF APPLICANT_A = WALKS ON WATER"  &&,
APPLICANT_A2="CAN SWIM UNDER WATER 12 MINUTES"
THEN SAY "YOU'RE HIRED "
ELSE  SAY "SOUNDS FISHY TO ME"

IF DISH_CONTENTS_A = 'DILL PICKLES' &&,
   DISH_CONTENTS_B = 'CHOCOLATE MOUSSE'
THEN SAY 'YUMMY'
ELSE SAY 'YUCK '
```

Figure 6.13. Examples of Boolean operators.

6.7 STYLE

Here are some suggestions regarding style:

- Place the IF, the THEN, and the ELSE on separate lines.

```
IF NAME = "POLLY"
THEN SAY "GRAF"
ELSE SAY "GLOTT"
```

- Indent each DO and its corresponding END equally.

```
IF A = 1
THEN
  DO
    SAY "A IS EQUAL TO 1"
    SAY "DID YOU KNOW THAT?"
  END
```

- Use identical comments on each DO and its corresponding END, especially when nesting DOs and ENDs.

```
/*doex02.cmd (Section 6.7)*/
  IF DAY = "SATURDAY" ¦ DAY = "SUNDAY"
  THEN
    DO /* WEEKEND */
      IF WEATHER = "FINE"
      THEN
        DO  /* WEATHER FINE */
            SAY "HEAD FOR TENNIS COURT"
        END /* WEATHER FINE */
      ELSE
        DO  /* WEATHER INCLEMENT */
            SAY "HEAD FOR SHOPPING MALL"
        END /* WEATHER INCLEMENT */
    END /* WEEKEND  */
  ELSE
    DO  /* WORK */
      SAY "HEAD FOR OFFICE"
    END /* WORK */
```

• Limit nesting to two or three levels. Use subroutines instead of confusing the reader with IF within IF within IF within IF within IF, and so on.

6.8 QUESTIONS/PROBLEMS

1. Is 43 = 4.3E1?

2. Is 43 = = 4.3E1?

3. Complete this program segment:

```
/*CH06P03Q.CMD*/
/* Won't work. Please fix it*/
NUMBER = +98765
IF NUMBER        +12345
THEN

    SAY "THE NUMBER IS 12345"
END
ELSE SAY "I DON'T KNOW WHAT IT IS EQUAL TO"
```

4. Write a program that will store the number 12 as a constant and store the number 13 as a constant. Then write the instructions that will compare the numbers and find them equal.

5. What does this program display?
```
A = 5
B = 4
SAY A = B
```

6. What does this program display? Try it to find out.

```
A = 2 + 2 = 2
SAY A
```

7. Write a program that will ask for a number (a temperature), then another number. Compare the two numbers. If the first is lower than the second, display 'rising'. If the second is lower than the first, display 'falling'. If the two numbers are equal, display 'steady'.

Chapter 7

STRING MANIPULATION:
THE PARSE INSTRUCTION

This chapter is about a REXX capability that sets it apart from all other languages. A language that shines in the area of string manipulation can really allow you to write concise, streamlined programs. I believe that REXX excels here. I urge you to really study this chapter and try it out on your system until you are completely comfortable with parsing in REXX.

Topics

87

7.1 GENERAL FORM OF THE PARSE INSTRUCTION

Refer to Figure 7.1 for a generalized form of the PARSE instruction. Notice that it consists of four parts: PARSE, UPPER, an origin, and a template. Let's look at each of these in turn.

PARSE [UPPER] origin template

origins   *templates*

ARG   list of variables
LINEIN   column delimiters
PULL   literal delimiters
SOURCE
VALUE
VAR
VERSION

Figure 7.1. The general form of the PARSE instruction.

• **PARSE.** The instruction starts with the keyword PARSE, although it may sometimes be left out, as we will see later.

• **UPPER.** UPPER is optional: If you specify it, the data will be converted to upper case. If you don't specify it, the data is left as it was, upper and lower mixed.

• **ORIGIN.** The origin is where the data comes from. Figure 7.1 contains a list of the possible origins. Note that PARSE works the same way regardless of the origin of the data.

• **TEMPLATE.** The template acts as a filter on the data, influencing the way the data is placed in the destination variable(s).

7.2 ABBREVIATIONS OF PARSE

Because an instruction like PARSE UPPER ARG is somewhat cumbersome, REXX allows you to abbreviate. You may say ARG instead of PARSE

UPPER ARG. In fact, you will rarely see PARSE UPPER ARG in any REXX program. The same goes for PARSE UPPER PULL. You may abbreviate that as PULL. Recall that PARSE ARG will *not* convert to upper case.

7.3 FUNCTION OF PARSING

Figure 7.2 is a schematic of how PARSE works. PARSE takes data from the origin, passes it through a template, and distributes the data into variables. Whenever you execute the PARSE instruction, all the variables are changed (with PARSE VAR the data comes from a source variable that is not changed). Some of the variables may receive a NULL value, that is, zero characters, but they are changed nevertheless.

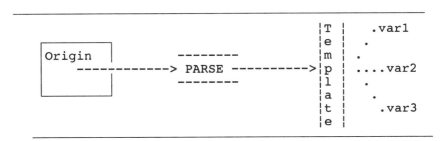

Figure 7.2. What PARSE does.

The template tells REXX exactly how to split up the data and put it into the variables in the template. The template may consist of the following:

- Just the variables (space is delimiter)
- Numbers designating columns (columns are delimiters)
- Literals (a specific character string is a delimiter)

7.4 PARSE ORIGINS

Let's look at the different origins of the data that is PARSEd (see Figure 7.3).

```
 origin of information              PARSE keyword

Command line -------------------> ARG
The REXX data queue/keyboard----> PULL
Keyboard -----------------------> LINEIN
Variable -----------------------> VAR
Literal/function----------------> VALUE
OS/2 info on how program
        was executed ------------> SOURCE
Version/release information ----> VERSION
```

Figure 7.3. Origins — where the information comes from on a PARSE.

- *Command line.* (PARSE ARG, ARG). When you execute the program you may place arguments, or items of data, on the same line as the command that executes the program. Your program receives these items through an ARG.

- *REXX data queue and keyboard.* (PARSE PULL, PULL). The REXX data queue is an internal data queue that OS/2 maintains for the benefit of REXX programs. PULL receives an item of data from the data queue, which is also used to receive information typed in at the keyboard.

- *Keyboard.* (PARSE LINEIN) You can receive whatever is typed in at the keyboard. There is no interaction with the data queue.

- *Variable.* (PARSE VAR) A variable may contain a string of characters consisting of any number of words, characters, spaces, or special characters. PARSE VAR allows you to break up that variable into several others.

- *Literal.* (PARSE VALUE) The data is specified in a literal or in a function instead of a literal. The keyword WITH is required in order to tell where the literal ends.

- *Internal information.* (PARSE SOURCE) You can use this to see which operating system you are running under: OS/2, TSO, or CMS.

- *Version/release*. (PARSE VERSION) You can find out what version of REXX you are running.

7.5 PARSING ARGUMENTS IN A MAIN PROGRAM

A "main program" is one that is executed from an OS/2 Window, OS/2 Full Screen, or the REXX program directory. In Figure 7.4 PARSE UPPER ARG receives anything you type in next to the REXX program name when you execute. Information is passed into the variables that you specify on the PARSE UPPER ARG instruction.

In the example in Figure 7.4 data is passed word by word; it is delimited by one or more spaces, with each word going into a different variable. You may not use commas between the variables on a PARSE ARG in a main program for a very good reason: it will not work. Please note that you may use as many variables as you want, while OS/2 batch files are limited to nine.

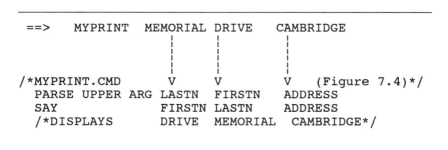

Figure 7.4. PARSE UPPER ARG receives information from the command line. The symbol = = > shows what was keyed in at the terminal.

PARSE UPPER ARG may be abbreviated as ARG, as shown in Figure 7.5, with the same results as in Figure 7.4.

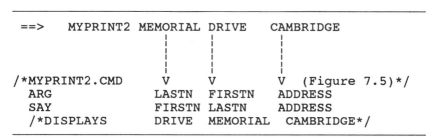

Figure 7.5. ARG receives information from the command line. The symbol = = > shows what was keyed in.

7.6 PARSING ARGUMENTS IN A FUNCTION OR SUBROUTINE

The PARSE ARG or ARG instruction is also used in a user-written function or subroutine. It acts like the PARSE ARG in a main program (see Figure 7.6). The main difference is that you *may* use commas between variables. In fact, I urge you to use them because that is how built-in REXX functions or subroutines do it. This subject is covered more fully in Chapter 14 on user-written functions/subroutines.

```
/*Parsarg.cmd (Figure 7.6)*/
CALL MYSUBR 1,2
SAY RESULT
EXIT

MYSUBR:
PARSE ARG NUMB1, NUMB2
RETURN NUMB1 + NUMB2
```

Figure 7.6. PARSE ARG in a user-written subroutine.

7.7 PARSING FROM THE DATA QUEUE AND KEYBOARD

Figure 7.7 shows the function of PULL. If there is nothing in the data queue, PARSE UPPER PULL and its abbreviation PULL receive any information you type in at the keyboard. Normally there is nothing in the data queue (unless you put it there with PUSH or QUEUE), so you can generally use this instruction to get information from the keyboard.

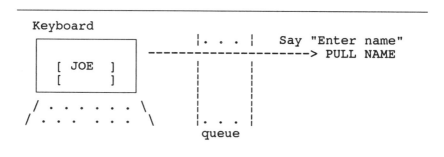

Figure 7.7. The function of the PULL instruction.

Figure 7.8 shows an example of how you might use PULL to get information from the keyboard.

```
/* parspul.cmd (Figure 7.8)*/
SAY "PLEASE ENTER YOUR NAME"
PULL NAME
SAY "THANK YOU, "    NAME
SAY " FOR ENTERING YOUR NAME "
```

Figure 7.8. Using PULL to get information from the keyboard.

7.8 PARSING FROM THE KEYBOARD ONLY

PARSE LINEIN will take information from the keyboard but not from the data queue. Use it when you don't want to interfere with the data queue. Figure 7.9 shows the function of PARSE LINEIN, and Figure 7.10 shows an example of its use.

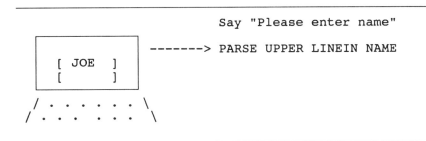

Figure 7.9. Another way of receiving information from the keyboard.

```
/*parslin.cmd (Figure 7.10)*/
SAY "PLEASE ENTER YOUR NAME"
PARSE UPPER LINEIN NAME
SAY "THANK YOU, "    NAME
SAY " FOR ENTERING YOUR NAME "
```

Figure 7.10. Using PARSE LINEIN to get information from the keyboard.

7.9 PARSING A VARIABLE

By parsing a variable, you can split up its contents into one or more other variables. Figure 7.11 shows an example of this.

```
/* parsvar.cmd (Figure 7.11)*/
NAME = "CAL A. MAZOO"
PARSE VAR NAME    FIRST MIDDLE LAST
SAY "YOUR MIDDLE INITIAL IS " MIDDLE
```

Figure 7.11. PARSE VAR.

7.10 PARSING A LITERAL: VALUE

In Figure 7.12 you will see an example of PARSE VALUE with a literal and an example with a function as well. REXX needs the keyword WITH so it can tell where the template begins. Using a literal doesn't seem to be very useful, but you may use a function instead. This figure uses the function DATE(), which gives the date in the form: 25 Dec 1994. We can split the date into three parts: Day, Month, and Year, by a PARSE VALUE.

```
/* parsval.cmd (Figure 7.12)*/
PARSE VALUE "THIS IS A SAMPLE" WITH A B C D
PARSE VALUE DATE() WITH DAY MONTH YEAR
SAY A
SAY B
SAY C
SAY D
SAY
SAY DAY
SAY MONTH
SAY YEAR
```

Figure 7.12. PARSE VALUE.

7.11 PARSE SOURCE

PARSE SOURCE asks OS/2 for information about the way the program was executed. There is an example of that in Figure 7.13. Please note that the TSO and the CMS versions of PARSE SOURCE work differently. They have a different number of variables.

You may use the variable names I have used or any others that are suitable. Figure 7.14 shows you what OS/2 may put in these variables when you execute the instruction.

```
/* parssor.cmd (Figure 7.13)*/

PARSE SOURCE OP_SYSTEM HOW_CALLED FILE_SPEC
SAY OP_SYSTEM
SAY HOW_CALLED
SAY FILE_SPEC
```

Figure 7.13. PARSE SOURCE on OS/2.

```
OP_SYSTEM        OS/2


HOW_CALLED       COMMAND, SUBROUTINE,
                 or FUNCTION.


FILE_SPEC        Your program's complete
                 file specification.
                 For example:
                 C:\REXXPRGS\TRYPARSE.CMD
```

Figure 7.14. What goes into the variables on the PARSE SOURCE instruction.

7.12 PARSE VERSION

You can find out what version of REXX you have. Figure 7.15 shows how. Try this out on your system to see which level of REXX you have and when it was created.

```
/* parsver.cmd (Figure 7.15)*/
PARSE VERSION LANGUAGE LEVEL DAY MONTH YEAR
SAY "MY LEVEL OF REXX IS " LEVEL
SAY "CREATED " DAY MONTH YEAR
```

Figure 7.15. PARSE VERSION.

7.13 THE TEMPLATE WITH JUST VARIABLES

The template is essentially a list of variables, into which PARSE puts data. By using different types of templates you can gain more control over how information is put into the variables.

Figure 7.16 shows a PARSE ARG with only variables in the template. Remember that the other forms of PARSE, PARSE PULL, PARSE VAR, and so forth, will work the same way. The information on the command line is placed in the variables shown in the instruction, with blanks delimiting what goes into each. One word goes into each variable (a word is separated from the next by spaces). In this example there are just as many words as variables, so each word goes into a different variable, and each variable gets a word. The words are placed in the variables in the same order they were entered.

Please don't use commas in a main program's ARG to delimit words. Use spaces instead. It is only on a function/subroutine that commas may be used on an ARG.

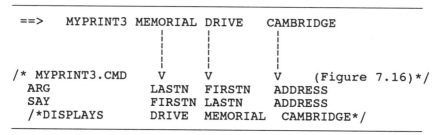

Figure 7.16. Just variables in the template.

7.14 MORE VARIABLES THAN WORDS

If you have extra variables on the instruction, they will contain nothing; they are made null. In Figure 7.17 FORTH contains nothing (null).

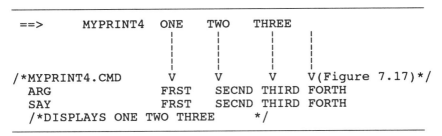

```
==>      MYPRINT4  ONE    TWO     THREE
                    |      |        |      |
                    |      |        |      |
                    |      |        |      |
                    |      |        |      |
/*MYPRINT4.CMD       V      V        V      V(Figure 7.17)*/
   ARG              FRST   SECND  THIRD  FORTH
   SAY              FRST   SECND  THIRD  FORTH
   /*DISPLAYS ONE TWO THREE        */
```

Figure 7.17. More variables than words.

7.15 MORE WORDS THAN VARIABLES

When there are more words than variables that can receive them, REXX puts the extra words in the last variable. In Figure 7.18 there are three variables and four items of data. The last two are put in the third variable.

```
==>    MYPRINT5     ONE    TWO    3  4
                     |      |     |  |
                     |      |     |  |
                     |      |     |  |
                     |      |     |  |
/* MYPRINT5.CMD       V      V     V  V (Figure 7.18)*/
   PARSE   ARG       FRST   SECND THIRD
   SAY               FRST   SECND THIRD
   /*DISPLAYS        ONE    TWO   3 4        */
```

Figure 7.18. More words than variables.

7.16 DROPPING EXTRA WORDS

If you know there are going to be extra items of information, you can throw them away by using a period instead of a variable. The period absorbs the data that goes into it and throws it away. Use the period to ignore extra words or items. There is an example of this in Figure 7.19. The period does not have to be last, so it can be used as a place holder.

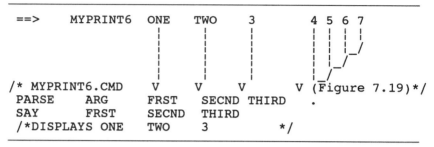

Figure 7.19. A period absorbing extra words.

7.17 A LITERAL IN A TEMPLATE

A literal character in a template will influence the way data is distributed into the variables. REXX will search for that literal character in the data. If it finds it, it will put all the data that is before the character into the variables that are before the literal character. Then it will place all the data that is after the character into the variables that are after the literal character.

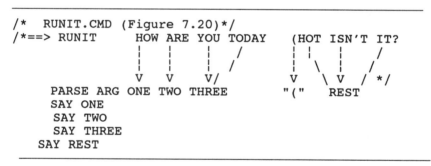

Figure 7.20. A literal in a template.

In Figure 7.20 REXX will search for the left parenthesis. When it finds it, it will split the *data* into two parts, the part before the parenthesis and the part after the parenthesis. Then it splits the *variables* into two parts the same way and then distributes the data. Anything before the left parenthesis goes into ONE, TWO, and THREE. Anything after goes into REST. What is unique about this is that the "before," or left side, has nothing to do with the "after," or right side. One side doesn't influence the other. It is as if there were two separate PARSE instructions. See Figure 7.21 for another example.

```
/*PARSARG2.CMD (Figure 7.21)          */
   PARSE UPPER ARG      QUESTION "?" ANSWER
   SAY "QUESTION" QUESTION
   SAY "ANSWER"   ANSWER

 /*EXECUTED WITH ==> PARSARG2 WHAT'S MY NAME? TONY*/

 /*DISPLAYS     QUESTION WHAT'S MY NAME      */
 /*             ANSWER TONY                  */
```

Figure 7.21. An example of PARSE ARG with a literal delimiter.

You might be wondering what happens if the data does not contain the literal character. If that happens, the variables to the right of the literal character are set to null.

A very important thing to note is that the literal string may consist of one or more characters. This enables you to search for a specific word or sequence of characters. Figure 7.22 shows an example.

```
/*PARSARG3.CMD (Figure 7.22)     */
   PARSE UPPER ARG      QUESTION "??" ANSWER
   SAY "QUESTION" QUESTION
   SAY "ANSWER"   ANSWER

 /*EXECUTED WITH ==> PARSARG3 WHAT'S MY NAME?? TONY*/

 /*DISPLAYS     QUESTION WHAT'S MY NAME      */
 /*             ANSWER TONY                  */
```

Figure 7.22. An example of PARSE ARG with a two-character literal delimiter.

Figure 7.23 is a useful example of something you might do with this facility. It illustrates how you can break up a file specification into its component parts. A typical file specification is put into the variable FILE_SPEC. Then in the first PARSE it is broken into two pieces: *drive* and *rest_of_name*. In the second PARSE rest_of_name is broken into directory, file_name and extension.

```
/* parsname.cmd (Figure 7.23)*/
/* breaks up a file specification into
component parts */
FILE_SPEC = "C:\REXXPRGS\MYPROG.CMD"
PARSE VAR FILE_SPEC DRIVE ":" REST_OF_NAME
PARSE VAR REST_OF_NAME "\" DIRECTORY     "\"
FILE_NAME "." EXTENSION
SAY 'The drive was:     '   DRIVE
SAY 'The directory was:'   DIRECTORY
SAY 'The file name was:'   FILE_NAME
SAY 'The extension was:'   EXTENSION
```

Figure 7.23. Breaking up a typical file specification using PARSE and literal strings.

7.18 A VARIABLE INSTEAD OF A LITERAL

You may want to change the literal delimiter you use. If so, you can put it in a variable. However, you must enclose the variable in parentheses, so REXX will have a way of knowing that this particular variable contains a literal delimiter. Figure 7.24 illustrates this. The variable SLSH could have contained any other literal delimiter.

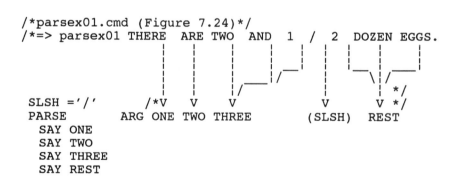

Figure 7.24. Using a variable instead of a literal.

Figure 7.25 shows a way of picking up the first character in a data string and using it as a delimiter later on in the same string. The PARSE picks up the first character, no matter what it is, and uses it as a delimiter later on in the same instruction.

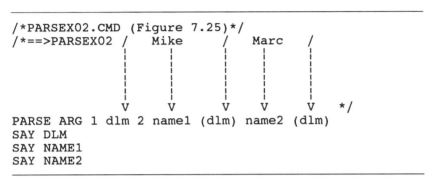

```
/*PARSEX02.CMD (Figure 7.25)*/
/*==>PARSEX02 /    Mike      /    Marc    /
                 |         |        |       |       |
                 |         |        |       |       |
                 |         |        |       |       |
                 |         |        |       |       |
                 V         V        V       V       V    */
PARSE ARG 1 dlm 2 name1 (dlm) name2 (dlm)
SAY DLM
SAY NAME1
SAY NAME2
```

Figure 7.25. Using the first character as a delimiter.

7.19 COLUMN DELIMITING WITH SINGLE NUMBERS

Here is another way of breaking apart the data that allows you to split the data at specific columns. This allows you to use fixed-format data, instead of variable-format data, as in the methods I showed you earlier. When you use this method, spaces between words do not mean anything.

There is something tricky about this — the numbers don't mean exactly what they seem to. To tell what columns go into a variable, look at the numbers on either side of it. The number on the left is the start column, the number on the right, minus 1, is the end column.

To understand what is happening in Figure 7.26, look at the numbers around VAR1. One is the number on the left, so that is the start column. Five is the number on the right, so 5 minus 1, or 4, is the end column. Columns 1 through 4 go into VAR1. Similarly, VAR2 receives columns 5 through 8, and VAR3 receives columns 9 through 12.

```
/*PARSEX03.CMD (Figure 7.26)*/
/*==> PARSEX03 ABCDEFGHIJKLMNOP

                ABCD        EFGH        IJKL
                 |           |           |
                 V           V           V   */
PARSE ARG 1 VAR1     5       VAR2    9   VAR3 13
SAY VAR1
SAY VAR2
SAY VAR3
```

Figure 7.26. Column delimiting with single numbers.

7.20 COLUMN DELIMITING WITH TWO NUMBERS

This method allows you to skip columns and to put the same columns into two variables. To determine which columns go into a variable, you do the same thing as in the previous method: look at the numbers around it. The number on the left is the start column, and the number on the right, minus 1, is the end column.

In Figure 7.27 VAR1 is surrounded by 1 and 5, so VAR1 gets the data in columns 1 through 4. VAR2 is surrounded by 7 and 9, so VAR2 gets the data in columns 7 and 8. VAR3 is surrounded by 11 and 13, so columns 11 and 12 go into VAR3.

```
/*PARSEX04.CMD (Figure 7.27)*/
/*==> PARSEX04 ABCDEFGHIJKLMNOP

                ABCD        GH          KL
                 |           |           |
                 V           V           V   */
    PARSE ARG 1 VAR1 5    7 VAR2 9    11 VAR3 13
    SAY VAR1
    SAY VAR2
    SAY VAR3
```

Figure 7.27. Column delimiting with two numbers.

Figure 7.28 shows how to put the same data into two variables VAR1 and VAR3.

```
/*PARSEX05.CMD (Figure 7.28)*/
/*==>PARSEX05 1234567890ABCDEF

                    12            4            12
                    |            |            |
                    |            |            |
                    V            V            V   */
   PARSE UPPER ARG 1 VAR1 3   4 VAR2 5   1 VAR3   3
   SAY VAR1
   SAY VAR2
   SAY VAR3
```

Figure 7.28. An example of PARSE ARG with a column delimiter, putting the same data into two variables.

7.21 QUESTIONS/PROBLEMS

1. If you execute this program with the command shown, what are the results?

```
/* CH07P01.CMD    */
ARG YOUR_NAME ADDRESS "/" JUNK
SAY "YOUR NAME IS " YOUR_NAME
SAY "YOU LIVE AT  " ADDRESS
/*
= = > CH07P01 JOHN 22 1/2 MAY ST LIMA PERU
*/
```

2. If you execute this program with the command shown, what are the results?

```
/* CH07P02.CMD*/
ARG  2 YOUR_NAME 5 6 ADDRESS 9
SAY "YOUR NAME IS " YOUR_NAME
SAY "YOU LIVE AT  " ADDRESS
/*
= = > CH07P02 JOHN 22 1/2 MAY ST LIMA PERU
*/
```

3. Write a program that accepts two ARGS: day of week and weather. If the weather is sunny or cloudy and it is Friday, display "Head for Golf Course!" But if it's Friday and raining, display "Head for office!"

4. Write a program that breaks up the information contained in a variable into three variables. Place this information in the first variable VAR1:

ABCDEFGHIJKLMNOP

Use the proper PARSE instruction to break up the first variable this way:

VAR2 gets columns 3 and 4
VAR3 gets columns 6 through 9
VAR4 gets columns 9 through 14
Display VAR2
Display VAR3
Display VAR4

Expected results:

CD
FGHI
IJKLMN

5. What would this say

```
/*CH07P05.CMD */
ARG N1 N2 N3
SAY N2 N3 N1
```

if it is executed this way?

= = > CH07P05 MARYELLEN SUE KAREN

6. This ARG, and this manner of execution, produces what display?

```
/* CH07P06.CMD */
ARG NUM1 NUM2 NUM3 .
TOTAL = NUM1 + NUM2 + NUM3
SAY TOTAL
```

= = = > CH07P06 10 20 30 40 50 60

7. Write a program that accepts three pieces of information from the command line and displays them in reverse order. If more than three are entered, display an error message. Expected results:

= = > CH07P07 peter paul mary
MARY PAUL PETER
= = > CH07P07 peter paul mary ringo
I said enter only three items please!

8. You want the user to type in three and only three items (words) of information, separated by spaces. What does your PULL look like?

9. Write a program that asks you to type in three words (only) and displays them in reverse order. Expected results:

= = = > CH07P09
= = = > a b c
    C B A
= = = > CH07P09
= = = > a b c d
    C B A

10. Write a front-end program for the ERASE OS/2 command, named BYEBYE.CMD. Have it ask, "Are you sure?" before deleting. If the file specification is "junk.dat," don't ask. Expected results:

= = = > BYEBYE abc.dat
  ARE YOU SURE? Y/N
  = = = > n
  NOT DELETED
= = = > BYEBYE junk.dat
  DELETED

11. Write a program that computes the percent of increase of one number over another. Ask for the two amounts from the keyboard. The formula is

% increase = 100 * ((new - old) / old)

Imagine your old salary was $21,203 and your new is $80,000. You would figure the % increase as

% increase = 100 * ((80000 - 21203) / 21203)

Expected results:

= = = > CH07P11
Please enter your old salary
= = = > 100
Please enter your new salary
= = = > 120
 % increase is 20

12. Ask for the weather from the keyboard and the day of the week. If it is raining, ask how many inches. If it is Friday and sunny or cloudy, display "Head for golf course." If it is Saturday and less than a half inch, display "Fishing pole, please." Expected results:

= = = > CH07P12
  WHAT IS THE WEATHER?
= = = > SUNNY
  WHAT DAY OF THE WEEK?
= = = > FRIDAY
= = = > CH07P12

  HEAD FOR GOLF COURSE
= = = > CH07P12
  WHAT DAY OF THE WEEK?
= = = > SATURDAY
  WHAT IS THE WEATHER?
= = = > RAINING
  HOW MANY INCHES OF RAIN?
  .4
FISHING POLE PLEASE

Please keep the logic of this problem simple. A simple series of conditions would be quite adequate. Otherwise it may take several hours to complete.

Chapter 8

DEBUGGING

In this chapter I will show you the OS/2 commands and REXX verbs that affect debugging and interactive trace. I will show you how to stop your program during execution and how to turn on debugging. I will explain what you can do during interactive debugging and point out the instructions you can place in your exec that control debugging.

Topics

8.1 Turning on Interactive Debugging
8.2 What You Can Do During Interactive Debug
8.3 Codes Displayed During Interactive Debug
8.4 Non-Interactive Tracing
8.5 REXX Error Codes
8.6 Questions/Problems

8.1 TURNING ON INTERACTIVE DEBUGGING

You can turn on interactive debugging and view everything your program is doing and interact with it. There are three ways to turn on interactive debugging: from the command line in an OS/2 Window or OS/2 Full Screen before executing your program, in the Presentation Manager Window, and inside the program.

BEFORE EXECUTING
Figure 8.1 shows how to turn on interactive debugging before executing your program from the command line. (This did not work with my release of OS/2 (2.1); later releases may correct this failure.) You are setting an OS/2 environment variable, which makes OS/2 turn on interactive debugging when

it starts the REXX interpreter. This will affect all subsequent executions of REXX programs, so be sure to turn it off when you no longer need it. Figure 8.2 shows how to turn it off.

```
SET RXTRACE = ON
```

Figure 8.1. Turning on interactive debugging in an OS/2 Window or OS/2 Full Screen.

```
SET RXTRACE = OFF
```

Figure 8.2. Turning off interactive debugging in an OS/2 Window or OS/2 Full Screen.

PRESENTATION MANAGER

If you are executing your program using the Presentation Manager it is very easy to turn on interactive debugging. The display created by interactive debugging can be scrolled and even saved in a file.

You get into the Presentation Manager by putting the word PMREXX before your program name when you execute it in an OS/2 Window or OS/2 Full Screen (Figure 8.3). You can turn on interactive debugging before the program starts or after.

Figure 8.3. Executing a program with Presentation Manager.

To turn on interactive debugging immediately, type PMREXX /T *program name*. Interactive debugging will be on the moment the program starts. To turn on interactive debugging after the program starts, wait until the Presentation Manager window appears, then click on OPTIONS to turn on interactive debugging (Figure 8.4). Then click on interactive trace (Figure 8.5). What interactive debugging looks like is shown in Figure 8.6.

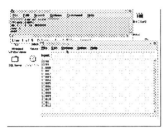

Figure 8.4. Starting up interactive debugging in a Presentation Manager window, part 1. Click on OPTIONS.

File   Edit   Options   Actions   Help
        Interactive trace on
        Set font   ▲

Figure 8.5. Starting up interactive debugging in a Presentation Manager window, part 2. Click on interactive trace.

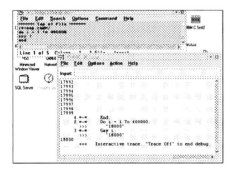

Figure 8.6. What interactive debugging looks like inside the Presentation Manager.

INSIDE THE PROGRAM

You can turn on interactive debugging by putting TRACE ?R or TRACE ?I inside your program. As soon as that statement is executed you will be in interactive debug.

8.2 WHAT YOU CAN DO DURING INTERACTIVE DEBUG

Interactive debug in REXX is truly amazing. Although your program is stopped, you can interact with it. You can view and change your program's variables and execute any instruction that would be legal inside the program. The only thing you may not do is change your program's statements. That will have to wait until you finish with interactive debug. Figure 8.7 lists some of the things you can do during interactive debug.

(ENTER)	single step execution
=	reexecute last command
TRACE ?	stop interactive debug
TRACE OFF	stop tracing
Any REXX verb	SAY "HI"
Any OS/2 command	"DIR"
Display variables	SAY NAME
Change variables	NAME = "MOE"
Assignment statement	NAME = "MOE"

Figure 8.7. What you can do during interactive debug.

When your program is in interactive debug, it stops after executing each instruction. You can then execute one instruction at a time just by pressing ENTER. This allows you to closely monitor your program's execution, since interactive debug gives you an automatic TRACE R, which displays the results of operations. Here are some of the things you can do during interactive debug:

- Execute the next instruction by pressing ENTER.
- Reexecute the last instruction that executed by typing "=". This is useful when you have just changed a variable and want to reexecute an instruction to see how it works this time.
- Display and change variables.
- Issue commands to OS/2 (enclosed in quotes, just as in REXX).
- End the program by typing EXIT.

- Display a line of your program with the SOURCELINE function: SAY SOURCELINE(line number).
- Display the entire program (this must be typed all on one line). DO I = 1 TO 9999;SAY SOURCELINE(I);END

8.3 CODES DISPLAYED DURING INTERACTIVE DEBUG

While your program is executing in interactive debug, REXX will display certain codes to tell you just what the display means. Figure 8.8 lists those codes.

```
*-* Original program line.

+++ Trace message.

>>> Result of an expression.   During TRACE R.

>.> Value assigned to a placeholder (period)
    during Parsing.

>C> The resolved name of a compound variable.

>F> Result of a function call.

>L> A literal.

>O> Result of an operation on two terms.

>P> Result of a prefix operation.

>V> Contents of a variable.
```

Figure 8.8. Codes displayed during interactive debug.

8.4 NON-INTERACTIVE TRACING

Figures 8.9 and 8.10 show some instructions you may put in your program that affect debugging. Most of these are non-interactive, that is your program does not stop and give you control. It continues to execute but displays certain items for you. You will most likely remove these instructions when your exec is ready for use. I have listed them in increasing order of things displayed.

If you put these instructions in your subroutines (Chapter 14), be aware that the main part of your program and its subroutines do not share tracing settings. The subroutines inherit trace settings from the main part of the program, but any change made to trace settings inside of a subroutine does not affect the main part of the program. This means that you may place these instructions in a subroutine to debug just the subroutine.

OS/2 displays OS/2 commands by default, so you don't have to do anything in order to see OS/2 commands. If you don't want to see OS/2 commands, you should put '@ECHO OFF' right after the initial comment in your programs.

```
Fewer things traced

^
|
|
|
|    TRACE   O (Off)        Nothing traced
|
|
|    TRACE   N (Normal)     OS/2 commands that fail
|    (The default)          REXX verbs that fail
|
|    TRACE   F (Failure)    OS/2 commands that don't exist
|                                or abend.
|
|    TRACE   E (Error)      OS/2 commands that don't work
|
|    TRACE   L (Labels)     Labels only
|
|    TRACE   A (All)        Labels
|                           Commands
|                           REXX verbs
|
|    TRACE   S (Scan)       Labels
|                           Commands
|                           REXX verbs
|                           But doesn't execute anything
|
|                           TRACE   R (Results)
|                           Labels
|                           Commands
|                           REXX verbs
|                           Any time a variable changes
```

Figure 8.9. Debugging instructions you can put in your program, part 1.

```
TRACE ?R (Results)  Labels
                    Commands
                    REXX verbs
                    Any time a variable changes
                    With interactive debug


TRACE ?I (Intermed)  Labels
                     Commands
                     REXX verbs
                     Any time a variable changes
                     Intermediate results
                     C = (4*3) + 2
                     With interactive debug
v

Most amount of things traced
```

Figure 8.10. Debugging instructions you can put in your program, part 2.

8.5 REXX ERROR CODES

Figure 8.11 contains a complete list of REXX syntax error codes, from 1 to 50, and their meaning. What is striking about this list is *that is all there is*. A language with so few error codes must be inherently simple.

```
 1  File table full (OS/2 only)
 2  Expression > 64000 characters (OS/2 only)
 3  Program is unreadable (in use by another process)
 4  Program interrupted
 5  Machine storage exhausted
 6  Unmatched /* or quote
 7  WHEN or OTHERWISE expected
 8  Unexpected THEN or ELSE
 9  Unexpected WHEN or OTHERWISE
10  Unexpected or unmatched END
11  Control stack full
12  Clause > 500 characters
13  Invalid character in data
14  Incomplete DO/SELECT/IF
15  Invalid hex constant
16  Label not found
17  Unexpected PROCEDURE
18  THEN expected
19  String or symbol expected
20  Symbol expected
21  Invalid data on end of clause
22  Invalid character string
23  Invalid SBCS/DBCS mixed string
24  Invalid trace request
25  Invalid sub-keyword found
26  Invalid whole number
27  Invalid do syntax
28  Invalid LEAVE or ITERATE
29  Environment name too long
30  Name or string > 250 characters
31  Name starts with numeric or "."
32  Invalid use of stem
33  Invalid expression result
34  Logical value not 0 or 1
35  Invalid expression
36  Unmatched "(" in expression
37  Unexpected "," or ")"
38  Invalid template or pattern
39  Evaluation stack overflow
40  Incorrect call to routine
41  Bad arithmetic conversion
42  Arithmetic overflow/underflow
43  Routine not found
44  Function did not return data
45  No data specified on function return
46  Invalid variable reference
47  Unassigned
48  Failure in system service
49  Interpreter failure
50  Unassigned
```

Figure 8.12. REXX error codes.

8.6 QUESTIONS/PROBLEMS

1. Your program is running in a Presentation Manager Window, apparently not doing anything, and won't stop. How can you start up interactive debugging to see what it is doing?

2. You are in interactive trace, single-stepping through the program. You have had enough. What do you type in to make the program run without any trace?

3. What is the OS/2 command that will turn on interactive debugging for your REXX programs?

4. Can you put "SET RXTRACE = ON" in your program to turn on interactive debug? Try it to find out.

5. Run your percent increase program with interactive trace on. During interactive trace turn on TRACE Intermediate. Watch how the variables are processed.

Chapter 9

TRAPPING ERRORS

This chapter will show you how to intercept error conditions that may occur during your program's execution. It will show you how to set up condition traps in your programs to trap syntax errors, command failures, undefined variables, errors while reading or writing files, and an interrupt.

Topics

9.1 FUNCTION OF THE TRAP

REXX allows you to set up a routine in your program to trap six exceptional conditions. If one of these conditions occurs, control jumps to its routine. You can take some action at that point and terminate the program if you wish.

The trap is physically located at the end of your program. Control must not *fall* into the trap; you must let REXX send control to the trap when an exception condition happens. To prevent control from falling into the trap,

119

you must place an EXIT just before the first trap. In order to activate the trap, you must include a statement near the beginning of your program that activates it.

9.2 GENERAL APPEARANCE OF THE TRAP

There are three kinds of traps:
- The trap that terminates (Figure 9.1). If the error condition happens, control goes into the trap, which terminates the program. It is activated by a SIGNAL and ends with an EXIT.
  — Can be used with ERROR, FAILURE, HALT,
       NOTREADY, NOVALUE, SYNTAX.
- The trap that continues (Figure 9.2). If the error condition happens, control goes into the trap, which returns control to the program. It is activated by a CALL and ends with a RETURN.
  — Can be used with ERROR, FAILURE, HALT,
       NOTREADY.
- The trap that continues, named anything you want (Figure 9.3). If the error condition happens, control goes into the trap, which returns control to the program. You may name the trap something other than the standard name. It is activated by a CALL and ends with a RETURN.
  — Can be used with ERROR, FAILURE, HALT,
       NOTREADY.

All three kinds of traps are physically located near the end of the program. They all need to be turned on or activated. This is done by a SIGNAL or CALL instruction in the body of the program. If the error condition happens before the SIGNAL or CALL is executed, the trap is not entered. If it happens after, the trap is entered.

```
SIGNAL ON condition
/* other instructions */

EXIT

condition:
/* handle condition */
/* other instructions */

EXIT
```

Figure 9.1. The general form of the trap that terminates.

```
CALL    ON condition
/* other instructions */

EXIT

condition:
/* handle condition */
/* other instructions */
RETURN
```

Figure 9.2. The general form of the trap that continues.

```
CALL    ON condition NAME routine_name
/* other instructions */

EXIT

routine_name:
/* handle condition */
/* other instructions */

RETURN
```

Figure 9.3. The general form of the trap that continues, named anything you want.

Condition may be one of the following:

- ERROR: OS/2 commands that don't work properly.
- FAILURE: OS/2 commands that don't exist.
- HALT: the user pressing CTRL and C, or CTRL and BREAK keys.
- NOTREADY: an error occuring while reading or writing a file.
- NOVALUE: using uninitialized variables.
- SYNTAX: REXX syntax errors, nonnumerics used in arithmetic, functions or subroutines not found.

9.3 TRAPPING COMMAND ERRORS

The ERROR trap gets control after known OS/2 commands finish executing but don't work properly. OS/2 gives back a non-zero return code from the command, which you can examine with the special variable RC. Figure 9.4 shows examples of what ERROR traps. If you have no FAILURE trap, ERROR traps that too.

ERROR may be used with SIGNAL or CALL. Figure 9.5 is an example of an ERROR trap with SIGNAL that terminates. Figures 9.6 and 9.7 are examples of ERROR traps with CALL that continue. If you don't have an ERROR trap, REXX displays the command that failed and continues with the program. To turn off the trap use SIGNAL OFF ERROR.

```
"DIR @.@.@"
"ERASE NOTTHERE.XXX"
```

Figure 9.4. Examples of what ERROR traps.

```
/* SIGERR.CMD (Figure 9.5)*/
SIGNAL ON ERROR
"DIR @.@.@"


EXIT
ERROR:
SAY "COMMAND ERROR"
SAY "ERROR ON LINE " SIGL
SAY "LINE CONTAINING ERROR IS "
SAY SOURCELINE(SIGL)
SAY "THE PROBLEM IS IN:"
SAY CONDITION("D")
SAY RC " WAS RETURN CODE FROM OS/2 COMMAND"
EXIT
```

Figure 9.5. An example of an ERROR trap that terminates.

```
/*callerr.cmd (Figure 9.6)*/
CALL   ON ERROR
"DIR @.@.@"
SAY "I HAVE RETURNED FROM THE TRAP"


EXIT
ERROR:
SAY "COMMAND ERROR"
SAY "ERROR ON LINE " SIGL
SAY "LINE CONTAINING ERROR IS "
SAY SOURCELINE(SIGL)
SAY "THE PROBLEM IS IN:"
SAY CONDITION("D")
SAY RC " WAS RETURN CODE FROM OS/2 COMMAND"
RETURN
```

Figure 9.6. An example of an ERROR trap that continues.

```
/*caller2.cmd (Figure 9.7)*/
CALL   ON ERROR NAME BADOS2CMD
"DIR @.@.@"
SAY "I HAVE RETURNED FROM THE TRAP"


EXIT
BADOS2CMD:
SAY "COMMAND ERROR"
SAY "ERROR ON LINE " SIGL
SAY "LINE CONTAINING ERROR IS "
SAY SOURCELINE(SIGL)
SAY "THE PROBLEM IS IN:"
SAY CONDITION("D")
SAY RC " WAS RETURN CODE FROM OS/2 COMMAND"
RETURN
```

Figure 9.7. An example of an ERROR trap that continues, named BADOS2CMD.

9.4 TRAPPING FAILURE

The FAILURE trap intercepts the severe failure of commands to OS/2. Figure 9.8 shows examples of what FAILURE can intercept. Essentially it is a command that does not exist. OS/2 gives back a 1041 return code that you can examine if you wish with the special variable RC.

FAILURE may be used with SIGNAL or CALL. Figure 9.9 is an example of a FAILURE trap with SIGNAL that terminates. Figures 9.10 and 9.11 are examples of FAILURE traps with CALL that continue.

If you don't have a FAILURE trap, REXX displays the command that failed and continues with the exec. To turn off the trap, use SIGNAL OFF FAILURE. If you don't have a FAILURE trap but do have an ERROR trap, the ERROR trap is used instead of FAILURE.

```
            "THIS IS NOT AN OS/2 CMD"
            "DIRE *.*"
```

Figure 9.8. An example of what FAILURE traps.

```
/*sigfail.cmd (Figure 9.9)*/
SIGNAL ON FAILURE
"THIS IS NOT AN OS/2 CMD"


EXIT
FAILURE:
SAY "COMMAND FAILURE"
SAY "ERROR ON LINE " SIGL
SAY "LINE CONTAINING ERROR IS "
SAY SOURCELINE(SIGL)
SAY "THE PROBLEM IS IN:"
SAY CONDITION("D")
SAY RC " WAS RETURN CODE FROM OS/2 COMMAND"
EXIT
```

Figure 9.9. An example of a FAILURE trap that terminates.

```
/*callfail.cmd (Figure 9.10)*/
CALL ON FAILURE
"THIS IS NOT AN OS/2 CMD"
SAY "I HAVE RETURNED FROM THE TRAP"


EXIT
FAILURE:
SAY "COMMAND FAILURE"
SAY "ERROR ON LINE " SIGL
SAY "LINE CONTAINING ERROR IS "
SAY  SOURCELINE(SIGL)
SAY "THE PROBLEM IS IN:"
SAY CONDITION("D")
SAY RC " WAS RETURN CODE FROM OS/2 COMMAND"
RETURN
```

Figure 9.10. An example of a FAILURE trap that continues.

```
/*callfai2.cmd (Figure 9.11)*/
CALL ON FAILURE NAME CMDFAIL
"THIS IS NOT AN OS/2 CMD"
SAY "I HAVE RETURNED FROM THE TRAP"


EXIT
CMDFAIL:
SAY "COMMAND FAILURE"
SAY "ERROR ON LINE " SIGL
SAY "LINE CONTAINING ERROR IS "
SAY SOURCELINE(SIGL)
SAY "THE PROBLEM IS IN:"
SAY CONDITION("D")
SAY RC " WAS RETURN CODE FROM OS/2 COMMAND"
RETURN
```

Figure 9.11. An example of a FAILURE trap that continues, named CMDFAIL.

9.5 TRAPPING A KEYBOARD INTERRUPT

If you press CTRL and C, then ENTER, or CTRL and BREAK, then ENTER while your program is executing, it will stop. You may trap that action if you wish by using a HALT trap. You will regain control in your program and can either terminate the program or continue executing it. I recommend that you not prevent the user from stopping the execution of the program but instead give a choice about whether or not to terminate.

Note that DOS works differently than OS/2. When you run a DOS batch file and interrupt it with CTRL and C, DOS asks 'TERMINATE BATCH JOB? Y/N.' OS/2 doesn't do this with batch files or REXX programs. You can, however, get the same effect in a REXX program if you have a HALT trap, such as the one shown in Figure 9.13.

HALT may be used with SIGNAL or CALL. Figure 9.12 is an example of a HALT trap with SIGNAL that terminates. Figures 9.13 and 9.14 are examples of HALT traps with CALL that continue. To turn off the HALT trap, use SIGNAL OFF HALT.

```
/*sighalt.cmd (Figure 9.12)*/
SIGNAL ON HALT
Say "Type in your name (interrupt here)"
Pull name
Say "Thank you, " name


EXIT
HALT:
SAY "DON'T INTERRUPT"
SAY "PROGRAM WAS ON LINE " SIGL
SAY "LINE CONTENTS "   SOURCELINE(SIGL)
EXIT
```

Figure 9.12. An example of a HALT trap that terminates.

```
/*callhalt.cmd (Figure 9.13)*/
CALL ON HALT
Say "Type in your name (interrupt here)"
Pull name
Say "Thank you, " name
SAY "I HAVE RETURNED FROM THE TRAP"


EXIT
HALT:
SAY "PROGRAM WAS ON LINE " SIGL
SAY "LINE CONTENTS "   SOURCELINE(SIGL)
SAY "TERMINATE REXX PROGRAM? Y/N"
PULL REPLY
IF REPLY = "Y" THEN EXIT
RETURN
```

Figure 9.13. An example of a HALT trap that gives a choice about terminating.

```
/*callhal2.cmd (Figure 9.14)*/
CALL ON HALT NAME BYE
Say "Type in your name (interrupt here)"
Pull name
Say "Thank you, " name
SAY "I HAVE RETURNED FROM THE TRAP"


EXIT
BYE:
SAY "PROGRAM WAS ON LINE " SIGL
SAY "LINE CONTENTS "    SOURCELINE(SIGL)
SAY "WANT TO STOP? Y/N"
PULL REPLY
IF REPLY = "Y" THEN EXIT
RETURN
```

Figure 9.14. An example of a HALT trap that gives a choice about terminating and uses the name BYE instead of HALT.

9.6 TRAPPING A READ OR WRITE ERROR

If an error occurs while you are reading or writing a file, you can trap it. You can't fix the error but can display a message.

NOTREADY may be used with SIGNAL or CALL. Figure 9.15 is an example of a NOTREADY trap with SIGNAL that terminates. To turn off the NOTREADY trap, use SIGNAL OFF NOTREADY.

```
/* signotr.cmd (Figure 9.15)*/
SIGNAL ON NOTREADY

/* instructions that read or write files such
as:*/
DO WHILE LINES("C:\REXXPRGS\TEST.DAT") > 0
   CALL LINEIN "C:\REXXPRGS\TEST.DAT"
   SAY 'LINE READ WAS ' RESULT
END


EXIT
NOTREADY:
SAY "ERROR ACCESSING FILE"
SAY "ERROR ON LINE " SIGL
SAY "LINE CONTAINING ERROR IS "
SAY SOURCELINE(SIGL)
SAY "THE PROBLEM IS IN:"
SAY CONDITION("D")
EXIT
```

Figure 9.15. An example of a NOTREADY trap that terminates.

9.7 TRAPPING NOVALUE

It is legal to use a variable that was never given a value — REXX just takes it as a literal. Trapping NOVALUE can be useful in debugging, but after your program is thoroughly tested, there is generally no need to leave a NOVALUE trap in it. Figure 9.16 contains examples of the use of uninitialized variables.

NOVALUE may be used with SIGNAL. Figure 9.17 is an example of a NOVALUE trap with SIGNAL that terminates. If you don't set up a NOVALUE trap, undefined variables are taken as literals and the program continues without interruption. To turn off the NOVALUE trap, use SIGNAL OFF NOVALUE.

```
SAY HELLO
X = Y
SAY "I HAVE " D "DOLLARS"
```

Figure 9.16. An example of what NOVALUE traps.

```
/* signov.cmd (Figure 9.17)*/
SIGNAL ON NOVALUE
SAY HELLO
/*other instructions*/


EXIT
NOVALUE:
SAY "PLEASE DEFINE YOUR VARIABLES"
SAY "ERROR ON LINE " SIGL
SAY "LINE CONTAINING ERROR IS "
SAY SOURCELINE(SIGL)
SAY "THE PROBLEM IS IN:"
SAY CONDITION("D")
EXIT
```

Figure 9.17. An example of a NOVALUE trap that terminates.

9.8   TRAPPING SYNTAX ERRORS

You may trap syntax errors in order to intercept things like illegal arithmetic, missing functions, and missing delimiters. Figure 9.18 contains examples of the type of error the syntax trap will catch.

SYNTAX may be used with SIGNAL. Figure 9.19 is a syntax error trap with SIGNAL that terminates. If you don't have a syntax trap, REXX displays the line in error and an error message, and stops your program. SIGNAL OFF SYNTAX turns off the trap.

```
Say "A" - "B"
X = (Cur - Prev / Prev
Call Notthere
```

Figure 9.18. Examples of syntax errors.

```
/*sigsyn.cmd (Figure 9.19)*/
SIGNAL ON SYNTAX
SAY "A" - "B"


EXIT
SYNTAX:
SAY "SYNTAX ERROR"
SAY "ERROR ON LINE " SIGL
SAY "LINE CONTAINING ERROR IS   "
SAY SOURCELINE(SIGL)
SAY "ERROR MESSAGE FROM REXX IS"
SAY ERRORTEXT(RC)
EXIT
```

Figure 9.19. An example of a syntax error trap that terminates.

9.9 WHAT YOU CAN PUT IN THE TRAP

You may put any REXX instruction or OS/2 command in your trap, but there are certain things that are particularly useful. Figure 9.20 illustrates several of these.

- The special REXX variable SIGL contains the line number of the statement that sent you to the condition trap. It may be used in any condition trap but is of little use in HALT traps.

- The function SOURCELINE(SIGL) gives the actual program statement that you wrote in the program. It may be used in any condition trap but is of little use in HALT traps.

- The function ERRORTEXT(RC) gives the message that REXX would normally display for the REXX error. It is normally used only in SYNTAX traps.

- The function CONDITION("D") displays the string in error, in ERROR, FAILURE, and NOVALUE traps, which can be useful in pinpointing the exact cause of the error.

- RC contains the return code from OS/2 commands. It is normally used only in ERROR and FAILURE traps.

```
label:
SAY "ERROR ON LINE " SIGL
SAY "LINE CONTAINING ERROR IS "
SAY SOURCELINE(SIGL)
SAY "THE PROBLEM IS IN:"
SAY CONDITION("D")
SAY "ERROR MESSAGE FROM REXX IS "
SAY ERRORTEXT(RC)
SAY RC " WAS RETURN CODE FROM OS/2 COMMAND"
EXIT
```

Figure 9.20. Examples of what you can put in the trap.

9.10 THE INFAMOUS "GO TO"

One form of the SIGNAL instruction acts like a GO TO (see Figure 9.21) —
it can send to a label, even without an error. This is the unconditional
transfer of control, or GO TO. It should not be used like a GO TO in
traditional programming languages. It is not needed in REXX, since REXX
is so completely endowed with structured programming constructs that it
handles all logic situations without using SIGNAL as a GO TO. If you do it,
I suggest you EXIT after the label you GO TO.

SIGNAL should not be used to get out of a loop because it destroys loop
control structures. REXX provides an orderly way of exiting from a loop
(LEAVE) that should be used instead. Figure 9.22 contains an example you
can try on your system. It will show you how SIGNAL destroys a loop control
structure.

```
/*signono.cmd (Figure 9.21)*/
/* other instructions */
SAY 'About to do a SIGNAL'
SIGNAL THE_END
/* other instructions that are not executed */
SAY 'This will not be executed'

THE_END:
SAY 'Have done a SIGNAL, about to exit'
EXIT
```

Figure 9.21. Using SIGNAL like a GO TO.

```
/* badsig.cmd (Figure 9.22)*/
/* shows how a SIGNAL destroys
   a loop control structure       */
Say "BEGIN"
Do I = 1 TO 5
   Say I
   If I = 2 then SIGNAL NEXT
   Say "A"
   NEXT:
   Say "B"
End
Say "END"
```

Figure 9.22. An example of how SIGNAL destroys a control structure.

9.11 QUESTIONS/PROBLEMS

1. ERRORTEXT(RC) is used in which type of trap?

2. Complete this program
```
/*CH09P02Q.CMD */
SIGNAL ON
"TURN DOWN VOLUME"
EXIT

SAY "COMMAND TO OS/2 FAILED"
```

3. Write a program that asks for a file name and then issues the OS/2 command DIR on it. Set up an ERROR trap to intercept the command that is not working. In the ERROR trap, display the line of the program in error and the error code from OS/2. Ask for the file name again, reexecute the command, and exit. Expected results:

```
= = = > CH09P03
    PLEASE ENTER FILE NAME
= = = > junk.dat
    CANNOT EXECUTE COMMAND
    OS/2 RETURN CODE IS 18
    LINE IN ERROR IS "DIR file_name"
    PLEASE REENTER
= = = > okfile.dat
    OKFILE.DAT      100 9-9-94 9:33a
```

Chapter 10

MATH

This chapter will concentrate on the way REXX does arithmetic. You will learn how to use REXX's arithmetic operators and how to change the precision for arithmetic operations.

Topics

10.1 WHEN IS MATH DONE?

```
A = 1 + 1

SAY 1 + 1
```

Figure 10.1. Examples of when math is done.

137

REXX will do math whenever it finds arithmetic operators and two or more numbers that are not enclosed in quotes or apostrophes. Figure 10.1 illustrates an assignment statement and a SAY instruction.

10.2 OPERATORS

The REXX operators shown in Figure 10.2 are like those in most other languages, with the possible exception of "%" for integer division and "//" for the remainder of a division. Please note that in REXX you must use operators, not words, you may not use "ADD," "SUBTRACT," and so forth. Figure 10.3 shows several examples of the arithmetic operators in action.

```
+         add

-         subtract

*         multiply

/         divide

%         integer divide

//        give remainder of division

**        raise to a power. (whole numbers only)
              negative exponents work

-         prefix on a number. (-1)
              take it as negative

+         prefix on a number. (+1)
              take it as positive

( )       to group items
```

Figure 10.2. Arithmetic operators in REXX.

```
/* mathex.cmd (Figure 10.3)*/

SAY  1  + 1          /*--> 2 */

SAY  2  - 1          /*--> 1  */

SAY  2  * 2          /*--> 4  */

SAY  4  / 2          /*--> 2  */

SAY  5  % 2          /*--> 2  */

SAY  5 // 2          /*--> 1  */

SAY  3 ** 2          /*--> 9  */

SAY  -1 * 2          /*--> -2 */

SAY  (4 + 2)  * 3    /*--> 18 */

SAY  4 + (2 * 3)     /*--> 10 */
```

Figure 10.3. Examples of the arithmetic operators.

10.3 PRECISION

REXX will normally carry out its arithmetic operations with a default precision of 9. If you give it more than 9 digits, it will have to do some rounding. For example, 1234567809 will be changed to 1234567810 and displayed as 1.23456781E+9. This is only a default, not a limit.

REXX can do math to any precision and with surprising speed. The only limitation is the amount of memory that is available on your system. I have tried with success a precision of 10,000 digits, but I must warn you that there is a very high overhead in such operations. Figure 10.4 illustrates REXX performing a division to 100 digits.

```
/* dig100.cmd (Figure 10.4)*/

SAY    2 / 3

/*displays   0.666666667
                 (9 digits)      */

NUMERIC DIGITS    100

SAY 2 / 3

/*displays
0.666666666666666666666666666666666666666666
  666666666666666666666666666666666666666666
  66666666666666666667    */
```

Figure 10.4. An example of REXX doing math to 100 digits of precision.

If you plan to experiment with high precision on your system, be aware that the example in Figure 10.5 will force you to suffer through the display of 10,000 threes! Interrupting the display will not make them go away.

```
NUMERIC DIGITS    10000

SAY 1 / 3
```

Figure 10.5. An example you shouldn't try unless you want to see 10,000 threes.

10.4 ROUNDING

When the precision is too small for the number that is being operated on, REXX will round the number so as not to lose any of the number's magnitude. REXX may lose some precision in the low-order digits, but, being low order, they don't matter very much.

You might want to try out the short program in Figure 10.6 to see the effect of rounding. I suggest you review the section on FUZZ to better understand how it is related to precision and rounding.

```
/* roundx1.cmd (Figure 10.6)*/
NUMERIC DIGITS 5 /* ENOUGH DIGITS*/
A = +11119
B = +11120

IF A = B
THEN SAY "EQUAL"
ELSE SAY "NOT EQUAL"
/* THEY WILL NOT BE EQUAL,
BECAUSE 11119 AND 11120 ARE NOT EQUAL */
SAY A
SAY B

NUMERIC DIGITS 4 /*NOT ENOUGH DIGITS */
A = +11119
B = +11120

IF A = B
THEN SAY "EQUAL"
ELSE SAY "NOT EQUAL"
/* THEY WILL BE EQUAL.
POSSIBLE ONLY IF ROUNDING DONE */
SAY A
SAY B
```

Figure 10.6. Examples of REXX doing rounding.

10.5 HOW ROUNDED NUMBERS ARE DISPLAYED

Whenever there are too many digits for the current precision, REXX will display numbers in exponential notation, using either scientific or engineering format, as shown in the next section. Figure 10.7 shows how rounded numbers are displayed.

```
/*roundx2.cmd (Figure 10.7)*/
NUMERIC DIGITS 4
A = 10001
B = 10009

SAY A + B
/* displays 2.001E+4 */
```

Figure 10.7. How rounded numbers are displayed.

10.6 CONTROLLING HOW LARGE NUMBERS ARE DISPLAYED

Anytime a number is larger than the precision setting allows, REXX will round it and display it in exponential notation. You have your choice of two kinds of display: SCIENTIFIC (the default) and ENGINEERING.

NUMERIC FORM SCIENTIFIC is the default and gives the answer shown in Figure 10.7 (2.001E+4). NUMERIC FORM ENGINEERING gives a number in the form 20.01E+3, as shown in Figure 10.8.

```
/*formex.cmd (Figure 10.8)*/
NUMERIC FORM ENGINEERING
NUMERIC DIGITS 4
A = 10001
B = 10009

SAY A + B
/* displays 20.01E+3 */
```

Figure 10.8. How rounded numbers are displayed with NUMERIC FORM ENGINEERING.

10.7 QUESTIONS/PROBLEMS

1. Write a program that will multiply two numbers. Ask the user for the two numbers, and set up a trap to intercept any error, such as invalid numbers.

2. Run this program to determine the effect of parentheses on arithmetic operations.

/*CH10P02.CMD*/
SAY (1 + 2) * 3
SAY 1 + (2 * 3)
SAY 1 + 2 * 3
What is displayed?

3. Create a simple program to calculate the effect of compound interest. Ask for the following items from the keyboard:
Principal
Percent of interest (yearly)
Number of years money kept in account
Compounding frequency (How many times per year is interest compounded? 1 = yearly; 12 = monthly; 52 = weekly; 365 = daily)
Perform the following calculations:
Compute the yearly rate of interest as yearly percent of interest / 100.
Compute r (the rate) as yearly rate of interest / compounding frequency.
Compute n (number of times compounded) as how many years X compounding frequency.
Compute final amount as principal X $((1 + r)^n)$.
Display final amount.
Keep this program, since you will be improving on it later.

Chapter 11

SELECT: THE CASE STRUCTURE

This chapter is about the REXX implementation of the CASE structure. You will see how to choose among several possible alternative actions with SELECT.

Topics

11.1 The Function of the SELECT
11.2 The Syntax of the SELECT
11.3 SELECT with Several Instructions and NOP
11.4 Several Instructions after the OTHERWISE
11.5 Questions/Problems

11.1 THE FUNCTION OF THE SELECT

SELECT is REXX's implementation of the structured programming construct CASE. It tests a series of conditions, one after the other, and as soon as it finds a true condition, it executes the instruction associated with it and exits from the structure. If none of the conditions are true, the OTHERWISE instruction is executed.

11.2 THE SYNTAX OF THE SELECT

Figure 11.1 shows an example of SELECT in its simplest form. Please examine it and notice the following points:

- SELECT, WHEN, OTHERWISE, and END are separate REXX instructions and should be placed on separate lines.
- Each WHEN introduces a comparison that will be tested.

- You may have as many WHENs as you wish.
- Each WHEN must have its THEN.
- Each THEN may have just one instruction (just like IF).
- The final END is required.
- The OTHERWISE is optional.

```
/*selex.cmd (Figure 11.1)*/
day = 5
SELECT
    WHEN    DAY = 1    THEN    SAY "MONDAY"
    WHEN    DAY = 2    THEN    SAY "TUESDAY"
    WHEN    DAY = 3    THEN    SAY "WEDNESDAY"
    WHEN    DAY = 4    THEN    SAY "THURSDAY"
    WHEN    DAY = 5    THEN    SAY "FRIDAY"
    WHEN    DAY = 6    THEN    SAY "SATURDAY"
    WHEN    DAY = 7    THEN    SAY "SUNDAY"
OTHERWISE
    SAY "UNKNOWN DAY"
END
```

Figure 11.1. An example of the SELECT.

11.3 SELECT WITH SEVERAL INSTRUCTIONS AND NOP

Figure 11.2 shows an example of SELECT that allows you to execute more than one instruction after a WHEN that comes true. Please notice the following points:

- The instructions are bounded by a DO and END.
- NOP means that no instruction is to be executed.

```
/*selex01.cmd (Figure 11.2)*/
DAY = 1
SELECT
  WHEN   DAY = 1
    THEN
      DO
        SAY "HAPPY"
        SAY "MONDAY"
      END
    WHEN   DAY = 5
    THEN
      DO
        SAY "TGI"
        SAY "FRIDAY"
      END
OTHERWISE NOP
END
```

Figure 11.2. An example of the SELECT allowing more than one instruction.

11.4 SEVERAL INSTRUCTIONS AFTER THE OTHERWISE

Figures 11.3 and 11.4 each show a different way to use more than one instruction after the OTHERWISE. I prefer the way shown in Figure 11.4 because it is more in keeping with the normal syntax of REXX IFs and WHENs. You may notice the following:

- The final END terminates the SELECT and the OTHERWISE.
- The DO END construction is not required in the OTHERWISE.

```
/*selex02.cmd (Figure 11.3)*/
DAY = 6
SELECT
   WHEN    DAY = 2      THEN   SAY "MONDAY"
   WHEN    DAY = 3      THEN   SAY "TUESDAY"
   WHEN    DAY = 4      THEN   SAY "WEDNESDAY"
   WHEN    DAY = 5      THEN   SAY "THURSDAY"
   WHEN    DAY = 6      THEN   SAY "FRIDAY"
OTHERWISE
   SAY "ENJOY"
   SAY "WEEKEND"
END
```

Figure 11.3. One way to execute several instructions after an OTHERWISE.

```
/*selex03.cmd (Figure 11.4)*/
DAY = 1
SELECT
   WHEN    DAY = 2      THEN   SAY "MONDAY"
   WHEN    DAY = 3      THEN   SAY "TUESDAY"
   WHEN    DAY = 4      THEN   SAY "WEDNESDAY"
   WHEN    DAY = 5      THEN   SAY "THURSDAY"
   WHEN    DAY = 6      THEN   SAY "FRIDAY"
OTHERWISE
   DO
     SAY "ENJOY"
     SAY "WEEKEND"
   END
END
```

Figure 11.4. Another way to execute several instructions after an OTHERWISE.

11.5 QUESTIONS/PROBLEMS

1. Correct this segment of code:
```
/*CH11P01Q.CMD with errors*/
NAME = "MIKE"
SAY "This won't work"
CASE
  WHEN "NAME" = "JOHN" THEN SAY "GRADE IS 78"
  WHEN  NAME  = "MARY" THEN SAY "GRADE IS 84"
  WHEN  NAME  = "MIKE" THEN SAY "GRADE IS 89"
  WHEN  NAME  = "MONA" THEN SAY "GRADE IS 91"
ELSE  THEN SAY "NOT ON ROSTER"
```


2. Are these two segments of code equivalent?
```
SELECT
  WHEN  NAME  = "ERIC" THEN SAY "GRADE IS 83"
  OTHERWISE  SAY "NOT ON ROSTER"
END
```


```
IF NAME = "ERIC"
THEN SAY "GRADE IS 83"
ELSE SAY "NOT ON ROSTER"
```

Chapter 12

EXECUTING OS/2 COMMANDS

This chapter concentrates on the manner in which you can talk to OS/2, the operating system that supports REXX. It will show you how to execute some of the more useful OS/2 commands in your REXX programs.

Please refer to Appendix B for a description of all the OS/2 commands you will need in this book.

Topics

12.1 How to Specify OS/2 Commands
12.2 How Does REXX Know a Command Is for OS/2?
12.3 Checking Whether OS/2 Commands Worked
12.4 Some Useful OS/2 Commands
12.5 Giving a Command to an Environment Other Than OS/2
12.6 Questions/Problems

```
'DIR'     /* good OS/2 command */

SAY RC    /* GIVES A 0          */

'DIRR'    /* COMMAND TO OS/2 */
          /* THAT OS/2 DOESN'T RECOGNIZE  */

SAY RC    /* GIVES A 1041       */
```

Figure 12.1. Examples of commands given to OS/2 — one that works and one that doesn't.

12.1 HOW TO SPECIFY OS/2 COMMANDS

REXX looks at the first word of each line of your program to see if it is a REXX verb (all listed in Appendix C). If REXX sees a word it doesn't understand at the beginning of a line, it assumes that it shouldn't try to understand it and passes it to OS/2. This is known as passing a command to the environment, or the operating system surrounding REXX.

There are only two things you can execute this way: OS/2 commands (major ones listed in Appendix B) and batch files with an extension of .BAT. If the execution is successful, it will place a zero in your REXX program's variable RC. If OS/2 cannot execute the command, it will place some other number in RC. Figure 12.1 shows two commands meant for OS/2, one that works and one that doesn't.

You can simplify the task of REXX by enclosing your OS/2 commands in apostrophes or quotation marks. Apostrophes are preferred, because some OS/2 commands use quotation marks and apostrophes won't interfere with them. It is important to understand that REXX cannot syntax check any OS/2 command; they all look good to REXX.

To summarize, here are some important points about executing by 'command name':
• The command name should always be in apostrophes or quotation marks.
• You can execute OS/2 commands.
• You can execute non-REXX batch files with an extension of .BAT.
• You cannot execute other REXX programs or REXX functions/subroutines this way.
• You cannot execute non-REXX batch files with an extension of .CMD.
• The special variable RC is always set when executing this way.
• The special variable RESULT is never set when executing this way.
• You may not use commas to separate parameters as you do with the REXX CALL (see below).
• After executing the command, batch file, or REXX program, your program continues executing. It does not terminate the way it happens inside of batch files.

When REXX passes a command to OS/2, it passes the entire line of your program that the command is on, including any literals, variables, or functions that are on the line. Figure 12.2 shows several examples of this.

```
/*PASSOS2.CMD (Figure 12.2)*/
Wild_card = '*.CMD'   /* set a variable*/
/* pass command with variable*/
'DIR ' Wild_card

/* pass command with a literal */
'DIR   *.CMD'

/* pass command with a literal, another way */
'DIR '   '*.CMD'
```

Figure 12.2. Passing variables and/or literals along with an OS/2 command.

You may also take advantage of REXX's string manipulation capabilities such as concatenation of data strings (Chapter 4) to combine literals and variables, as shown in Figure 12.3.

```
/*PASSOS2A.CMD (Figure 12.3)*/
Extension  = '.CMD'   /* set a variable*/
/*command with literal and variable
 concatenated using the broken
 vertical bar symbol*/
'DIR' '*' ¦¦ Extension
```

Figure 12.3. Using concatenation to pass variables and literals along with an OS/2 command.

USE UPPER OR LOWER CASE

It doesn't matter if you use upper case or lower case in your OS/2 commands. Both ways work equally well.

12.2 HOW DOES REXX KNOW A COMMAND IS FOR OS/2?

See Figures 12.4 through 12.7. REXX looks at every line of the program to decipher each command or instruction. If it sees quotes, apostrophes, or even parentheses around the first word in the sentence, and the instruction is not an assignment, it will pass the command to OS/2. An unknown command that is not in quotes or apostrophes will also be passed to OS/2, but this action will be less efficient than if apostrophes or quotes were used.

A variable that starts a line and that is not involved in an assignment is assumed to contain an OS/2 command, as in the example BYE in Figure 12.6.

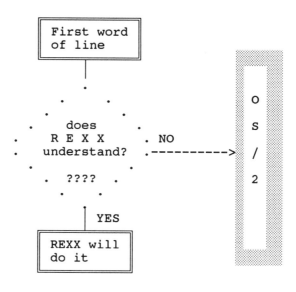

Figure 12.4. REXX decides if a command should go to OS/2.

1	Is it assignment? - do assignment.	A = 3 SAY = "BARK"
2	Is it REXX verb? - execute REXX verb	SAY "ahh"
3	Is it comparison without IF? - return a 1 or 0. (Unusual).	"abc"= "def"
4	Is command in quotes? - give to OS/2.	'DIR'
5	Is command in parentheses? - give to OS/2. (Unusual).	(ERASE)
6	Does variable start the line? - give to OS/2. (Unusual).	CMD="DIR" CMD
7	Is it out of quotes, parens, variables, but unknown to REXX? - give to OS/2.	SOY "Hello" DIR

Figure 12.5. How REXX decides if a command is for OS/2.

```
'ERASE ABC.DATA'        /* OK. OS/2 executes it */

'ERASER ABD.DATA'       /* NG. OS/2 rejects  it */

'DIRXX'                 /* NG.  OS/2 rejects  it */

'HEY BUD'               /* NG. OS/2 rejects  it */

(DIR)                   /* OK.  OS/2 executes it */

BYE = "EXIT"            /* this is done by REXX */
BYE                     /* OK. OS/2 closes window */

ERASER ABC.DATA         /* NG.  OS/2 rejects it  */

SOY "HELLO"             /* NG.  OS/2 rejects it
                              (so did REXX)      */
```

Figure 12.6. Examples of commands that REXX sends to OS/2 (not necessarily good commands — they may or may not work).

```
ERASE = "SCRATCH ABC.DATA"      /* assignment, OK */

'ERASE' = "SCRATCH ABC.DATA"    /* comparison, NG */
                                /* bad for REXX, bad for OS/2*/
SAY "ERASER"                    /* SAY, OK          */

CALL SUBROUTINE1                /* subroutine, OK */
```

Figure 12.7. Examples of commands that don't go to OS/2 and that REXX tries to execute (not necessarily good REXX commands — they may or may not work).

12.3 CHECKING WHETHER OS/2 COMMANDS WORKED

OS/2 will do its best to execute the commands your REXX program passes to it. If it is successful, OS/2 will display any information requested and place a zero in your program's special reserved variable RC. You can check this variable after executing any OS/2 command to see if it worked. Figure 12.8 shows one way you might do this.

```
/*CHEKRC.CMD (Figure 12.8)*/
SAY 'About to try a good OS/2 command '
'DIR'
SAY 'Return code from good command was ' RC

SAY 'About to try a bad OS/2 command '
'DIRE'
SAY 'Return code from bad command was ' RC
```

Figure 12.8. Checking to see if OS/2 commands have worked.

Another way to check whether an OS/2 command has worked is to use an ERROR or FAILURE trap (Chapter 9.)

12.4 SOME USEFUL OS/2 COMMANDS

I have included some of the most useful OS/2 commands here for convenience, with examples of their use in a REXX program. This does not attempt to be a complete listing of all OS/2 commands, but only those that you would be most likely to find in a REXX program.

'CALL'

'CALL *file name*' executes a batch file, whether it is written in REXX or the older batch file language. This may not be used to execute REXX functions/subroutines (Chapters 13 and 14). For that, you must use the REXX verb CALL.

Here is a comparison of the 'OS/2 CALL' and the REXX CALL, so as to avoid confusion between the two. You may want to compare these with the 'command name' method of execution explained above in Section 12.1.

The OS/2 'CALL':
— is in apostrophes or quotes when found in a REXX program.
— always sets the special variable RC.
— never sets the special variable RESULT.
— returns control to the program in which it was found, after the other program is executed.
— can execute old-style batch files written with batch language and named with .BAT or .CMD extensions.

— can execute REXX programs, provided they do not have commas delimiting their ARG variables and provided they end with an EXIT.

— cannot successfully execute REXX subroutines, written with an ARG and variables delimited by commas, and ending with a RETURN (Chapter 14).

The REXX CALL:

— is used only in REXX programs.

— is not in apostrophes or quotes.

— never sets the variable RC.

— sets the variable RETURN, provided you are calling a REXX subroutine that passes back data with a RETURN.

— returns control to the statement after itself, after the other program is executed.

— executes REXX subroutines, written with an ARG and variables delimited by commas, and ending with a RETURN (Chapter 14).

— cannot correctly execute old-style batch files written with batch language and named with a .BAT extension (use 'command name' instead).

— can execute REXX programs that do not have commas delimiting their ARG variables and that end with an EXIT, but I recommend that you don't try to use RESULT, and don't try to pass parameters delimited by commas.

'CD *directory*'

Changes the default directory, so OS/2 will search in that directory for programs and data.

'CD' (Change Directory) changes to the root directory of the current disk drive.

'CD \REXXPRGS' changes to the directory REXXPRGS.

'CD \GAMES\FOOTBALL' changes to the directory FOOTBALL within the directory GAMES. Example of use:

```
/*CDEXAMP.CMD (Section 12.3)*/
'CD \REXXPRGS'
'DIR *.CMD'
```

'CLS'

CLS clears the screen in an OS/2 Window or OS/2 Full Screen. The REXX function SYSCLS does this too (Chapter 13). Example of use:

```
/*TRYCLS.CMD (Section 12.3)*/
'CLS'
Say 'Please type in your name'
Pull name
Say 'Thank you, ' name
```

'COPY'

'COPY *input file output file*' creates a copy of an existing file. If the output file exists, it will replace it. If the output file does not exist, it will be created. Example of use:

```
/*COPYEXMP.CMD (Section 12.3)*/
Say 'Please type in the "from" file name'
Pull input_file
Say 'Please type in the "to" file name'
Pull output_file
'COPY ' input_file output_file
```

Here is a slightly better way to copy. It checks first to see if the file exists before mindlessly destroying an existing file. It uses the Stream function, covered in the chapter on reading and writing files (Chapter 18).

```
/*COPYEXM2.CMD (Section 12.3)*/
Say 'Please type in the "from" file name'
Pull input_file
Say 'Please type in the "to" file name'
Pull output_file
If Stream(output_file,'C','QUERY EXISTS') = ''
Then 'COPY ' input_file output_file
Else
   DO
      Say 'File' output_file
      Say 'exists. OK to delete it? Y/N'
      pull reply
      if reply = 'Y'
      then 'COPY ' input_file output_file
   END
```

'disk drive'

'*disk drive*' changes the default disk drive.
'C:' changes to the C drive.
'A:' changes to the A drive.   Example of use:

```
/*DDRIVE.CMD (Section 12.3)*/
Say 'Please place a disk in the A drive'
'A:'
'DIR '
```

'ERASE'

'ERASE *file specification*' deletes a file.
'ERASE TEMP.DAT' deletes the file TEMP.DAT.   Example of use:

```
/*ERASEIT.CMD (Section 12.3)*/
Say 'Please type in a file name to delete'
Pull say_good_bye_file
'ERASE ' say_good_bye_file
If RC = 0
then say 'File ' say_good_bye_file ' erased'
```

'EXIT' (The OS/2 command)

Ends a program and closes an OS/2 Window or OS/2 Full Screen. Be sure
to enclose it in apostrophes or quotation marks, or REXX will interpret it as
the REXX EXIT, which means just end the program. Example of use:

```
/*TRYEXIT.CMD (Section 12.3)*/
'CLS'
Say 'Please type in your name'
Pull name
Say 'Thank you, ' name
'EXIT'
```

'MD'

'MD *directory*' (Make Directory) creates a directory inside of the current one.
'MD \FOOTBALL' creates the directory FOOTBALL inside of the current one. If the current one was GAMES, it creates FOOTBALL within GAMES. Example of use:

```
/* shows how you might create a directory */
'CD \GAMES'
'MD \FOOTBALL'
IF RC = 0
THEN Say 'Directory FOOTBALL created'
ELSE Say 'Cannot create directory ' FOOTBALL
```

'RD'

'RD *directory*' (Remove Directory) deletes a directory (which must not contain files) inside of the current one.
'RD \FOOTBALL' deletes the directory FOOTBALL inside of the current one. If the current one was GAMES, it deletes FOOTBALL within GAMES. Example of use:

```
/* shows how you might delete a directory */
'CD \GAMES'
'RD \FOOTBALL'
IF RC = 0
THEN Say 'Directory FOOTBALL deleted'
ELSE Say 'Cannot delete directory ' FOOTBALL
```

12.5 GIVING A COMMAND TO AN ENVIRONMENT OTHER THAN OS/2

It is possible to have other environments besides OS/2, but OS/2 is the only one covered in this book. An environment is a command processor. REXX has the ability to pass commands to any command processor that registers itself with OS/2 and tells OS/2 that it can accept commands from REXX programs. How to set up other environments is beyond the scope of this book.

Suppose that there is a command processor named NETCNTRL and that it has registered with OS/2 as an environment. Then you would execute the following REXX verb to communicate with NETCNTRL: ADDRESS NETCNTRL. After that all non-REXX commands will be passed to NETCNTRL, and not to OS/2. To go back to passing non-REXX commands to OS/2, use the REXX verb ADDRESS CMD. An example of this is shown in Figure 12.9.

```
/*how to pass commands*/
Say 'Going to pass commands'
Say 'to the hypothetical environment NETCNTRL'
ADDRESS NETCNTRL /* will not give an error, */
          / *even if NETCNTRL doesn't exist*/
/* hypothetical command being sent*/
/* to NETCNTRL*/
'LOGON MYUSER'
Say 'Returning to OS/2'
ADDRESS CMD
'DIR'
```

Figure 12.9. Hypothetical environment NETCNTRL receiving commands from a REXX program.

12.6 QUESTIONS/PROBLEMS

1. Will this line of instruction be passed to the environment?

PULL var1 var2 var3

2. Will this line of instruction be passed to the environment?

BARK "PLEASE ENTER NAME"

3. If this command works, what will be in RC?

"ERASE ABC.DAT"

Chapter 13

BUILT-IN FUNCTIONS

Functions are a built-in feature of REXX, which supports a very large number of functions that can greatly simplify your programming. This chapter will introduce you to REXX's functions, and it will classify them by their purpose. It will show you two ways to use REXX functions: as functions and as subroutines. Finally, it will tell you how to use the functions that are found only in the OS/2 environment.

Topics

13.1 How Functions Work
13.2 Functions Classified by Type
13.3 The More Important Functions
13.4 Functions Found Only on OS/2
13.5 Using Functions as Subroutines
13.6 Questions/Problems

13.1 HOW FUNCTIONS WORK

A function acts mathematically or does string manipulation on the data passed to it (see Figure 13.1).

```
/*fun01.cmd (Figure 13.1)*/
SAY LENGTH("ABCDE")              /* 5        */


CALL LENGTH "ABCDE"
SAY RESULT                       /* 5        */


SAY TIME()                       /*11:21:43*/
SAY DATE()                       /*25 Dec 1994*/
SAY REVERSE("ABCDEF")            /*FEDCBA   */
SAY RIGHT("ABCDE",3)             /*CDE      */


CALL RIGHT "ABCDE",3
SAY RESULT                       /*CDE      */
```

Figure 13.1. Examples of functions.

Functions may be used in two ways:
- By letting REXX substitute the result of the function's processing for the function invocation, for example:

> SAY LENGTH("ABCDEF") /*becomes SAY 6, which then displays a "6" on the monitor*/
>
> SAVE_LENGTH = LENGTH(NAME)   /* assignment */
>
> SAY "NAME CONTAINS ",
> LENGTH(NAME) " LETTERS"   /* substitution */
>
> SAY "DOUBLING YOUR NAME'S LENGTH GIVES",
> LENGTH(NAME) * 2 "LETTERS"/* arith. expression */

Notes:
  — There must not be a space between the name of the function and the parenthesis.
  — The result of the function is not available in the variable RESULT.

— Separate parameters with commas, not spaces, as in
LEFT("ABCD",2).

• By using the reserved variable RESULT to obtain the result of the function's processing, for example:

```
CALL LENGTH "ABCDEF"
SAY RESULT        /* result contains a 6, which is displayed */

CALL LENGTH "ABCDEF"
SAVE_LENGTH = RESULT      /* assignment */

CALL LENGTH NAME
SAY "NAME CONTAINS ",
    RESULT " LETTERS"     /* substitution*/

CALL LENGTH NAME
SAY "DOUBLING YOUR NAME'S LENGTH GIVES",
    RESULT * 2 " LETTERS "
       /* arithmetic expression */
```

Notes:
— You must do a CALL if you wish to receive the result of the function in the variable RESULT.
— Separate parameters with commas, not spaces, as in
  CALL LEFT "ABCD",2.
— Parentheses are not used.

Some functions have defaults and don't need anything passed to them. Figure 13.2 shows several examples of this.

```
/*fun02.cmd (Figure 13.2)*/
SAY TIME()      /*11:22:33          */

CALL TIME
SAY RESULT      /*11:22:33          */

SAY DATE()      /*22 Jun 1994       */

CALL DATE
SAY RESULT      /*22 Jun 1994       */
```

Figure 13.2. Examples of functions that don't need data passed to them.

13.2 FUNCTIONS CLASSIFIED BY TYPE

To make it easier to find the particular function you need, I have classified the functions by their type.

Character. These act on data as strings, not as numbers. The first group comprises those that examine:

ABBREV	Is it an abbreviation?
ARG	Get info from command line or CALL.
DATATYPE	Is it numeric or character? Covered below.
FIND	Locates a string in another string.
INDEX	Locates a string in another string.
LASTPOS	Locates a string in another string.
LENGTH	Gives number of characters in the string.
POS	Locates a string in another string. Covered below.
SYMBOL	Determines if it is a variable or literal.
WORD	Gives the nth word in a string.
WORDINDEX	Locates a word in a string.
WORDLENGTH	Gives the length of a word in a string.
WORDPOS	Locates a phrase in a string.
WORDS	Counts words in a string.

Those that change:

CENTER	Centers a string.
COMPARE	Compares two strings.
COPIES	Reproduces a string.
DELSTR	Removes characters from a string.
DELWORD	Removes words from a string.
INSERT	Inserts characters into a string.
JUSTIFY	Aligns to the right.
LEFT	Gives the leftmost characters of a string.
REVERSE	Turns a character string around.
RIGHT	Gives the rightmost characters of a string.
SPACE	Inserts spaces into a string.
STRIP	Strips blanks or characters from a string.
SUBSTR	Gives a portion of a string. Covered below.
SUBWORD	Gives some of the words in a string.
TRANSLATE	Converts characters to other characters.

Those that convert:

C2D	Character to decimal
C2X	Character to hexadecimal
D2C	Decimal to character
D2X	Decimal to hexadecimal
X2C	Hexadecimal to character
X2D	Hexadecimal to decimal

Numeric. Those that act on numbers only:

ABS	Drops the sign
FORMAT	Gives back a number with a fixed number of decimal positions
MAX	Determines the highest number of a series
MIN	Determines the lowest number of a series
RANDOM	Gives a series of unpredictable numbers
SIGN	Determines if a number is positive or negative
TRUNC	Adds or deletes decimal positions

Informational. Those that return information about the operating system or about REXX options:

ADDRESS	Tells what the current environment is.
CONDITION	Gives information about errors.
DATE	Gives current date.
DIGITS	Gives current NUMERIC DIGITS setting.
ERRORTEXT	Gives a REXX syntax error message corresponding to the number of the error message.
FORM	Gives current NUMERIC FORM setting.
FUZZ	Gives current NUMERIC FUZZ setting.
QUEUED	Counts the number of lines available in the REXX data queue. Covered below.
SOURCELINE	Gives the text of the program corresponding to a line number.
TIME	Gives current time.

CMS only. Those that work only in the CMS operating system: (not covered here)

DIAG	Gives command to CP.
DIAGRC	Gives command to CP and returns a return code.

OS/2 only, available at once. Those that work only under OS/2 without anything special needing to be done:

BEEP	Sounds a tone in the speaker. Covered below.
B2X	Convert binary to hexadecimal.
CHARIN	Reads a character from a file. See Chapter 18.
CHAROUT	Writes a character to a file. See Chapter 18.
CHARS	Tells how many characters have not yet been read in a file. See Chapter 18.
DIRECTORY	Tells the current directory and optionally changes it. Covered below.
ENDLOCAL	Restores drive, directory and environment variables in effect before last SETLOCAL. Covered below.
FILESPEC	Analyzes a file specification and tells whichever of the following is requested: Drive, Path, File name. Covered below.
LINEIN	Reads a line (record) from a file. See Chapter 18.
LINEOUT	Writes a line (record) to a file. See Chapter 18.
LINES	Tells how many lines (records) have not yet been read in a file. See Chapter 18.
RXFUNCADD	Makes certain other OS/2 functions available for use (listed in Appendix D).
RXFUNCDROP	Makes certain other OS/2 functions unavailable for use (see RXFUNCADD).
RXFUNCQUERY	Tells if certain other OS/2 functions are available for use (see RXFUNCADD).
RXQUEUE	Creates and deletes private data queues. See Chapter 16.

SETLOCAL	Saves drive, directory and environment variables currently in effect.
STREAM	Opens, closes files, gives current status information about files. See Chapter 18.
X2B	Converts hexadecimal to binary.

OS/2 only, must be preregistered. Available only if you tell OS/2 you need them: (see text, Section 13.4) and Figure 13.10.

RXMESSAGEBOX	Under Presentation Manager only. Displays a question and answer box. Covered below.
SYSCLS	Clears the screen. Same as OS/2 command 'CLS'. Covered below.
SYSCREATEOBJECT	Creates an instance of an object class. beyond the scope of this book.
SYSCURPOS	May not be used under Presentation Manager. Tells the current cursor position and optionally moves the cursor to a specific position. Covered below.
SYSCURSTATE	May not be used under Presentation Manager. Removes the cursor from the screen or brings it back.
SYSDEREGISTEROBJECTCLASS	
	Deregisters an object class. Beyond the scope of this book.
SYSDESTROYOBJECT	
	Destroys an existing Workplace Shell object. Beyond the scope of this book.
SYSDRIVEINFO	Tells the current drive, its capacity and available space. Covered below.
SYSDRIVEMAP	Tells the letters of the drives that are available. Covered below.
SYSDROPFUNCS	Drops all these functions.
SYSFILEDELETE	Deletes a file. Same as OS/2 command ERASE. Covered below.
SYSFILESEARCH	Searches through a file and finds all lines (records) that match a given character string.

SYSFILETREE	Searches through directories and finds all files that match a given file specification.
SYSGETEA	Returns the extended attribute of a file.
SYSGETKEY	Goes immediately to the keyboard and gets the next character that was typed in, in the keyboard buffer. Does not wait until you press ENTER. Covered below.
SYSGETMESSAGE	Retrieves a help message from OS/2, given the message's number. Covered below.
SYSINI	Retrieves and changes variable information maintained by OS/2, known as profile variables.
SYSMKDIR	Creates a directory. Same as OS/2 command 'MD'.
SYSOS2VER	Tells the version of OS/2 that is being used.
SYSPUTEA	Puts an extended attribute on a file.
SYSQUERYCLASSLIST	Tells the names of currently registered object classes. Beyond the scope of this book.
SYSREGISTEROBJECTCLASS	Registers an object class. Beyond the scope of this book.
SYSRMDIR	Deletes a directory. Same as OS/2 command 'RD'.
SYSSEARCHPATH	Searches through a file path to find a file. Tells the file specification.
SYSSETICON	Associates an icon with a file.
SYSSETOBJECTDATA	Opens an instance of an object or changes the settings of an existing object. Beyond the scope of this book.
SYSSLEEP	Suspends execution of the program for a specified number of seconds. Covered below.
SYSTEMPFILENAME	Asks OS/2 to give you a file name you can safely use as a temporary file. It is one that does not currently exist.

SYSTEXTSCREENREAD
> Reads characters from the screen. May not be used with the Presentation Manager.

SYSTEXTSCREENSIZE
> Tells the size of the screen. May not be used with the Presentation Manager.

SYSWAITNAMEDPIPE
> Waits for a given length of time for a pipe to become available. Beyond the scope of this book.

TSO only. Those that work only in the TSO system: (not covered here)

LISTDSI	Gives dataset information
OUTTRAP	Captures display output of TSO commands
SYSDSN	Gives dataset information
SYSVAR	Gives information about execution and system status

Unclassifiable

| VALUE | Examines a literal as if it were a variable; examines a variable and processes its contents as another variable |

13.3 THE MORE IMPORTANT FUNCTIONS

The full list of REXX functions can be found in Appendix D. I will explain only a few here.

DATATYPE (Figure 13.3). This one allows you to check all numbers typed in at the terminal for validity. You need to do this, because any attempt to do arithmetic with character data will give you a REXX syntax error.

```
/*dtex01.cmd (Figure 13.3)*/
 /*DATATYPE(string)
   Result is NUM if a valid REXX number.
   CHAR otherwise.

   SAY DATATYPE(123)  --> NUM
   SAY DATATYPE(ABCD) --> CHAR      */


  /* REXX make sure person enters a number */
  SAY "PLEASE ENTER A NUMBER "
  PULL NUMBER
  IF DATATYPE(NUMBER) = "NUM"
  THEN SAY "ONE HALF OF THAT IS " NUMBER / 2
  ELSE
      do
        Say "You must enter a number"
        Exit
      end
```

Figure 13.3. Example of making sure a valid number is entered.

LENGTH (Figure 13.4). This will tell you the total number of characters in the string. If a variable is used, the contents of the variable are examined.

```
/*lex01.cmd (Figure 13.4)*/
 /* LENGTH(string)
    Counts the characters in string.*/

   SAY "PLEASE ENTER YOUR NAME"
   PULL NAME
   SAY "YOUR NAME CONTAINS"
   SAY LENGTH(NAME) " CHARACTERS"
```

Figure 13.4. The LENGTH function.

POS (Figure 13.5). This can be used to determine if a character is present.

```
/*pos01.cmd (Figure 13.5)*/
/* POS(needle,haystack[,start-pos])
    Returns the starting position of
    needle in haystack.
    If not there, a 0 is returned
    If start-pos specified,
    search starts at that position.    */

    SAY POS('C','ABCDEF')  /*--> 3*/
```

Figure 13.5. The POS function.

QUEUED() (Figure 13.6). This will return the number of lines that are currently available in the data queue. Chapter 16, which is on the data queue, will provide some examples of its use.

```
/*qex01.cmd (Figure 13.6)*/
/* QUEUED()
    The number of lines available in the data queue.*/

    PUSH 'ABCDEF'
    SAY QUEUED()  /*--> 1 */
```

Figure 13.6. The QUEUED function.

SUBSTR (Figure 13.7). This will give you a portion of a string.

```
/*subex01.cmd (Figure 13.7)*/
/* SUBSTR(string,start-pos,length)

    Returns a portion of a string
    beginning at start-pos, for length.    */

    SAY SUBSTR('ABCDEF',3,2)  /*--> CD */
```

Figure 13.7. The SUBSTR function.

TRANSLATE. This function provides a convenient way to convert to upper case. Figure 13.8 shows how you might convert to upper case.

```
/*trxex01.cmd (Figure 13.8)*/
name_1 = 'Sue'
name_2 = 'SUE'
if translate(name_1) = translate(name_2)
then say 'now they are equal'
```

Figure 13.8. Converting to upper case.

X2D and D2X. These two functions convert from one numbering system to another. X2D converts from hexadecimal to decimal, and D2X converts from decimal to hexadecimal. Please see Figure 13.9 for an example of how you might create a hexadecimal addition program using REXX functions.

```
/*d2xex01.cmd (Figure 13.9)*/
/*REXX Hex  adder */
ARG HEX1 HEX2
DEC1 = X2D(HEX1)
DEC2 = X2D(HEX2)
DECSUM = DEC1 + DEC2
SAY "HEX SUM IS: " D2X(DECSUM)
```

Figure 13.9. Doing Hex addition using functions.

13.4 FUNCTIONS FOUND ONLY ON OS/2

Please look at the list of functions in Section 13.2 that are available only under OS/2. There is a very large number of them. Also, please notice that there are two types — those that are available now, automatically, without any further ado, and those that you have to do something special if you want them. I know you can't wait to use these functions, so I will tell you right now what you have to do in order to use them. Add statements similar to those shown in Figure 13.10 to the beginning of your program. These statements will register the optional REXX function that you intend to use and make it available in your program. This is conceptually like loading the function into memory so it can be available for your use.

```
/* showload.cmd (Figure 13.10) */
/* shows how to register a function with OS/2
   so that you can use it in your program

   change "syscls" shown below to the function name
   that you are actualloy using
*/

function_to_load = "syscls"
call rxfuncadd function_to_load,'rexxutil',,
    function_to_load
/* now you can use the function in this program*/
CALL SYSCLS
Say "SYSCLS has been loaded"
```

Figure 13.10. Suggested statements that will make available a built-in REXX function that needs preregistering. Change the name shown "syscls" to the actual function name that you are using in your program.

BEEP (Figure 13.11). BEEP sounds a tone in the speaker. You can use this to warn of error, alert the person at the keyboard that something is to be typed in, or to play a tune. The format is

CALL BEEP frequency, milliseconds

```
/*TRYBEEP.CMD (Figure 13.11)*/
CALL BEEP 600, 200  /* will sound a 600 Hertz
(cycles per second) tone for two tenths of a
second */
Say 'Please type in your name'
PULL name
IF name = ''
then
  do
    CALL BEEP 170, 1200
    Say 'You did not type in a name.'
    Say 'Please type it in now'
    PULL name
  end
```

Figure 13.11. Program that uses the BEEP function.

Here is a fun program that allows you to play a tune if you are somewhat tolerant of imperfect pitch (Figure 13.12.)

```
/*tune.cmd (Figure 13.12, 13.25)*/
say "type in a number 1 - 0.  E to end"
key = ''
do until Translate(key) = "E"
   key = sysgetkey()

      if key = 1 then call beep 262,200
      if key = 2 then call beep 294,200
      if key = 3 then call beep 330,200
      if key = 4 then call beep 349,200
      if key = 5 then call beep 392,200
      if key = 6 then call beep 440,200
      if key = 7 then call beep 494,200
      if key = 8 then call beep 523,200

end
```

Figure 13.12. A primitive piano.

DIRECTORY (Figure 13.13). Tells the current directory and optionally changes it. The following example will illustrate both capabilities.

```
/*dirtest.cmd (Figure 13.13)*/
desired_directory = 'c:\rexxprgs'
say 'Current directory is  ' directory()
say 'Desired directory is' desired_directory
if translate(directory()) =,
   translate(desired_directory)
then say 'Already in correct directory'
else call directory desired_directory
```

Figure 13.13. A program that uses the DIRECTORY function.

ENDLOCAL (Figure 13.14). Restores the drive, directory, and environment variables that were in effect before last SETLOCAL.

```
/*locltest.cmd (Figure 13.14)*/
say 'Current directory is ' directory()
call setlocal
say 'Changing to  root'
'cd \'
say 'Now it is ' directory()
say 'Going back to original'
call endlocal
say 'Went back to ' directory()
```

Figure 13.14. Using the SETLOCAL and DIRECTORY functions.

FILESPEC (Figure 13.15). Analyzes a file specification and tells whichever of the following is requested: drive, path, name of the file.

```
/*fispec.cmd (Figure 14.15)*/
file = 'c:\rexxprgs\test.dat'
say filespec('drive',file) /* c:        */
say filespec('path',file)  /* \rexxprgs\ */
say filespec('name',file)  /* test.dat   */
```

Figure 13.15. The FILESPEC function.

SETLOCAL . See ENDLOCAL, above.

RXMESSAGEBOX (Figures 13.16 – 13.18). Works under Presentation Manager only. Displays a question and answer box. Try the following two programs, TESTPM1 and TESTPM2, to see exactly what a message box looks like. You'll need to execute your program with the Presentation Manager like this:
PMREXX TESTPM1

```
/* testpm1.cmd (Figure 13.16)*/
/*    if    presentation    manager    is    available,
function_to_load = "rxmessagebox"
call rxfuncadd function_to_load,'rexxutil',,
     function_to_load
display message box */
if address() = 'PMREXX'
then
  do
    call rxmessagebox "Want to Continue",,
         "Continue?","yesno","hand"
    say result
  end
```

Figure 13.16. Using the RXMESSAGEBOX function.

```
/* testpm2.cmd (Figure 13.17)*/
/* if presentation manager is available,
   call subroutine BOX.CMD to display
   message box,
   otherwise start up presentation manager,
   then run program BOX.CMD to display
   message box
*/
if address()  = 'PMREXX'
then
   do
     say 'In presentation manager'
     call 'box'
   end
else
   do
      say 'Not in presentation manager'
      'pmrexx box'
   end
```

Figure 13.17. Program that starts up the Presentation Manager if it hasn't already been started.

```
/* box.cmd (Figure 13.18)
  displays message box.
  works in presentation manager only
*/
function_to_load = "rxmessagebox"
call rxfuncadd function_to_load,'rexxutil',,
     function_to_load
call rxmessagebox "Want to continue",,
     "Continue?","yesno","hand"
say result
if result = 6
then say 'Thank you for replying yes'
else say 'Your reply was no'
return
```

Figure 13.18. A user-written function that displays a message box.

SYSCLS (Figure 13.19). Clears the screen. This does the same thing as the OS/2 command 'CLS'.

```
/*clearit.cmd (Figure 13.19)*/
function_to_load = "syscls"
call rxfuncadd function_to_load,'rexxutil',,
     function_to_load
function_to_load = "syssleep"
call rxfuncadd function_to_load,'rexxutil',,
     function_to_load
say 'Going to clear screen with OS/2 command'
call syssleep 5
'CLS'
say 'Going to clear it with function'
call syssleep 5
call syscls
say 'notice any difference?'
call syssleep 1
```

Figure 13.19. Clearing the screen two different ways.

SYSCURPOS (Figures 13.20 and 13.21). May not be used under Presentation Manager. Tells the current cursor position and optionally moves the cursor to a specific position.

```
/*trycur1.cmd (Figure 13.20)*/
/* tells where cursor is */
/* do not use under presentation manager */
function_to_load = "syscurpos"
call rxfuncadd function_to_load,'rexxutil',,
     function_to_load
say syscurpos()
```

Figure 13.20. Determining the cursor position.

```
/*trycur2.cmd (Figure 13.21)*/
/* tells where cursor is */
/* do not use under presentation manager */
say syscurpos()
/* then change it to row 5, column 10 */
function_to_load = "syscurpos"
call rxfuncadd function_to_load,'rexxutil',,
     function_to_load
call syscurpos  5, 10
say syscurpos()
```

Figure 13.21. Changing the cursor position.

SYSDRIVEINFO (Figure 13.22). Tells the current drive, its capacity, and available space.

```
/*trydriv.cmd (Figure 13.22)*/
function_to_load = "sysdriveinfo"
call rxfuncadd function_to_load,'rexxutil',,
     function_to_load
say sysdriveinfo('c:')
```

Figure 13.22. Obtaining disk drive information.

SYSDRIVEMAP (Figure 13.23). Tells the letters of the drives that are available.

```
/*trydrivm.cmd (Figure 13.23)*/
function_to_load = "sysdrivemap"
call rxfuncadd function_to_load,'rexxutil',,
     function_to_load
say sysdrivemap()
```

Figure 13.23. Obtaining the letters of the drives that are currently available.

SYSFILEDELETE. Deletes a file. Same as OS/2 command ERASE, except that it doesn't display an error message when the file doesn't exist. Try the program in Figure 13.24.

```
/*trydel1.cmd (Figure 13.23)*/
function_to_load = "sysfiledelete"
call rxfuncadd function_to_load,'rexxutil',,
     function_to_load
say 'Using erase command'
say 'Going to delete file that is not there',
    '(error message)'
'erase tempdel.del'
say 'now it is there, trying to delete again'
'copy c:\rexxprgs\trydel1.cmd    tempdel.del'
'erase tempdel.del'

say 'Using sysfiledelete function'
say 'Going to delete file that is not there',
    '(no error message)'
call sysfiledelete 'tempdel.del'
say 'now it is there, trying to delete again'
'copy c:\rexxprgs\trydel1.cmd    tempdel.del'
call sysfiledelete 'tempdel.del'
```

Figure 13.24. Deleting a file two different ways.

SYSGETKEY (Figure 13.25). Goes immediately to the keyboard and gets the next character that was typed in, in the keyboard buffer. Does not wait until you press ENTER. This program, already shown with BEEP above, will illustrate how SYSGETKEY works.

```
/*tune.cmd (Figure 13.12, 13.25)*/
function_to_load = "sysgetkey"
call rxfuncadd function_to_load,'rexxutil',,
     function_to_load
say "type in a number 1 - 0.  E to end"
key = ''
do until Translate(key) = "E"
   key = sysgetkey()

        if key = 1 then call beep 262,200
        if key = 2 then call beep 294,200
        if key = 3 then call beep 330,200
        if key = 4 then call beep 349,200
        if key = 5 then call beep 392,200
        if key = 6 then call beep 440,200
        if key = 7 then call beep 494,200
        if key = 8 then call beep 523,200

end
```

Figure 13.25. Finding out the key just pressed and using it in a program.

SYSGETMESSAGE (Figure 13.26). Retrieves a help message from OS/2, given the message's number. Try this program, using other numbers instead of 49.

```
/*getmsg.cmd (Figure 13.26)*/
function_to_load = "sysgetmessage"
call rxfuncadd function_to_load,'rexxutil',,
     function_to_load
say sysgetmessage(49)
```

Figure 13.26. Example of SYSGETMESSAGE.

SYSSLEEP (Figure 13.27). Suspends execution of the program for a specified number of seconds. Try this one:

```
/*snooze.cmd (Figure 13.27)*/
function_to_load = "syssleep"
call rxfuncadd function_to_load,'rexxutil',,
     function_to_load
say 'zzzzzzzz'
call syssleep 5
say 'hi again'
```

Figure 13.27. Example of the SYSSLEEP function.

13.5 USING FUNCTIONS AS SUBROUTINES

All REXX functions can be used as subroutines. This means that you may do a CALL and use the reserved variable RESULT. Both methods produce the same answers. The choice of which to use is a matter of personal preference or style.

Here are some suggestions on when to use functions as subroutines:

• When no answer or result is needed.
• When you need the result more than once. This lets REXX perform the function just once and results in more efficiency. Example:

```
/*fun03.cmd (Section 13.5)*/
SAY "PLEASE ENTER YOUR NAME"
PULL NAME
CALL LENGTH  NAME
IF RESULT < 1
THEN SAY "YOU DIDN'T ENTER YOUR NAME"
ELSE SAY "NAME IS" RESULT "CHARACTERS LONG"
```

13.6 QUESTIONS/PROBLEMS

1. True or false: There must be a space after the name of the function and before the parenthesis when you use a function.

2. When you call a built-in function with CALL, where is the answer given?

3. Accept two numbers from the keyboard, and check to be sure they are valid. Subtract one from the other. Drop the sign of the answer, and display the answer. Expected results:

= = = > CH13P03 100 20
   80
= = = > CH13P03 20 100
   80

4. Using a function, create a program that will convert one character string to another. Set it up so that if you type in:

  GREAT

it will print out:

  BUENO.

5. Write a program that will accept a hex number, a plus or minus sign, and another hex number; then add or subtract based on the sign. Display the answer in hex. Expected results:

= = = > CH13P05 e - 2
   C
= = = > CH13P05 e + 2
   10

6. Here is a working example of a program that will convert all the letters in a string of characters to lower case. Modify it so that it converts from lower case to upper case. (Be aware that the REXX PARSE UPPER instruction will do the same thing.)

```
/*CH13P06Q.CMD converts upper to lower*/
instring = "THIS WAS IN UPPER CASE"
upper_alpha = "ABCDEFGHIJKLMNOPQRSTUVWXYZ"
lower_alpha = "abcdefghijklmnopqrstuvwxyz"
outstring = translate(instring,lower_alpha,upper_alpha)
Say "Here is the converted string"
Say outstring
```

Chapter 14

USER-WRITTEN FUNCTIONS/SUBROUTINES

This chapter will show you how to create and use both the internal and external types of functions and subroutines.

Topics

14.1 Considerations in Writing Functions/Subroutines
14.2 What Are Internal Functions/Subroutines Like?
14.3 What Are External Functions/Subroutines Like?
14.4 Search Order for Functions/Subroutines
14.5 Style
14.6 Questions/Problems

14.1 CONSIDERATIONS IN WRITING FUNCTIONS/SUBROUTINES

All built-in REXX functions may be used as functions or subroutines. Figure 14.1 shows such a case. The result of the function is substituted for the function.

```
/*uwfs01.cmd (Figure 14.1)*/
 SAY LENGTH("ABCDE")
 /* 5 IS DISPLAYED */
```

Figure 14.1. A built-in function being used as a function.

185

Figure 14.2 shows a built-in function used as a subroutine. The result of the function is available in the special variable RESULT.

```
/* uwfs02.cmd (Figure 14.2)*/
CALL LENGTH "ABCDE"
SAY RESULT
/* 5 IS DISPLAYED */
```

Figure 14.2. A built-in function being used as a subroutine.

I don't see any difference between built-in functions and built-in subroutines. The "difference" is in the way they are invoked, or called. I strongly suggest that you write your own functions so they can be used as either functions or subroutines, just as IBM did. It isn't hard to accomplish this. These points should be followed in writing your functions/subroutines so that they will look and act like IBM's:

- Pass information to them through an ARG.

- Give back an answer on the RETURN statement, even if it is only the null string (").

- Avoid sharing variables with the main part of the program. Don't take this as absolute, however, because sharing variables with the main part of the program may sometimes be more convenient.

If you write your functions/subroutines this way, you may use them either internally or externally with very little change. In addition, your programs will be more modular and robust.

A REXX function/subroutine can be internal, physically contained in the same program, or external, a separate program. REXX will look internally first, then for a built-in, then externally. You may force REXX to look first for built-in and then externally by putting the name of the function/subroutine in quotes. SAY "MYSUBR"(12345) would accomplish this. SAY MYSUBR(1234) would make REXX search internally, then for a built-in, then externally.

Figure 14.3 contains an example of a custom-made function/subroutine that will replace any character string with another. It makes use of several built-in functions to accomplish this. Please type it in and try it on your system.

```
/*uwfs03.cmd (Figure 14.3)*/
Call replchar "N", "D", "NANCY LOVES YOGURT"
say result              /* DANCY LOVES YOGURT */

EXIT

/* Function/Subroutine begins here */
REPLCHAR:
ARG BAD_CHAR, GOOD_CHAR, STRING
DO LENGTH(STRING)
 WHICH_BAD_CHAR    = POS(BAD_CHAR,STRING)
 IF WHICH_BAD_CHAR = 0 THEN RETURN STRING
 LENGTH_BAD_CHAR   = LENGTH(BAD_CHAR)
 STRING =,
  SUBSTR(STRING,1,WHICH_BAD_CHAR-1) ||,
       GOOD_CHAR,
  ||   SUBSTR(STRING, WHICH_BAD_CHAR + LENGTH_BAD_CHAR)
RETURN STRING
```

Figure 14.3. An example of a custom-written function/subroutine you might create to change any character in a string to any other character.

14.2 WHAT ARE INTERNAL FUNCTIONS/SUBROUTINES LIKE?

Refer to Figure 14.4 for the general form of the function/subroutine. See Figure 14.5 for an example of invoking a function/subroutine as a subroutine and Figure 14.6 for an example of invoking one as a function. Notice the following points about user-written internal functions/subroutines:

- They are contained within the program, usually at the physical end, after an EXIT statement, so that control will not fall through into the subroutines.

- They are defined by a label, which is its first statement.

- Data is usually passed to the function/subroutine through its ARG statement. The ARG statement functions like the ARG in the main program, but you should use commas to separate the different items of data.

- After computing the answer, place it on the RETURN statement. This passes the answer back to the statement that called the function/subroutine.

- An internal function/subroutine inherits these settings from the main program: ADDRESS, NUMERIC DIGITS, and FUZZ. However, any change that the internal function/subroutine makes to these settings affects only itself. REXX restores the settings at the RETURN, so that the main program will see them just as it left them.

- If you want to know the line number of the statement that called the function/subroutine, examine the special variable SIGL.

```
/* main part of program here */
 invoke function/subroutine
           .
           .
 EXIT

 /* Function/Subroutine begins here */
 label:
 /*comment explaining purpose*/
 ARG var1, var2, var3, var4 . . .
 /*compute answer here */
 RETURN answer
```

Figure 14.4. The general form of an internal function/subroutine (label and answer will be different, depending on the particular program).

```
/*uwfs04.cmd (Figure 14.5)*/
/*REXX main program*/
  CALL ADDEMUP 1,2           /* invoking with CALL */
  SAY RESULT                 /* answer in RESULT   */
  EXIT                       /* don't drop into it */

 /* Function/Subroutine begins here */
 ADDEMUP:                    /* label is name        */

 ARG NUM1,NUM2              /*pick up info on args */
 ANSWER =    NUM1 + NUM2
 RETURN ANSWER              /* give back answer    */
                            /* on RETURN           */
```

Figure 14.5. An example of an internal function/subroutine invoked as a subroutine.

```
/*uwfs05.cmd (Figure 14.6)*/
 /*REXX main program*/

 SAY  ADDEMUP(1,2)          /* invoking as functt*/
 EXIT                       /* don't drop into it*/

 /* Function/Subroutine begins here */
 ADDEMUP:                   /* label is name        */

 ARG NUM1,NUM2             /*pick up info on args*/
 ANSWER =    NUM1 + NUM2
 RETURN ANSWER             /* give back answer    */
                           /* on RETURN (requird)*/
```

Figure 14.6. An example of an internal function/subroutine invoked as a function.

The PROCEDURE statement after the label prevents sharing of variables. (See Figures 14.7 and 14.8.) Variables are shared if you don't specify PROCEDURE (Figures 14.4 and 14.5).

```
/*uwfs06.cmd (Figure 14.7)*/
 /*REXX main program*/
 CALL ADDEMUP 1,2           /* invoking with CALL*/
 SAY RESULT                 /* answer in RESULT  */
 EXIT                       /* don't drop into it*/

 /* Function/Subroutine begins here */
 ADDEMUP: PROCEDURE         /* label is name       */
                            /* don't share varbls */
 ARG NUM1,NUM2              /*pick up info on args*/
 ANSWER =   NUM1 + NUM2
 RETURN ANSWER              /* give back answer    */
                            /* on RETURN           */
```

Figure 14.7. An example of an internal function/subroutine that doesn't share variables, invoked as a subroutine.

```
/*uwfs07.cmd (Figure 14.8)*/
 /*REXX main program*/

 SAY  ADDEMUP(1,2)          /* invoking as funct */
 EXIT                       /* don't drop into it*/

 /* Function/Subroutine begins here */
 ADDEMUP: PROCEDURE         /* label is name       */
                            /* don't share varbls */
 ARG NUM1,NUM2              /*pick up info on args*/
 ANSWER =   NUM1 + NUM2
 RETURN ANSWER              /* give back answer    */
                            /* on RETURN (requird)*/
```

Figure 14.8. An example of an internal function/subroutine that doesn't share variables, invoked as a function.

If you use PROCEDURE and need to share selected variables, you may use EXPOSE (see Figure 14.9).

```
/*uwfs08.cmd (Figure 14.9)*/
 /*REXX main program*/

 CALL ADDEMUP 1,2            /* invoking with CALL*/
 SAY RESULT                  /* answer in RESULT  */
 SAY NUM2                    /* this var shared   */
 EXIT                        /* don't drop into it*/

 /* Function/Subroutine begins here */
 ADDEMUP:                    /* label is name     */
 PROCEDURE EXPOSE NUM2       /* share only num2   */
 ARG NUM1,NUM2              /*pick up info on args*/
 ANSWER =   NUM1 + NUM2
 RETURN ANSWER              /* give back answer   */
                            /* on RETURN          */
```

Figure 14.9. An example of an internal function/subroutine that shares only one variable.

Using PROCEDURE allows you to create functions/subroutines that may be executed recursively, that is, they may execute themselves. Figure 14.10 illustrates how you may compute the factorial of a number.

```
/*uwfs09.cmd (Figure 14.10)*/
 /*REXX main program*/

 CALL FACTORIAL 4           /* invoking with CALL*/
 SAY RESULT                 /* RESULT =     24   */
 EXIT                       /* don't drop into it*/

 /* Function/Subroutine begins here */
 FACTORIAL:                 /* label is name     */
 PROCEDURE                  /* don't share vars  */
 ARG NUM1                  /*pick up info on args*/
 IF NUM1 = 0 THEN RETURN 1
 CALL FACTORIAL NUM1 - 1   /* call self         */
 RETURN RESULT * NUM1      /* give back answer  */
                           /* on RETURN         */
```

Figure 14.10. An example of an internal function/subroutine that invokes itself.

14.3 WHAT ARE EXTERNAL FUNCTIONS/SUBROUTINES LIKE?

Let's see how external functions/subroutines are different from internal ones:

- External user-written functions/subroutines are contained in a separate program.
- OS/2 must be able to find the function/subroutine just as it found the main program that calls the function/subroutine.
  — Either the function/subroutine must be in the same search path as the main program, or you must give the complete file specification for the function/subroutine when calling it.

- When the function/subroutine is in the same search path as the program calling it (the main program), you place the name of the function/subroutine optionally inside of quotes or apostrophes after the REXX verb CALL. See Figure 14.11. This way is neat and convenient, but the subroutine and main program must be in the same path. (They normally are.)

```
/*MAINPROG.CMD (Figure 14.11)*/
/*It is assumed you execute this program this way:
MAINPROG*/
/* function/subroutine had better be in same search path
as main program*/
call extfunc '1'
say result
/* or: */
call 'extfunc' '1'
say result
exit
- - - - - - - - - separate program- - - - - - -
/*extfunc.cmd (Figure 14.11)*/
/* a sample external function/subroutine that goes with
MAINPROG.CMD
and MAINPRO2.CMD*/
arg number
if datatype(number) = 'NUM'
then return number + 1
else return ''
```

Figure 14.11. How to call a function/subroutine when it is in the same search path as the main program.

- When the functions/subroutine is not (or might not be) in the same search path as the program calling it (the main program), you place the complete file specification of the function/subroutine inside of quotes or apostrophes after the REXX verb CALL. See Figure 14.12. This way gives you independence. You don't have to know or care if the function/subroutine is in the same search path as the main program. But you have to know the drive and directory of subroutines. (You normally do.)

```
/*MAINPRO2.CMD (Figure 14.12)*/
/* doesn't matter if function/subroutine is in
same search path as main
program*/
call 'c:\rexxprgs\extfunc' '1'
say result
```

Figure 14.12. How to call a function/subroutine when it is not in the same search path as the main program.

- There is no PROCEDURE statement in an external function/subroutine (Figure 14.13). All variables are automatically insulated from those of the calling program.

- A label is not used to define the external function/subroutine (Figure 14.14).

- Settings of ADDRESS and NUMERIC are not inherited from the caller; they revert to the system default.

```
/*mainpro3.cmd (Figure 14.13)*/

    CALL "ADDEMUP" 1,2          /* invoking with CALL*/
    SAY RESULT                  /* answer in RESULT  */
    EXIT

 - - - - - - - - - - separate program- - - - - - - - -
    /*ADDEMUP.CMD (Fig 14.13)  filename is func name */
    ARG NUM1,NUM2              /*pick up info on args*/
    ANSWER =   NUM1 + NUM2
    RETURN ANSWER             /* give back answer   */
                             /* on RETURN          */
```

Figure 14.13. An example of an external function/subroutine invoked as a subroutine.

```
/*mainpro4.cmd (Figure 14.14)*/
  /*REXX MAIN PROG */
  SAY  "ADDEMUP"(1,2)      /* invoking as function*/
  EXIT

- - - - - - - - - - separate program- - - - - - - - -
  /*ADDEMUP.CMD (Fig 14.13)  file name is func name*/
  ARG NUM1,NUM2            /*pick up info on args */
  ANSWER =   NUM1 + NUM2
  RETURN ANSWER           /* give back answer    */
                          /* on RETURN           */
```

Figure 14.14. An example of an external function/subroutine invoked as a function.

There are, of course, quite a few similarities with internal functions/subroutines (compare Figures 14.15 and 14.16):

• Both use an ARG to pick up the data passed to them.

• Commas are used to separate the items on the ARG.

• Both end with a RETURN that passes back the answer to the caller.

```
/*mainpro5.cmd (Figure 14.15)*/
  /* REXX Exec that uses internal subroutine */
  FIRST      = 100
  SECOND     = 120

  /* CALL AS SUBROUTINE */
  CALL WHICH_GREATER    FIRST  ,  SECOND
  SAY "THE GREATER IS      " RESULT
  /* USE AS FUNCTION */
  SAY "THE GREATER IS       "
  SAY  WHICH_GREATER(FIRST, SECOND)
  EXIT

  WHICH_GREATER:
  ARG NUM1, NUM2
  IF DATATYPE(NUM1) = "NUM" & DATATYPE(NUM2) = "NUM"
  THEN NOP
  ELSE RETURN ""
  IF NUM1 = NUM2 THEN RETURN ""
  IF NUM1 > NUM2 THEN RETURN 1
  IF NUM2 > NUM1 THEN RETURN 2
```

Figure 14.15. An example of an internal function/subroutine to decide which number is greater.

```
/*mainpro6.cmd (Figure 14.16)*/
  /* REXX Exec that uses external subroutine */
  FIRST    = 100
  SECOND   = 120

  /* CALL AS SUBROUTINE */
  CALL "WHICHGTR"        FIRST  ,  SECOND
  SAY "THE GREATER IS     " RESULT

  /* USE AS FUNCTION */
  SAY "THE GREATER IS     "
  SAY  "WHICHGTR"(FIRST, SECOND)
  EXIT
- - - - - - - s e p a r a t e   p r o g r a m  - - - - -

/*WHICHGTR.cmd  (Figure  14.16)  in  your  REXXPRGS
directory*/
 ARG NUM1, NUM2
 IF DATATYPE(NUM1) = "NUM" & DATATYPE(NUM2) = "NUM"
 THEN NOP
 ELSE RETURN ""

 IF NUM1 = NUM2 THEN RETURN ""
 IF NUM1 > NUM2 THEN RETURN 1
 IF NUM2 > NUM1 THEN RETURN 2
```

Figure 14.16. An example of an external function/subroutine to decide which number is greater.

14.4 SEARCH ORDER FOR FUNCTIONS/SUBROUTINES

Here is the order in which OS/2 will search for functions/subroutines:

• If there are no quotes or apostrophes around the name, OS/2 will search for
  - An internal function first,
  - then a built-in,
  - then an external.

• If the function/subroutine name is in quotes or apostrophes, OS/2 will search for
  - A built-in first,
  - then an external.

14.5 STYLE

I don't like complex programs. I feel that complex processing should be broken down into manageable portions. Functions/subroutines make this easy. Here are some recommendations regarding style.

- Design the program so the logic consists of a main logic area and many functions/subroutines — for example:

DO UNTIL TIME_TO_STOP = "YES"
  CALL SUBR11
  CALL SUBR2
  CALL SUBR3
END
EXIT
SUBR1:
/* subroutine instructions */
RETURN
SUBR2:
/* subroutine instructions */
RETURN
SUBR3:
/* subroutine instructions */
RETURN

- Write external functions/subroutines that can be shared by all in your installation.

- Use a function/subroutine as a function or as a subroutine, whichever is more convenient.
CALL BEEP 400, 200
SAY LENGTH("ABCD")

- If possible, hide variables in internal functions/subroutines by means of the PROCEDURE verb.

- If invoking an external function/subroutine, put the name in quotes.

- Use commas to separate items passed to a function/subroutine.

- Use commas to separate variables on the ARG of a function/subroutine.

- If writing a long function/subroutine, put a comment on the RETURN statement that repeats the name of the function/subroutine.

14.6 QUESTIONS/PROBLEMS

1. True or false: In REXX, user-written functions/subroutines may be used either as functions or subroutines.

2. True or false: If you use the function/subroutine as a function, you do it this way: function-name(data).

3. True or false: If you use the function/subroutine as a subroutine, you do it this way:

 CALL function-name data

and the answer comes back in RESULT.

4. Write an internal function/subroutine that will concatenate two items passed to it (without spaces). Invoke it as a function, then as a subroutine. Check automatically within the program that both ways produce the same result. Expected results:

= = = > CH14P04 cat dog
INVOKED AS FUNCTION: CATDOG
INVOKED AS SUBROUTINE: CATDOG
RESULTS ARE EQUAL

5. Redo the percent increase problem as an external subroutine, naming it PERCENTI (see Problem 12 in Chapter 7). Have it accept two parameters (that is, arguments): first, old salary; second, new salary. Have it return the percent increase on the RETURN statement. Check both numbers for numeric. If either is not valid, display a message and return a zero.

 Write another program to test this one by calling it as a function, then as a subroutine. Place both in the same directory.

6. Using the solution to Problem 4, write your concatenate function/sub-routine as an external function/subroutine (leave the internal function/sub-routine where it is). Call the external function/subroutine in such a way that you are sure to invoke the external, not the internal function/subroutine. Prove that you invoked the external, not the internal.

7. Create a metric conversion external function/subroutine named Metric. It will accept two arguments: UNIT and QUANTITY. UNIT has these possible values:

  LITER   QUART   MILE   KILOMETER.

It returns a number equivalent to QUANTITY in the other measuring system, based on this table:

1 liter	= 1.057 quarts
1 quart	= .946 liters
1 mile	= 8/5 kilometers
1 kilometer	= .625 miles

Also, write a main program that invokes this as a function. Expected results:

```
= = > CH14P07M  kilometer 1000
   625 MILES
```

Chapter 15

LOOPING

This chapter will acquaint you with REXX's loop control structure, DO. REXX implements the repetition control structure perfectly, allowing many options on the DO. You will see how to repeat and step a variable, set the condition for ending the loop, loop without limit, exit properly from the loop, and how to skip back to the beginning of the loop.

Topics

15.1   THE DO AND END

The DO control structure always begins with a DO and ends with an END (see Figure 15.1). Between the DO and the END will be found the instructions that are to be executed repeatedly. The loop can be controlled by the addition of modifiers.

199

```
                                    modifiers
     DO      modifiers
             instruction           WHILE
             instruction           UNTIL
     END                           variable =
                                   FOREVER
                                   FOR
                                   number
```

Figure 15.1. The general form of the DO and END.

15.2 THE DO WHILE

WHILE continues the loop as long as something is true. It checks before doing the loop the first time and may not execute it even once. See Figure 15.2 for the general form of the DO WHILE and Figure 15.3 for an example.

```
     DO WHILE something is true
          instructions
     END
```

Figure 15.2. The DO WHILE.

```
     DO WHILE TIME() < "17:01:00"
       SAY "WORK"
     END
```

Figure 15.3. An example of DO WHILE.

15.3 THE DO UNTIL

UNTIL loops up to the moment when something becomes true. It checks at the END but doesn't check before the first time. It will normally do the loop at least once. Figure 15.4 shows an example of the DO UNTIL.

```
DO UNTIL TIME() > "17:00:00"
  SAY "WORK"
END
```

Figure 15.4. An example of DO UNTIL.

Figure 15.5 shows a practical use for the DO UNTIL, asking for valid information from the person at the keyboard.

```
/*doex03.cmd (Figure 15.5)*/
 /* REXX sample. Loop until satisfied with reply */
  Valid_reply = ""
  DO Until Valid_reply = "YES"
     Say "Please enter a number "
     Pull Number
     If Datatype(Number) = "NUM"
     Then Valid_reply = "YES"
  End

  Say "Thank you for entering a valid number "
```

Figure 15.5. An example of looping until a valid number is entered.

15.4 STEPPING THROUGH A VARIABLE

Figure 15.6 illustrates stepping through a variable up to a limit. This puts a 1 into I, and adds 1 to I every time it goes through the loop. When I is more than 10, the loop stops. You may use any variable name you want instead of I. If you want to add 2 each time, specify BY 2: DO I = 1 TO 10 BY 2.

```
DO I = 1 TO 10
        SAY "NUMBER OF TIMES THRU LOOP " I
END
```

Figure 15.6. Stepping through a variable.

If you wish, you may put the same variable on the END as on the DO. This makes REXX confirm that you have matched your DOs and ENDs properly (see Figure 15.7).

```
DO I = 1 TO 10
        SAY "NUMBER OF TIMES THRU LOOP " I
END I
```

Figure 15.7. Stepping through a variable, ending the loop with the same variable it began with.

As shown in Figure 15.8, you may also step through a variable without a limit. You will have to stop the loop with LEAVE.

```
DO I = 1
   SAY I
   IF I > 1000 THEN LEAVE
END
```

Figure 15.8. Stepping through a variable without limit.

Please note that if you ask REXX to do something impossible like DO I = 1 TO 10 BY -2, it will just ignore you and not do the loop even once (see Figure 15.9).

```
DO I = 1 TO 10 BY -2
   SAY "YOU WON'T SEE THIS"
END
```

Figure 15.9. Asking REXX to do the impossible. This will not be executed.

15.5 LOOPING FOREVER

You may loop without any limit at all with FOREVER. However, you do have to get out sometime and so will have to use LEAVE. LEAVE exits gracefully from the loop. Do not use SIGNAL to do this.

Figure 15.10 shows an example of FOREVER and LEAVE. Notice that LEAVE sends control after the END.

```
DO FOREVER
   IF TIME() > "12:01:00" THEN LEAVE
   SAY "IS IT LUNCH YET?"
END
   <
```

Figure 15.10. Looping FOREVER.

15.6 LOOPING A FIXED NUMBER OF TIMES

FOR provides a way to limit the number of times a loop will be stepped through. If you have a FOR, the loop will be executed that many times, unless another limiting condition comes true first. Figure 15.11 illustrates FOR.

```
DO I = 1000 TO 2000 BY .5 FOR 50
   ..
END
```

Figure 15.11. Looping a fixed number of times with FOR.

Specifying a constant provides another way to loop a fixed number of times. Figure 15.12 illustrates this.

```
DO 10
    /* statements go here */
END
```

Figure 15.12. Looping a fixed number of times.

15.7 LOOPING DEPENDING ON A VARIABLE

You may loop depending on the value in a variable — that is, as many times as the number in the variable. Figure 15.13 illustrates this.

```
SAY "HOW MANY TIMES TO LOOP?"
PULL HOW_MANY
DO HOW_MANY
    /* statements go here */
END
```

Figure 15.13. Looping depending on a variable.

15.8 SKIPPING BACK TO THE BEGINNING

You may want to skip back to the beginning of the loop. ITERATE says "never mind the rest of the loop," skips the rest, and goes back to the DO for another pass around the loop. Figures 15.14 and 15.15 illustrate the use of ITERATE.

```
     ┌─────────────┐
     v             │
DO I = 1 TO 10     │
                   ^
    IF I = 1 THEN ITERATE
    SAY I
END
```

Figure 15.14. Skipping back to the beginning.

```
/*doex04.cmd (Figure 15.15)*/
          DO I = 1 TO 14
              IF I = 13 THEN ITERATE
              SAY "I IS " I
          END
  /*  the output is I IS 1
                    I IS 2
                    I IS 3
                    I IS 4
                    I IS 5
                    I IS 6
                    I IS 7
                    I IS 8
                    I IS 9
                    I IS 10
                    I IS 11
                    I IS 12
                    I IS 14              */
```

Figure 15.15. An example of skipping "unlucky" 13.

ITERATE goes back to the beginning of the repetitive loop it is in. In Figure 15.16 control goes back to the DO I even though the ITERATE is in a nonrepetitive DO END sequence.

```
/*doex05.cmd (Figure 15.16)*/
  DO I = 1 TO 7
    IF I = 3
    THEN
      DO
        SAY "GOING TO ITERATE"
        ITERATE
      END
      SAY I
  END I
  /* Produces this output:
      1
      2
      GOING TO ITERATE
      4
      5
      6
      7       */
```

Figure 15.16. ITERATE takes you out of repetitive loops.

If the loop increments a variable, you may specify the variable on the ITERATE, as in Figure 15.17.

```
/*doex06.cmd (Figure 15.17)*/
 DO I = 1 TO 7
   IF I = 3
   THEN
     DO
       SAY "GOING TO ITERATE"
       ITERATE I
     END
     SAY I
 END I
  /* Produces this output:
     1
     2
     GOING TO ITERATE
     4
     5
     6
     7
 */
```

Figure 15.17. You may specify a control variable on ITERATE.

If you are in a nested loop and you ITERATE, you go to the beginning of the inner loop, as shown in Figure 15.18.

```
/*doex07.cmd (Figure 15.18)*/
 DO I = 1 TO 3
    SAY "IN I" I
    DO J = 1 TO 3
      IF J = 2 THEN ITERATE
      SAY "IN J" J
    END J
 END I
  /* Produces this output:
     IN I 1
     IN J 1
     IN J 3
     IN I 2
     IN J 1
     IN J 3
     IN I 3
     IN J 1
     IN J 3        */
```

Figure 15.18. An ITERATE in a nested loop goes back to the beginning of the nested loop.

If you are in a nested loop, you can specify the control variable of the inner or outer loop. You will skip back to the beginning of whichever one you specify, as illustrated in Figures 15.19 and 15.20.

```
/*doex08.cmd (Figure 15.19)*/
 DO I = 1 TO 3
    SAY "IN I" I
    DO J = 1 TO 3
      IF J = 2 THEN ITERATE I
      SAY "IN J" J
    END J
 END I
 /* Produces this output:
      IN I 1
      IN J 1
      IN I 2
      IN J 1
      IN I 3
      IN J 1
 */
```

Figure 15.19. Specifying a control variable on an ITERATE in a nested loop takes you back to the beginning of whichever loop you specify.

```
/*doex09.cmd (Figure 15.20)*/
 DO I = 1 TO 3
    SAY "IN I" I
    DO J = 1 TO 3
      IF J = 2 THEN ITERATE J
      SAY "IN J" J
    END J
 END I

 /* Produces this output:
      IN I 1
      IN J 1
      IN J 3
      IN I 2
      IN J 1
      IN J 3
      IN I 3
      IN J 1
      IN J 3
 */
```

Figure 15.20. Specifying a control variable on an ITERATE in a nested loop takes you back to the beginning of whichever loop you specify.

15.9 JUMPING OUT OF A LOOP

LEAVE terminates a repetitive loop (see Figures 15.21, 15.22, and 15.23).

```
DO FOREVER
   IF TIME > "17:00:00" THEN LEAVE
END
```

Figure 15.21. Ending a repetitive loop with LEAVE.

```
DO I = 1 TO 10000
   IF I = 200 THEN LEAVE
END
```

Figure 15.22. Ending a repetitive loop with LEAVE.

```
DO I = 1    /* note: no limit */
   IF I = 200 THEN LEAVE
END
```

Figure 15.23. Ending a repetitive loop with LEAVE.

LEAVE terminates the repetitive loop it is in. In Figure 15.24 control goes after the END I even though the LEAVE is in a DO END sequence.

```
/*doex10.cmd (Figure 15.24)*/
 DO I = 1 TO 100
    SAY I
    IF I = 3
    THEN
     DO
       SAY "GOING TO LEAVE"
       LEAVE
     END
 END I

 /* Produces this output:
     1
     2
     3
     GOING TO LEAVE
 */
```

Figure 15.24. LEAVE takes you out of repetitive loops.

If the loop increments a variable, you may specify the variable on the LEAVE, as in Figure 15.25.

```
/*doex11.cmd (Figure 15.25)*/
 DO I = 1 TO 7
    SAY I
    IF I = 3
    THEN
     DO
        SAY "GOING TO LEAVE"
        LEAVE I
     END
 END I

 /* Produces this output:
      1
      2
      3
      GOING TO LEAVE
 */
```

Figure 15.25. You may specify a control variable on LEAVE.

If you are in a nested loop and you LEAVE, you cancel the loop you are in, as shown in Figure 15.26.

```
/*doex12.cmd (Figure 15.26)*/
  DO I = 1 TO 3
     SAY "IN I" I
     DO J = 1 TO 3
       IF J = 2 THEN LEAVE
       SAY "IN J" J
     END J
  END I

  /* Produces this output:
       IN I 1
       IN J 1
       IN I 2
       IN J 1
       IN I 3
       IN J 1
  */
```

Figure 15.26. LEAVE in a nested loop terminates the loop it is in.

If you LEAVE a nested loop, you can specify the control variable of the inner or outer loop. You will terminate whichever one you specify, as illustrated in Figures 15.27 and 15.28.

```
/*doex13.cmd (Figure 15.27)*/
  DO I = 1 TO 3
     SAY "IN I" I
     DO J = 1 TO 3
       IF J = 2 THEN LEAVE J
       SAY "IN J" J
     END J
  END I

  /* Produces this output:
       IN I 1
       IN J 1
       IN I 2
       IN J 1
       IN I 3
       IN J 1
  */
```

Figure 15.27. Specifying a control variable on a LEAVE in a nested loop takes you out of whichever loop you specify.

```
/*doex14.cmd (Figure 15.28)*/
 DO I = 1 TO 3
    SAY "IN I" I
    DO J = 1 TO 3
      IF J = 2 THEN LEAVE I
      SAY "IN J" J
    END J
 END I

 /* Produces this output:
     IN I 1
     IN J 1
 */
```

Figure 15.28. Specifying a control variable on a LEAVE in a nested loop takes you out of whichever loop you specify.

15.10 STYLE

• Where possible end a loop with the same variable that you began it with.

    DO I = 1 TO 10
     /* instructions */
    END I

• Use comments to match DOs and ENDs.

    DO UNTIL TIME() > "14:00:00"
     /* instructions */
    END /* until time */

• Make the main line of your program a DO loop.

    DO UNTIL REPLY = "END"
     /* instructions */
    END /* until */

• If you need to exit from a loop, use LEAVE.

    DO 1000
     /* instructions */
            IF condition THEN LEAVE
    END /* 1000 */

- Nest loops if you wish, but not more than three levels.

```
DO I = 1 to 10
    DO J = 1 TO 10
        DO K = 1 TO 10
            SAY I J K
        END K
    END J
END I
```

- Don't change the loop control variable.

```
DO I = 1 TO 10
  /* instructions */
  I = 4 /* don't do this */
END I
```

15.11 QUESTIONS/PROBLEMS

1. What is the missing word?

```
DO FOREVER
  SAY "WHAT NUMBER AM I THINKING OF. 1-10"
  PULL NUMBER
  IF NUMBER = 7
  THEN
  SAY "STILL HAVEN'T GOT IT"
END
SAY "GOOD GUESS. GOING TO TRY THE LOTTERY NEXT?"
```

2. Write a program that asks the user to enter a series of numbers, but never the same one twice in a row. Limit it to 10 numbers.

3. Write an external subroutine to compute the square root of a number passed to it. Name it SQRT.CMD. It will accept one ARG: the number. Validate the number. If negative, or not numeric, display a message and return a zero. Make your guess one-half of the number.
Repeat this loop 50 times.
  Make new guess = (guess + (number / guess)) / 2
  Make guess = new guess
End-repeat

Return the new guess to the caller.   Write a main program that calls this function/subroutine. Execute the main program.

4. Set secret number equal to 13. Write a program to keep asking the user to enter a number from 1 to 20 until the secret number is guessed. Limit the loop to 10 guesses. Expected results:

```
= = = >  CH15P04
   PLEASE ENTER YOUR GUESS, FROM 1 TO 20
= = = > 2
   WRONG
= = = > 7
   WRONG
= = = > 13
   RIGHT
```

5.   Improve on your compound interest program written in Chapter 10, Question 3. The added requirements are listed below under "Enhancements." Create a simple program to calculate the effect of compound interest. Ask for the following items from the keyboard:

Principal
Percent of interest (yearly)
Number of years money kept in account
Compounding frequency (How many times per year is interest compounded? 1 = yearly; 12 = monthly; 52 = weekly; 365 = daily)
Perform the following calculations:
Compute the yearly rate of interest as yearly percent of interest / 100.
Compute r (the rate) as yearly rate of interest / compounding frequency.
Compute n (number of times compounded) as how many years X compounding frequency.
Compute final amount as principal X $((1 + r)^n)$.
Display final amount.

Enhancements. Put the dialogue with the person, calculations, and display into a loop that will repeat until you type in "NO." After getting the amounts from the keyboard, verify the following:
If principal is blank, end the loop.
If percent blank, or years blank, or years over 100, or principal not numeric, or percent not numeric, or years not numeric, then start the loop over again.

Chapter 16

QUEUING DATA WITH REXX

This chapter will tell you how the REXX Data Queue works, how to put things onto it, and how to take them off. You will learn how to create a private, named data queue of your own and how to do process-to-process communication using it.

Topics

16.1 What Is the Data Queue?
16.2 How Do You Put Things into the Data Queue?
16.3 How Do You Take Things from the Data Queue?
16.4 Description of the Data Queue
16.5 Clearing the Data Queue
16.6 Creating a Private Data Queue
16.7 Questions/Problems

16.1 WHAT IS THE DATA QUEUE?

The Data Queue is a temporary buffer-like storage area managed by REXX and OS/2. It stores data in memory where it is readily available to your program. Data is stored in a queue-like fashion, like a line, or queue, at a bank teller. There are two kinds: the SESSION queue and named private queues.

The SESSION queue is created automatically the moment you start running any REXX program and is available to any other REXX program you may CALL or execute from within your program, and to REXX programs you execute later in the same OS/2 Window or OS/2 Full Screen. It lasts only as long as your OS/2 Window or OS/2 Full Screen; it is deleted when you close the OS/2 Window or OS/2 Full Screen, and all the data in it is lost. (It is not passed to OS/2 for execution, either.)

215

The private, named Data Queue allows you to isolate and protect the SESSION queue and to exchange data with *another* OS/2 Window or OS/2 Full Screen (this is called process-to-process communication, covered later in this chapter).

Both types of Data Queue work similarly, but you can use only one at a time. If you create and use a private Data Queue, the SESSION queue goes off stage for a while and cannot be accessed.

16.2 HOW DO YOU PUT THINGS INTO THE DATA QUEUE?

The first part of Figure 16.1 shows some instructions that put information into the Data Queue (whichever type you are using). In addition, anything you type at the keyboard is placed in the Data Queue (unless you do a PARSE LINEIN or the function LINEIN with no arguments, which will prevent the data from getting into the Data Queue).

```
/*dqex01.cmd (Figure 16.1)*/
/* putting things into the data queue*/
PUSH   'This is being pushed (LIFO)'
CALL LINEOUT 'QUEUE:','Queued by LINEOUT'
QUEUE 'This is being queued (FIFO)'

/* now display them*/
DO QUEUED()
   PULL LINE_IN_QUEUE
   SAY   LINE_IN_QUEUE
END
```

Figure 16.1. Instructions that put information into the Data Queue.

16.3 HOW DO YOU TAKE THINGS FROM THE DATA QUEUE?

The second part of Figure 16.2 shows commands that take information from the Data Queue. I should point out that PARSE LINEIN and the function LINEIN with no arguments take information directly from the keyboard and not from the Data Queue.

```
/*dqex02.cmd (Figure 16.2)*/
/* first put some things into the queue*/
PUSH 'First line ' TIME()
PUSH 'Second line ' TIME()

/* now take them out of the queue*/
PULL LINE_IN_QUEUE
SAY 'Received with PULL: ' LINE_IN_QUEUE
CALL LINEIN('QUEUE:')
LINE_IN_QUEUE = RESULT
SAY 'Received with LINEIN' LINE_IN_QUEUE
```

Figure 16.2. Instructions that take information from the Data Queue.

16.4 DESCRIPTION OF THE DATA QUEUE

In Figure 16.3 the REXX Data Queue shown is a temporary holding area your program can use to save data in. Data moves from the "top" of the Data Queue to the "bottom." To aid your understanding and recall, imagine the data carried to the bottom by the force of gravity.

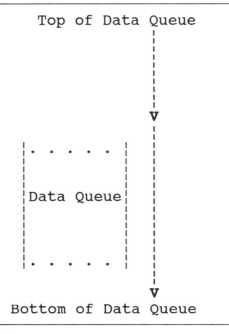

Figure 16.3. The REXX Data Queue, Part 1.

In Figure 16.4 data moves one "line" at a time. Each line in the Data Queue corresponds to one line entered at the keyboard, or one REXX instruction being executed. Each line of data that is put on the Data Queue may contain a null — that is, zero characters, or one or more character strings.

Each PUSH or each time you press ENTER places one line in the Data Queue; each PULL retrieves a line.

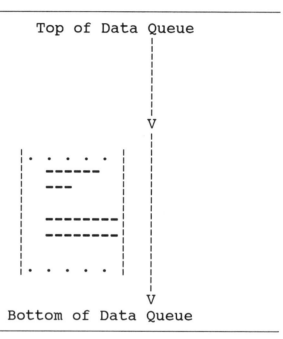

Figure 16.4. The REXX Data Queue, Part 2.

FIFO (First In, First Out) commands put lines of data into the program Data Queue, as shown in Figure 16.5. They will later be PULLed in the order they were put in. QUEUE is a FIFO command.

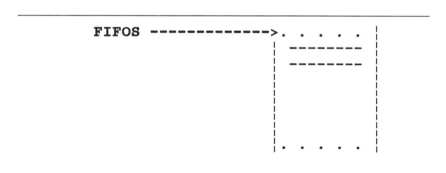

Figure 16.5. The REXX Data Queue, Part 3.

LIFO (Last In, First Out) commands put data into the Data Queue where shown in Figure 16.6. PUSH is a LIFO command. Whatever is put into the Data Queue LIFO will be the first thing to reach the bottom. Data will be later PULLed in reverse order to that in which it was put in.

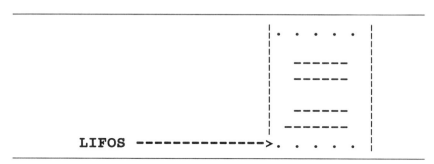

Figure 16.6. The REXX Data Queue, Part 4.

In Figure 16.7 data is taken out of the Data Queue at the "bottom." Any instruction such as PULL, that takes data out of the Data Queue takes it from here (except PARSE LINEIN and the function LINEIN with no arguments).

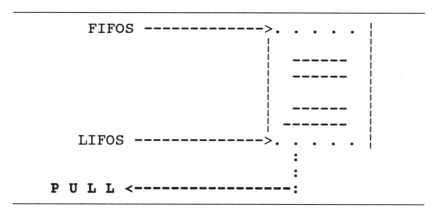

Figure 16.7. The REXX Data Queue, Part 5.

As shown in Figure 16.8, REXX will tell you how many lines are in the Data Queue with the function QUEUED(), which tells you the total number of lines available. QUEUED() can't count what you type in at the keyboard because you can't type it in until the program does a PULL, which immediately grabs what you type in.

```
SAY QUEUED()
/* "4" */
```

Figure 16.8. The REXX Data Queue, Part 6.

In Figure 16.9, PARSE LINEIN and the function LINEIN without any parameters cause the program to stop and wait for you to type in something.

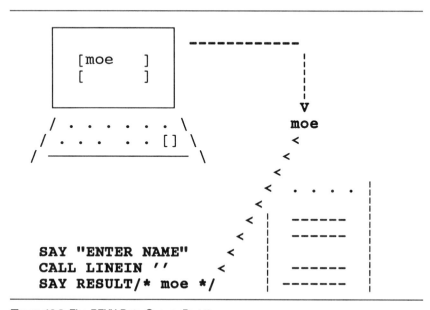

Figure 16.9. The REXX Data Queue, Part 7.

The program in Figure 16.10 shows how LINEIN works:

```
/* trylin2.cmd (Figure 16.10)*/
/* see if linein goes right to the keyboard
buffer without looking in the data queue
*/
Push time() /*something in queue now*/
say 'Please enter your name, I will read it
with linein'
call linein ''
say result
/* can also do it this way:
parse linein name
say name
*/
say 'thank you,' name
do queued() /* clear out the queue*/
   pull .
end
```

Figure 16.10. Example of LINEIN.

As shown in Figure 16.11, if the Data Queue is empty and you try to take something out of it (with a PULL, for example), the program stops and you will then have to type something in in order for the program to continue.

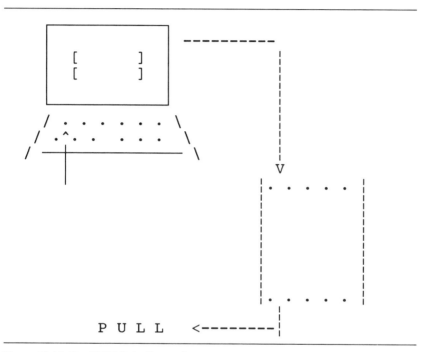

Figure 16.11. The REXX Data Queue, Part 8.

The program in Figure 16.12 shows what happens when you try to take something from an empty Data Queue.

```
/* trypull1.cmd (Figure 16.12)*/
/* nothing in data queue, so goes to keyboard
*/

say 'Please enter your name'
pull name
say 'thank you,' name
```

Figure 16.12. What happens when you try to take something from an empty Data Queue.

The program in Figure 16.13 shows what happens when you try to use PULL to get input from the keyboard, but there is already something in the Data Queue.

```
/* trypull2.cmd (Figure 16.13)*/
/* show how pull looks first in the data queue
      if there's something there, it gets that,
      not what you type in
*/

push TIME()
say 'Please enter your name'
pull name
say 'thank you,' name
```

Figure 16.13. What happens when you try to use the Data Queue to dialogue with the keyboard, but there is already something in the Data Queue..

16.5 CLEARING THE DATA QUEUE

To be sure there is nothing left in the Data Queue that you are using, you may use the code shown in Figure 16.14.

```
Do QUEUED()
    Pull .
END
```

Figure 16.14. An example of code you might use to ensure that there is nothing left in the Data Queue that you are using.

16.6 CREATING A PRIVATE DATA QUEUE

There are two benefits to this: *isolation* and *process-to-process communication,* and one drawback: the *need to delete it.*

ISOLATION

If you create and use a private, named Data Queue you will isolate the SESSION queue, and protect whatever is in it. Figure 16.15 shows how the old Data Queue is bypassed and protected. PULLs pull from the new private Data Queue, not the old SESSION one. Keyboard input goes into the new queue unless you use PARSE LINEIN or the function LINEIN without any parameters. Deleting your private Data Queue will set things back the way they were before you created it, and anything you put into the *new* Data Queue will be deleted when you delete it. Be sure to delete your private Data Queue when you are finished with it.

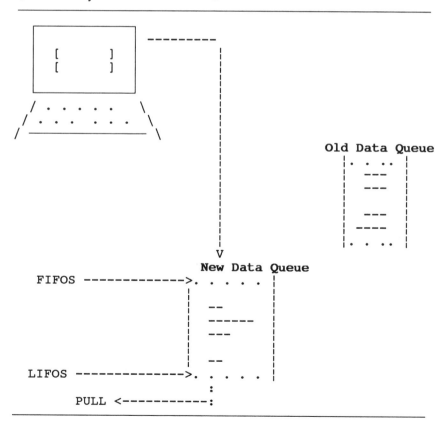

Figure 16.15. The effect of creating a new queue.

Figure 16.16 shows how you can create a new queue. This will allow you to isolate anything that was in the old queue. All your PUSHES and PULLS will now affect the new queue. This queue will outlast your program, your OS/2 Window or OS/2 Full Screen, and even outlast a boot! So you've got to make a solemn promise to me that you'll delete the queue when you are finished; if you don't, it will always be there to haunt you.

```
/* newq.cmd (Figure 16.16)*/
/* creates a new queue,
   puts some data into it
*/
/* don't forget the name of the queue...*/
do queued() /* clear old queue*/
  pull .
end /* do */
queue_name = 'Q'
/* delete first in case it exists */
call rxqueue 'delete', queue_name
call rxqueue 'create', queue_name
call rxqueue 'set',    queue_name
say 'now using the new queue'
date = date()
say 'Going to put date into the new queue'
push date
say 'now there are' queued()
say 'things in the new queue'
/* new queue outlasts the program
   unless you delete it as shown */
Pull thing_in_new_queue
Say 'this was in new queue'
Say thing_in_new_queue
call rxqueue 'delete', queue_name
```

Figure 16.16. Creating a private Data Queue.

PROCESS-TO-PROCESS COMMUNICATION

Your named private queue may be used to pass information to another REXX program that is executing in a different OS/2 Window or OS/2 Full Screen. To try this out, execute the program shown in Figure 16.17 in an OS/2 Full Screen. It will loop around and wait for data from the other program. Then while the first program is still executing, open another OS/2 Window or OS/2 Full Screen and execute the program shown in Figure 16.18. With ALT plus ESC go back and forth between the sessions and you will see how data is sent from one program to another. Here is the sequence of events:

1. Open an OS/2 Full Screen by double clicking on the OS/2 System Icon, double clicking on the Command Prompts Icon, and double clicking on the OS/2 Full Screen Icon.
2. Execute QWAIT02 in the OS/2 Full Screen by changing to its directory and typing in QWAIT02.
3. While QWAIT02 is executing, press ALT + ESC repeatedly until you are back to your open OS/2 Window.
4. Execute the program Q01.
5. While Q01 is executing, press ALT + ESC repeatedly until you are back to your open OS/2 Full Screen.
6. Watch how data is exchanged between the OS/2 sessions.
7. Close the OS/2 Full Screen.

```
/* qwait02.cmd (Figure 16.17)*/
/* loops around and waits to see if anything
   ever comes into the queue named 'Q'.
   if it does, displays it
   Run this in one window,
   then run Q01 in another window.
   This automatically closes
   its session window and deletes
   the named queue,
   so just let it run without stopping it
*/
/* same queue name as in other program */
do queued() /* clear out old queue*/
  pull .
end /* do */
queue_name = 'Q'
call rxqueue 'set',    queue_name
do 90
  say 'waiting.....'
  call syssleep 1
  say queued() 'Items in the queue named' queue_name
  pull data_in_queue
  say 'retrieved this data from queue'
  say data_in_queue
end
say 'qwait02.cmd ending'
call rxqueue 'delete', queue_name
do queued() /* clear out new queue*/
  pull .
end
'EXIT'
```

Figure 16.17. Process-to-process communication. The first program to be executed.

```
/* q01.cmd (Figure 16.18)*/
/* creates a new queue,
   puts some data into it
   run this while the program QWAIT02
   is running in another Window
*/
/* never forget the name of the queue...*/
say 'there are ' queued()
say 'things in the old queue'
date = date()
say 'Going to put date into the old queue'
push time
/* when a program starts, it automatically uses old
queue */
do queued()/* clear out old queue */
  pull .
end /* do */
say 'now there are ' queued()
say 'things in the old queue'
queue_name = 'Q'
call rxqueue 'delete', queue_name
call rxqueue 'create', queue_name
call rxqueue 'set'   , queue_name
say 'now using the new queue'
time = time()
say 'Going to put time' time 'into the new queue'
push date
say 'now there are ' queued() ' things in the new
queue named ' queue_name
/* new queue outlasts the program */
```

Figure 16.18. Process-to-process communication. The second program to be executed.

16.7 QUESTIONS/PROBLEMS

1. What will this line of a REXX program do?
SAY QUEUED()

2. There is nothing in the Data Queue, and your program says PULL. What happens?

3. Your program does 10 PUSHes, and 9 PULLs. What happens?

4. Your program does 9 PUSHes, and 10 PULLs. What happens?

Chapter 17

COMPOUND VARIABLES

This chapter will explain how compound variables are used in REXX and how you can use them to simulate random access memory.

Topics

17.1 WHAT IS A COMPOUND VARIABLE?

Compound variables are *two-part* variables, with the parts separated by a period (see Figure 17.1). WEEKDAY.A is a compound variable. REXX treats the two parts of a compound variable differently. The part on the left is known as the *stem*; the part on the right is known as the *extension*. REXX examines the extension first to see if it is a variable. If it is, REXX substitutes its value, but if it isn't, it is a literal and doesn't change. Then REXX looks at the *combination* of stem and extension and treats that as one variable. Let's follow REXX step by step as it processes the compound variables WEEKDAY.1 and WEEKDAY.A in Figure 17.1.

1. It examines the extension 1.
2. It sees that 1 is not a variable, but a literal.
3. It treats WEEKDAY.1 as a variable and sets it to MONDAY.
4. A is set to 1.
5. REXX examines WEEKDAY.A.
6. It checks to see if A is a variable; it is.
7. It retrieves the value of A, which is 1.
8. REXX is now looking at the compound variable WEEKDAY.1.
9. It then uses WEEKDAY.1 as a variable in the instruction.
10. It looks to see if WEEKDAY.1 is a variable; it is.
11. It retrieves the value of WEEKDAY.1, which is MONDAY.

```
/*compoun1.cmd (Figure 17.1)*/

WEEKDAY.1        = "MONDAY"
A = 1
SAY WEEKDAY.A
/* displays MONDAY */
```

Figure 17.1. An example of the use of a compound variable.

Compound variables are like subscripted variables in BASIC, FORTRAN, and COBOL. Figure 17.2 compares subscripted variables in those traditional languages with REXX compound variables. Both program segments do exactly the same thing: set four occurrences of the subscripted variable DAY with the days of the week, then step through the occurrences with a loop.

```
Traditional              REXX

(BASIC)
DAY(1) = "MON"           DAY.1 = "MON"
DAY(2) = "TUE"           DAY.2 = "TUE"
DAY(3) = "WED"           DAY.3 = "WED"
DAY(4) = "THU"           DAY.4 = "THU"

FOR I = 1 TO 4           DO I = 1 TO 4
   PRINT DAY(I)             SAY DAY.I
NEXT I                   END I
```

Figure 17.2. A comparison of traditional subscripted variables and REXX compound variables.

Compound variables are different from subscripted variables because the extension may be a variable that contains *letters,* not just numbers. I promise you that REXX will not bark at you if your "subscript" is someone's name. Just try that with traditional languages! Figure 17.3 shows how that is done.

```
/*compoun2.cmd (Figure 17.3)*/
Student = "JOE"

Grade.Student = 98.2
Student = "CURLY"
Grade.Student = 89

Student = "MOE"

Grade.Student = 77

Say "Whose grade do you want? (Joe, Curly,
Moe)"
Pull Who

Say "The grade for " Who " is " Grade.Who
```

Figure 17.3. Extensions on REXX compound variables can contain letters.

Figure 17.4 is an example of what you might do with extensions that contain letters. It creates a kind of instant lookup, where all the information is retained in REXX variables in memory. For an interesting demonstration of what REXX can do, I invite you to type in this program very carefully and execute it. You will see how it instantaneously retrieves the information you have typed in.

```
/*compoun3.cmd (Figure 17.4)*/
/*random access memory */
DO 100 /*ask names and phones*/
  SAY "WHAT IS YOUR NAME? ('END' TO STOP) "
  PULL NAME
  IF NAME = "END" THEN LEAVE
  SAY "THANK YOU," NAME ",WHAT IS YOUR PHONE?"
   PULL PHONE_NUM
   IF DATATYPE(PHONE_NUM) <> "NUM"
   THEN SAY "REJECTED, NOT GOOD NUMBER "
   ELSE PHONE.NAME = PHONE_NUM
END /*ASK NAMES */

/* NOW ALLOW PERSON TO INQUIRE */
DO 100 /*RETRIEVE PHONES*/
  SAY "WHOSE PHONE DO YOU WANT TO KNOW?" ,
      " ('END' TO STOP)"
  PULL NAME
  IF NAME = "END" THEN LEAVE
     IF SYMBOL('PHONE.NAME') <> "VAR"
     THEN  SAY "THAT NAME NOT NOW IN MEMORY"
  ELSE SAY NAME" HAS PHONE NUMBER:" PHONE.NAME
END /*RETRIEVE PHONES*/
```

Figure 17.4. An example of a program that uses compound variables to create a form of random access, or content-addressable memory.

17.2 STEPPING THROUGH THE EXTENSIONS

If you use numbers in your extensions, you can easily vary the extension with a DO loop. Figure 17.6 shows an example of how you might step through values of the extension A in a loop. This example will set WEEKDAY.1 through WEEKDAY.7 with the names of the days and then display all seven days.

```
/*compoun4.cmd (Figure 17.6)*/

WEEKDAY.1          =  "MONDAY"
WEEKDAY.2          =  "TUESDAY"
WEEKDAY.3          =  "WEDNESDAY"
WEEKDAY.4          =  "THURSDAY"
WEEKDAY.5          =  "FRIDAY"
WEEKDAY.6          =  "SATURDAY"
WEEKDAY.7          =  "SUNDAY"

DO A = 1 TO 7
   SAY WEEKDAY.A
END
```

Figure 17.6. Stepping through values of the extension.

Figure 17.7 shows how you can use a compound variable as an array and how you can fill it with values and then display those values.

```
/*compoun5.cmd (Figure 17.7)*/
/* loads an array with lines typed in */

Do I = 1 to 20
    Say "please enter a line "
    Pull Element.I
End


/* Unloading the array */
Do I = 1 to 20
    Say Element.I
End


/* Unloading the array in reverse order*/
Do I = 20 to 1 by -1
    Say Element.I
End
```

Figure 17.7. An example of loading and unloading an array.

17.3 CHANGING THE STEM

The stem is the first part of a compound variable. If you change the stem, you are changing every single element in the array, even elements that haven't been created yet. What you are actually doing is setting a default value for any possible uninitialized variable based on the stem (see Figure 17.8). Notice that you include the period when changing the stem.

```
/*compoun6.cmd (Figure 17.8)*/
WEEKDAY.     =      "UNKNOWN"

SAY WEEKDAY.99     /*UNKNOWN*/

WEEKDAY.1    =      "SUNDAY"

SAY WEEKDAY.1      /*SUNDAY*/

SAY WEEKDAY.98     /*UNKNOWN*/
```

Figure 17.8. Changing the stem.

17.4 USING TWO OR MORE EXTENSIONS

You may use more than one extension with compound variables. This is like multidimensional arrays in traditional programming languages. Figure 17.9 shows a possible use of multiple subscripts. If you decide to try this one out on your system, I suggest you reduce the number of days, hours, and channels to a manageable limit, or plan on bringing a sleeping bag to the terminal!

```
/*compoun7.cmd (Figure 17.9)*/
DO DAY = 1 TO 7
  DO HOUR = 1 TO 24
    DO CHANNEL = 2 TO 70
        SAY "PLEASE ENTER THE NAME OF"
        SAY "THE TV PROGRAM"
        SAY "FOR DAY:" DAY
        SAY "FOR HOUR:" HOUR
        SAY "FOR CHANNEL:" CHANNEL
        PULL PROG.DAY.HOUR.CHANNEL
    END CHANNEL
  END HOUR
END DAY

SAY "WHICH DAY'S PROGRAMMING WOULD ",
    "YOU LIKE TO ASK ABOUT?"
PULL DAY
SAY "WHICH HOUR'S PROGRAMMING WOULD ",
    "YOU LIKE TO ASK ABOUT?"
PULL HOUR
SAY "WHICH CHANNEL'S PROGRAMMING WOULD ",
    "YOU LIKE TO ASK ABOUT?"
PULL CHANNEL

SAY "THE PROGRAM THAT IS ON AT THAT TIME"
SAY "IS: " PROG.DAY.HOUR.CHANNEL
```

Figure 17.9. An example of a three-level array using compound variables.

17.5 QUESTIONS/PROBLEMS

1. Write a program with a loop that sets NUMBER.1 through NUMBER.10 to the numbers 101 through 110; then loop through the array, displaying the contents of NUMBER.1 through NUMBER.11 — yes, NUMBER.11 — to see what happens.

Chapter 18

READING AND WRITING FILES

This chapter will introduce you to the concept of reading and writing files in REXX programs. It will show how to read from and write to disk files and other devices on your computer.

Topics

18.1 THE FILES YOU CAN READ AND WRITE TO

You can read and write files on your hard disk and on your floppy disks. You can also read and write other types of devices that I will call generically "files." The full list follows:

COM1:	Communications port 1
COM2:	Communications port 2
KBD:	The keyboard
LPT1:	Printer 1
LPT2:	Printer 2
PRN:	Current default printer
STDERR:	Device for error messages (screen)

STDIN: Standard input device (the keyboard, generally)
STDOUT: Standout output device (the screen, generally)
disk files   Specify the name of the file.

18.2 BEFORE READING OR WRITING

You do not have to open or close a file explicitly on OS/2. The first time you read or write, OS/2 will open a file if necessary, and when you end your program it will close the file. But since there may be times when you want to do it yourself, I'll show you how to do it. Figure 18.1 shows how to open a file and how to tell if the action was successful.   Opening it with the keyword OPEN allows you to both read and write to the file. If you want to allow reading only and not writing, use OPEN READ instead of OPEN. If you want to allow writing only and not reading, use OPEN WRITE.

```
/*openfile.cmd (Figure 18.1)*/
/* opens a disk file */
Disk_file = 'c:\rexxprgs\samp1.dat'
CALL STREAM disk_file,'C','OPEN'
If result = 'READY:'
then say disk_file 'opened successfully'
else say  disk_file 'could not be opened'
```

Figure 18.1. Opening a disk file.

Figure 18.2 shows how to close a file and how to tell if you were able to close it successfully.

```
/*closfile.cmd (Figure 18.2)*/
/* closes a disk file */
Disk_file = 'c:\rexxprgs\samp1.dat'
CALL STREAM disk_file,'C','CLOSE'
SELECT
  When result = 'READY:'
  then say disk_file 'closed successfully'
  When result = ""
  then say  disk_file 'was already closed'
  otherwise  say   disk_file  'could  not  be
closed, unknown reason'
END
```

Figure 18.2. Closing a disk file.

Even more important than opening a file is checking to see if the file exists before trying to use it. This is important because

- if you are going to read the file it must exist, and
- if you are going to write to it, and it exists you should know it.

Figure 18.3 shows how to determine if a disk file exists. Another way is shown in Figure 18.4, which checks to see if the file is ready to be used in input or output; if it is ready for use, it must exist!

```
/*exists.cmd (Figure 18.3)*/
/* tells if a disk file exists or not */
Disk_file = 'c:\rexxprgs\samp1.dat'
If STREAM(disk_file,'C','QUERY EXISTS') = ""
then say  disk_file 'does not exist'
else say  disk_file 'exists as specified'
```

Figure 18.3. Determining if a disk file exists.

```
/*okuse.cmd (Figure 18.4)*/
/*tells if a disk file is ready for use or
not*/
Disk_file = 'c:\rexxprgs\samp1.dat'
If STREAM(disk_file,'S') = 'READY'
then say  disk_file 'can be used in reading or
writing'
else say  disk_file 'cannot be used in reading
or writing'
say "going to open it now"
call STREAM disk_file,'C','OPEN READ'
If STREAM(disk_file,'S') = 'READY'
then say  disk_file 'can be used in reading or
writing'
else say  disk_file 'cannot be used in reading
or writing'
```

Figure 18.4.   Determining if a disk file is ready for use in input/output.

18.3   READING ONE CHARACTER AT A TIME

You can read one character at a time from any of the files or devices mentioned in Section 18.1. This is done with the function CHARIN. The first time you do a CHARIN it gives you the first character in the file. If you continue to do CHARIN over and over again you will receive all the characters in the file, including all system control characters, end-of-line and end-of-file delimiters. If you are reading from a device other than a disk file, and there is no character available just yet, the program will wait until there is one available. Figure 18.5 shows how you might read a disk file one character at a time. It will stop after reading 100 characters.

```
/*read01.cmd (Figure 18.5)*/
/* read 100 characters, one character at a
time from a disk file */
/* does it exist? */
Disk_file = 'c:\rexxprgs\samp1.dat'
If STREAM(disk_file,'C','QUERY EXISTS') = ""
then
  do
     say  disk_file 'does not exist'
     exit
  end

Do 100
    Char_read = CHARIN(disk_file)
    Say 'Just read the character' Char_read
end
```

Figure 18.5. Reading from a disk file one character at a time.

When do you stop? You can't keep reading forever. You'll run out of characters at some time or other. With devices other than disk files, for example the communications port, you can choose to stop after a certain length of time when an error condition is raised (SIGNAL ON NOTREADY, Chapter 9) or when a predetermined character is read. If you are reading a disk file, you can use the CHARS function to tell when you reach the end. Figure 18.6 shows an example of how to use the CHARS function.

```
/*read02.cmd (Figure 18.6)*/
/* read one character at a time from a disk
file, until no more characters */
/* does it exist? */
Disk_file = 'c:\rexxprgs\sampl.dat'
If STREAM(disk_file,'C','QUERY EXISTS') = ""
then
  do
     say  disk_file 'does not exist'
     exit
  end

Do while CHARS(disk_file) > 0
    Char_read = CHARIN(disk_file)
    Say 'Just read the character' Char_read
end
```

Figure 18.6. Reading one character at a time from a disk file.

In case you are tempted to skip checking if the file exists, I can assure you that the CHARS(disk_file) > 0 condition shown in Figure 18.6 will come to your rescue. If the file doesn't exist, there will be zero characters remaining to be read! I would rather have you check for the file's existence first — it's a much better programming practice.

May I make another suggestion? Use a NOTREADY trap in any program that reads or writes files. This will intercept any error condition with the file and tell you about it. All you need to do is add the program statements that are marked in bold in Figure 18.7. Please include them in all programs that do input or output.

```
/*read03.cmd (Figure 18.7)*/
/* read one character at a time from a disk
file, until no more characters */
/* shows NOTREADY trap */
SIGNAL ON NOTREADY
/* does it exist? */
Disk_file = 'c:\rexxprgs\samp1.dat'
If STREAM(disk_file,'C','QUERY EXISTS') = ""
then
   do
      say  disk_file 'does not exist'
      exit
   end

Do while CHARS(disk_file) > 0
    Char_read = CHARIN(disk_file)
    Say 'Just read the character' Char_read
end

EXIT
NOTREADY:
Say 'File error condition has occured on line
' sigl
Say 'Program statement is ' sourceline(sigl)
Say 'Program terminated'
EXIT
```

Figure 18.7. Trapping an error condition while reading or writing.

18.4 WRITING ONE CHARACTER AT A TIME

This is very similar to reading one character at a time. If you are writing to a disk file, you will have to supply your own end of line and end of file characters. Figure 18.8 is a program that writes a word to a file one character at a time.

```
/*writ02.cmd Figure 18.8)*/
/* write a word, one character at a time, to a disk
file */
SIGNAL ON NOTREADY
/* does it exist? */
Disk_file = 'c:\rexxprgs\sampl.tmp'
If STREAM(disk_file,'C','QUERY EXISTS') = ""
then nop
else 'erase' disk_file

Call charout disk_file, 'M'
Call charout disk_file, 'a'
Call charout disk_file, 'r'
Call charout disk_file, 'i'
Call charout disk_file, 'e'

/* close it */
call stream disk_file ,'C', 'CLOSE'

/* did it work?*/
'type ' disk_file
'erase' disk_file

EXIT
NOTREADY:
Say 'File error condition has occured on line ' sigl
Say 'Program statement is ' sourceline(sigl)
EXIT
```

Figure 18.8. Writing a word to a file, one character at a time.

18.5 READING ONE LINE AT A TIME

You can read one line, or record, at a time from any of the files or devices mentioned in Section 18.1. This is done with the function LINEIN. The first time you do a LINEIN it gives you the first line in the file. If you continue to do LINEIN over and over again, you will receive all the lines in the file. If you are reading from a device other than a disk file, and there is no data available just yet, the program will wait until there is one available. Figure 18.9 shows how you might read a disk file one line at a time.

```
/*read04.cmd (Figure 18.9)*/
/* read one line at a time from a disk file,
until the end */
SIGNAL ON NOTREADY
/* does it exist? */
Disk_file = 'c:\rexxprgs\samp1.dat'
If STREAM(disk_file,'C','QUERY EXISTS') = ""
then
  do
     say  disk_file 'does not exist'
     exit
  end

Do while LINES(disk_file) > 0
   Line_read = LINEIN(disk_file)
   Say 'Just read the line' Line_read
end

EXIT
NOTREADY:
Say 'File error has occured on line' sigl
Say 'Program statement is ' sourceline(sigl)
Say 'Program terminated'
EXIT
```

Figure 18.9. Reading from a disk file one line at a time.

18.6 WRITING ONE LINE AT A TIME

This is very similar to reading one line at a time. Figure 18.10 is a
program that writes three sentences to a file one line at a time.

```
/*writ05.cmd (Figure 18.10)*/
/* write three sentences, one at a time, to a
disk file */
SIGNAL ON NOTREADY
/* does it exist? */
Disk_file = 'c:\rexxprgs\samp1.tmp'
If STREAM(disk_file,'C','QUERY EXISTS') = ""
then say  disk_file 'does not exist,
creating'
else
  do
     say  disk_file 'exists, deleting'
     'erase ' disk_file
  end

Call lineout disk_file, 'REXX is fun'
Call lineout disk_file, 'I like OS/2 REXX'
Call lineout disk_file, 'I will use REXX for
all my programs'

/* close it */
Call stream disk_file , 'C', 'CLOSE'

/* did it work?*/
'type ' disk_file
'erase ' disk_file

EXIT
NOTREADY:
Say 'File error condition has occured on line
' sigl
Say 'Program statement is ' sourceline(sigl)
Say 'Program terminated'
EXIT
```

Figure 18.10. Writing three sentences to a disk file.

18.7 QUESTIONS/PROBLEMS

1. Create a program that reads the file SAMP1.DAT one line (record) at a time. Display each line.

2. Copy the file SAMP1.DAT to the file SAMP1.DEL using LINEIN and LINEOUT.

3. Improve on Problem 2. Check to see if the file SAMP1.DEL exists. If it exists, delete it before copying.

4. Using output redirection (see Section 3.10), put the output of a DIR *.CMD OS/2 command into a datafile named DIRTEMP.TMP. Using file IO, read the file DIRTEMP.TMP. Examine each line of the file DIRTEMP.TMP. If any line contains the string 'SAYHI.CMD', display the line.

5. Modify the previous problem. Instead of displaying the line containing 'SAYHI.CMD', display the contents of the file SAYHI.CMD.

Chapter 19

THE INTERPRET INSTRUCTION

This chapter will help you to understand the functioning of the INTERPRET instruction and suggest some possible uses for it.

Topics

19.1 What INTERPRET Does
19.2 Questions/Problems

19.1 WHAT INTERPRET DOES

INTERPRET makes REXX process an expression as an instruction by asking it to "Have another look." The string formed by the expression is reexamined by REXX, which then executes it as a REXX instruction.

Please note that the VALUE function is similar. Before using INTERPRET, check to see if the VALUE function is more suitable. Figure 19.1 shows how two variables containing "SAY" and "HELLO" are examined by the INTERPRET instruction, which then executes the instruction SAY HELLO.

```
/*intrpt1.cmd (Figure 19.1)*/

INSTR = "SAY"
VAR = "HELLO"
/*becomes SAY HELLO interpret executes that */
INTERPRET INSTR VAR
```

Figure 19.1. An example of how INTERPRET processes an expression, or string.

251

Figure 19.2 shows what would happen if you simply tried to execute the two variables as an instruction. They would be passed to OS/2, which would not recognize the SAY as an OS/2 command.

```
/*intrpt2.cmd (Figure 19.2)*/
INSTR = "SAY"
VAR = "HELLO"
INSTR VAR                /*becomes SAY HELLO     */
                         /*but REXX passes it to */
                         /*the environment,      */
                         /*which rejects it      */
                         /*"command not found"   */
```

Figure 19.2. An example showing what happens if you don't use INTERPRET.

Figure 19.3 shows a way of making REXX use a variable that was not in the original program but is made up of something that was typed in at the terminal.

```
/*intrpt3.cmd (Figure 19.3)*/
SAY "PLEASE ENTER YOUR NAME"
PULL NAME
SAY "THANK YOU," NAME "NOW ENTER YOUR PHONE"

PULL PHONE

INTERPRET NAME "=" PHONE
/*if name was JOE, it assigns the variable JOE
 the value of his phone*/

SAY "WHOSE PHONE DO YOU WANT TO RETRIEVE?"
SAY "ENTER NAME"
PULL NAME

INTERPRET "SAY " NAME

/*if name was JOE,
  it executes the instruction SAY JOE*/
```

Figure 19.3. An example of making REXX find the value of a variable that was not in the original source program. A variable equal to the name typed in is created.

19.2 QUESTIONS/PROBLEMS

1. Create a quick calculator program. Use **INTERPRET** to execute an expression that is typed in, then display the result and name it CH19P01. It will be used this way:

= = > CH19P01 1 + 1

It will then display "2."

Chapter 20

CONVERTING FROM BATCH FILES

This chapter will help you to transfer your Batch File programming skills to the world of REXX. You will see how to use REXX to do the things you used to do with Batch Files. You will find here most Batch File features and the way to program them in REXX.

Topics

20.1 Why Convert?
20.2 Considerations in Converting
20.3 Batch File Features and How to Convert
20.4 When You Don't Want to Convert

20.1 WHY CONVERT?

Why should you convert to REXX from OS/2 Batch Files? After all, your old Batch Files still work on OS/2, so you aren't forced to convert. There are several reasons:
- REXX is much more flexible than Batch Files.
- REXX is a clearer language.
- REXX is found in several other programming environments besidcs OS/2.
- REXX is the standard procedure language on all IBM systems.
- IBM will eventually stop adding new features to Batch Files.
- IBM may stop supporting Batch Files altogether.

20.2 CONSIDERATIONS IN CONVERTING

Conversion of one language to another requires a knowledge of both languages and how they function. This book is about REXX, not Batch Files, and so I will not explain Batch File features in detail.

Practically all Batch File features have their REXX counterpart. The only feature that will require some work is the FOR that performs the same action on several files designated by their names or a wild card character. To help with that conversion I have created two programs that duplicate the action of the FOR (see Figures 20.1 and 20.2). You may copy the programs and use them, or incorporate them into larger REXX programs.

Both REXX and Batch Files contain OS/2 commands. This chapter does not discuss how to convert OS/2 commands, because they don't need conversion. OS/2 commands in REXX need only to be enclosed in apostrophes or quotation marks. This chapter will discuss only Batch File language elements and their corresponding REXX features.

There is really an immense difference between Batch Files and REXX. Batch File language has less than ten verbs, while REXX has about twenty-five. Batch Files have absolutely no built-in functions, while REXX has about 75. Since Batch Files are simpler than REXX, it should be very easy to duplicate all the functions of a Batch File in REXX.

A reminder — Batch Files may have an extension of either .BAT or .CMD. REXX programs must have an extension of .CMD. And don't forget the comment required at the beginning of REXX programs: /*something*/.

20.3 BATCH FILE FEATURES AND HOW TO CONVERT

I am going to show you several language elements of Batch Files and their REXX equivalents. I remind you that many equivalences are only approximate and that you should test your programs before letting unsuspecting persons use them.

ALT 7 (sound speaker)   REXX Equivalent: CALL BEEP
The character combination ALT plus the keypad number 7 sounds the computer's speaker every time you display it. It is used to call attention to an error condition or to remind a person to type something in.

Here is an example that will sound the speaker and display the word Error:

REM ALT 7 Error

The way you would do this in REXX is

Say 'Error'
Call BEEP 400,200

@command   REXX equivalent: '@command'
Putting the "at" sign in front of an OS/2 command suppresses the display of that command as it executes.

Here is an example that will suppress the display of the word ECHO as it executes: (The command ECHO OFF suppresses the display of subsequent OS/2 commands.)

@ECHO OFF

The way you would do this in REXX is

'@ECHO OFF'

@ECHO Hi   REXX equivalent: Say 'Hi' '
The command ECHO displays a message on the screen. The "at" sign in front of it suppresses the display of the command.

Here is an example that will display the word Hi.

@ECHO Hi

The way you would do this in REXX is

Say 'Hi'

@ECHO .   REXX cquivalent: Say "
The command ECHO displays a message on the screen. The period means that it should display a blank line.

Here is an example that will display a blank line.

@ECHO .

The way you would do this in REXX is

Say "

FOR   See text and Figures 20.1 and 20.2
There is really no REXX equivalent for FOR, so I have created two programs
you can use instead of FOR. One is used with *wild card* characters, the other
with a *list of files*. Creating one program to handle both wild card characters
and a list of files would have meant an extremely complex program, so I have
created two.

Figure 20.1 can be used instead of the wild card character FOR. To adapt
it to your needs you have to change only two things: the wild character
specification, (you'll use things like '*.DAT', '*.*' and 'PROG*.CMD')
and the command to be executed (you'll use things like PRINT and ERASE).

```
/*dofor01.cmd (Figure 20.1)*/
/* does the same thing as the wild card type of FOR
command:
for %%i in (*.cmd) do type %%i
a batch file command that does
a dir *.cmd and then for each
file that matches, does a TYPE
*/

/*substitute your wild card here */
dir_spec = '*.cmd'
/*substitute your command here*/
command_to_execute = 'type'

/*no need to change anything else */
if command_to_execute = '' then signal no_command

'dir'       dir_spec       '> dir.fil'
do while lines('dir.fil') > 0
  call do_command linein('dir.fil')
 end

Call stream 'dir.fil', 'C', 'CLOSE'
'erase dir.fil'
exit

do_command:
arg file_name extension .

if file_name = '' then return

full_name_of_file = file_name || '.' || extension
if stream(full_name_of_file,'C','QUERY EXISTS') =  ""
then return

say command_to_execute full_name_of_file
command_to_execute full_name_of_file
call SYSSLEEP 2
return
no_command:
say 'A  command  must  be  supplied  in  the  variable
command_to_execute'
exit
```

Figure 20.1. Program that does the same thing as the FOR batch file command with a wild card.

Figure 20.2 can be used with the list of files. To adapt it to your needs you just need to change the list of files and the command to be executed.

```
/*dofor02.cmd (Figure 20.2)*/
/*does the same thing as the list of files type of
FOR command:
for %%i in (trycls.cmd cdexamp.cmd) do type %%i
a batch file command that displays
each of the files in the parens
*/

/* substitute your list of files here */
list_of_files  = 'trycls.cmd cdexamp.cmd'
/*substitute your command here*/
command_to_execute = 'type'

if command_to_execute = "" then signal no_command

files_to_do = list_of_files

do until files_to_do = ""

  parse var files_to_do file_being_done files_to_do
    call do_command file_being_done

end
exit

do_command:
arg file_name .

if file_name = ""
then return

say command_to_execute file_name
command_to_execute file_name

return

no_command:
say  'A  command  must  be  supplied  in  the  variable
command_to_execute'
exit
```

Figure 20.2 Program that does the same thing as the FOR batch file command with a list of files.

GOTO EXIT   REXX equivalent: EXIT

The way you end a Batch File when you are not at the physical end is to GOTO a label generally named :EXIT. Then you have to place the label :EXIT on the very last line of your program (nothing after it!).

Here is an example that will end the program:

GOTO EXIT
(more instructions here)
:EXIT

The way you would do this in REXX is

EXIT

^G   REXX Equivalent: CALL BEEP

The character combination ALT plus the keypad number 7 appears in your program as ^G. This causes a sound in the computer's speaker every time you display it. It is used to call attention to an error condition or to remind a person to type something in.

Here is an example that will sound the speaker and display the word Error:

REM ^G Error

The way you would do this in REXX is

Say 'Error'
Call BEEP 400,200

IF EXIST   REXX Equivalent: IF STREAM

IF EXIST checks to see if a file exists. If so, it executes a command you specify.

Here is an example that will check to see if the file TMP.DAT exists and if it does will erase it:

IF EXIST TMP.DAT ERASE TMP.DAT

The way you would do this in REXX is

 IF STREAM('TMP.DAT','C','QUERY EXISTS') < > ""
THEN 'ERASE TMP.DAT'

IF %1 = = REXX Equivalent: Use variables on an ARG.
%1 signifies the first word passed to a program when it is executed.
Assuming the program is named MYPROG then MARIE is the first word
passed to the program when it is executed this way: MYPROG MARIE
BETH SUE.

Here is an example that will check to see if the first word passed to it is
an uppercase Y and if it is will erase a file named TMP.DAT.

IF %1 = =Y ERASE TMP.DAT

The way you would do this in REXX is
ARG VAR1 VAR2
IF VAR1 = 'Y' /*person can type in upper or lower case Y*/
THEN 'ERASE TMP.DAT'

IF %1 = = . REXX Equivalent: Use variables on an ARG.
%1 signifies the first word passed to a program when it is executed. The
period signifies "nothing," in other words, there was nothing passed to the
program when it was executed.

Here is an example that will check to see if nothing was passed to it and
if so will go to a label named :MSG.

IF %1 = = . GOTO MSG
(More instructions)
:MSG

The way you would do this in REXX is
ARG VAR1 VAR2
IF VAR1 = "
THEN Signal msg
(More instructions)
MSG:

IF "%1" = = "" REXX Equivalent: Use variables on an ARG.
%1 signifies the first word passed to a program when it is executed. The two
consecutive quotation marks signify "nothing," in other words, there was
nothing passed to the program when it was executed.

Here is an example that will check to see if nothing was passed to it and
if so will go to a label named :MSG.

IF "%1" = = "" GOTO MSG
(More instructions)
:MSG

The way you would do this in REXX is
ARG VAR1 VAR2
IF VAR1 = "
THEN Signal msg
(More instructions)

IF ERRORLEVEL   REXX equivalent: If RC >
ERRORLEVEL tests the return code from an OS/2 command after it is
executed. It checks for a 2 and anything higher.
   Here is an example that will check to see if a command returned a 2 or
higher. If so it will go to a label named :MSG.

IF ERRORLEVEL 2 GOTO MSG
(More instructions)
:MSG

The way you would do this in REXX is
IF RC > 1
THEN SIGNAL MSG
(More instructions)
MSG:

GOTO label   REXX equivalent: SIGNAL label
GOTO sends control to a label.
   Here is an example that will go to a label named HERE.

GOTO HERE
(More instructions)
:HERE

The way you would do this in REXX is
SIGNAL HERE
(More instructions)
HERE:

PAUSE   REXX equivalent: Say and Pull
PAUSE stops the program and displays a message followed by "PRESS ANY KEY TO CONTINUE." You can press almost any key to continue.

Here is an example that will display the messages "Turn on printer," "PRESS ANY KEY TO CONTINUE" and will stop the program until you press a key.

PAUSE Turn on printer

The way you would do this in REXX is
Say 'Turn on printer'
Say 'Press ENTER to continue'
Pull .

REM   REXX equivalent: Say
REM allows you to put a comment in your program. It is, however, displayed when the program executes.

Here is an example that will display "REM My program."

REM My program

The way you would do this in REXX is
Say 'REM My program'

@REM   REXX equivalent: Say
@REM allows you to put a comment in your program. It is not displayed when the program executes.

Here is an example that will not display anything:

@REM My program

The way you would do this in REXX is
/*My program*/

Named Parameters   REXX equivalent: Use value function (Appendix D)
Named parameters are the nearest thing to variables in Batch Files. You can
make up and use names at will. They need to be used with care, however,
because they are really global variables affecting any other program that
executes! This means that if you use and set a named parameter called
PATH it will affect the DOS or OS/2 environment variable PATH!

Here is an example that will display the current value of the PATH
environment variable:

ECHO %PATH%

The way you would do this in REXX is
Say value('PATH',,'OS2ENVIRONMENT')

Here is an example that will change the current value of the PATH
environment variable:

SET PATH = C:\REXXPRGS

The way you would do this in REXX is
'SET PATH = C:\REXXPRGS'

SHIFT
There is absolutely no equivalent in REXX for SHIFT, nor is there anything
like it in any other programming language beyond Venus! Changing the
meaning of a variable to that of another by subtracting one from the number
of the variable is extinct programming methodology and has no match in
REXX.

20.4 WHEN YOU DON'T WANT TO CONVERT

There may be times when converting from Batch Files to REXX is not
convenient. At trying times such as these you may want to simply put Batch
File statements in your REXX program, without changing them. You can
very easily do this, but be sure to enclose them in apostrophes or quotes, since
the Batch File statements are OS/2 commands and OS/2 commands must be
enclosed in apostrophes or quotes. Figure 20.1 shows the OS/2 commands
ECHO, PAUSE and FOR contained in a REXX program.

```
/*sample1.cmd*/
"@ECHO Please enter file spec or wild card to
delete"
Pull file_spec
"PAUSE OK to delete " file_spec "? ENTER to
delete, CTRL + C to cancel"
"FOR %%I in  (" file_spec ") DO ERASE %%I"
```

Figure 20.1. REXX program containing batch file commands.

Appendix A

PROBLEMS AND SOLUTIONS

CHAPTER 2

1. What is another name for a REXX program?

A: Exec.

2. REXX programs must be written in _____ format.

A: ASCII, text, or DOS.

3. REXX programs must have the extension _____.

A: .CMD

4. A REXX program must be executed in a _____.

A: OS/2 Window, OS/2 Full screen, REXX program directory.

5. What is the minimum shortest example of the item required at the beginning of each REXX program?

A: /**/

6. Which has true programming variables, REXX or Batch files?

A: REXX.

CHAPTER 3

1. Perform the initial setup described in Section 3.1, Part 1 of this chapter.

2. Perform the steps described in Section 3.1, Part 2 of this chapter.

3. Create a REXX program named TRY1.CMD using the Extended Editor. Place the following statements in the program. A comment containing the name of the program and the REXX statement: Say 'This is a test: does REXX work?'

A:
```
/*TRY1.CMD*/
Say 'This is a test: does REXX work?'
```

4. Execute the program in an OS/2 Window.

5. Execute the program in OS/2 Full Screen.

6. Execute the program using the Presentation Manager.

7. If you use a word processor to create your program, what must you be careful about?

A: To create an ASCII, text, or DOS file.

CHAPTER 4

1. What must a REXX program always start with?

A: /*.........*/

2. What word or instruction in REXX means to display on the monitor?

A: SAY.

3. What does this program do?
```
/*ch04p03.cmd*/
X = 10
Y = 20
Z = Y - X
SAY "THE ANSWER IS " Z
```

A: It displays
     THE ANSWER IS 10
on the terminal.

4. Do these have correct syntax?

  A. SAY "HELLO";SAY "GOODBYE"

  B. SAY "HELLO";
     SAY;
     "GOODBYE"

  C. COMPUTE;   C = 3 + 4

A: A. Yes.
  B. No.
     SAY,
     "GOODBYE"
  C. No.
     COMPUTE: C = 3 + 4

5. True or false: A label is the target of an instruction that transfers control to it.

A: True.

6. True or false: The instruction EXIT must always be the very last line in the program.

A: False. Not needed if it would be the last line.

7. Will REXX try to execute this linc?
BARK "HELLO"

A: No. REXX doesn't understand the word "BARK," so it gives it to OS/2.

8. Write a program to execute the OS/2 commands:

PATH

DIR *.CMD /P

Include the comment:
This is a sample program

A:
```
/* ch04p08.cmd */
'PATH'
'DIR *.CMD /P'
/*  this is a sample program */
```

9. What does this program do?
```
/*ch04p09.cmd*/
SAY Greeting
```

A: Displays "GREETING" on the terminal. GREETING is a literal without quotes.

10. What does this program do?
```
/*ch04p10.cmd*/
GREETING = "HELLO"
SAY GREETING
```

A: Displays "HELLO" on the terminal. The literal "HELLO" is put into the variable GREETING. The contents of the variable GREETING are displayed on the terminal.

11. Can you tell what this does? Try it out if you don't know.
```
/*ch04p11.cmd*/
GREETING = "HAPPY HALLOWEEN"
SAY GREETING
DROP GREETING
SAY GREETING
```

A: Displays "HAPPY HALLOWEEN" on the terminal, then "GREETING." The literal "HAPPY HALLOWEEN" is put into the variable GREETING. The contents of the variable GREETING are displayed on the terminal. The variable GREETING is undefined, that is, changed back to a literal without quotes. The literal GREETING is displayed on the terminal.

12. What does this display on the screen?
```
/*ch04p12.CMD*/
SAY '323334'X
```

A: 234

13. Write a program that displays these lines exactly as shown:

3 + 1 is 4

'3 + 1 is 4'

O'brien

A:
```
/* ch04p13.cmd*/
Say "3 + 1 is 4"
Say "'3 + 1 is 4'"
Say "O'brien"
```

14. Which variable names are invalid and why?
   A. 1_time_only
   B. PrOgRaMmEr_nAmE
   C. prog_name
   D. input-data
   E. Say

A: A begins with a number; D contains a hyphen; E is valid but not recommended.

15. What does this program print out?

```
/*ch04p15.cmd*/
MESSAGE = MESSAGE
SAY MESSAGE
EXIT
```

A: MESSAGE

16. In a program, assign the number 10 to a variable. Assign the number 20 to another variable. In one instruction display the total of the two.

A:
```
/* ch04p16.cmd  */
Number1 = 10
Number2 = 20
Say number1 + number2
```

17. First assign the variable DRIVE the value of your hard disk drive letter. Then execute the OS/2 command DIR followed by a disk drive letter:

DIR   disk drive letter

A:
```
/* CH04P17.CMD*/
DRIVE = "C:"
'DIR ' DRIVE
```

18. When this prints out, will there be a blank between Sam and Antha?
SAY "SAM"   ¦ ¦   "ANTHA"

A: No, because ¦ ¦ means string together without blanks.

19. When this prints out, how many blanks will there be between Kelly and Beth?

SAY "KELLY"   "BETH"

A: One. Just putting two things next to each other with one or more blanks gives ONE blank.

CHAPTER 5

1. Write a program that accepts an extension like .BAT, .CMD, .DAT from the command line when the program is executed. Use the extension in an OS/2 DIR command: DIR *.*extension*.

```
A:
/*CH05P01.cmd*/
ARG EXTENSION
'DIR *.'EXTENSION
/*  or
'DIR *. ¦¦ 'EXTENSION
*/
```

2.   Write a program that asks for an extension like .BAT, .CMD, .DAT, then reads it in when it is typed in. Use the extension in an OS/2 DIR command: DIR *.*extension*.

```
A:
/*CH05P02.cmd*/
Say 'Please type in an extension'
PULL EXTENSION
'DIR *.'EXTENSION
/*  or
'DIR *. ¦¦ 'EXTENSION
*/
```

3.   Redo the first problem in this chapter, but suppress the display of the OS/2 command DIR.

```
A:
/*CH05P03.cmd*/
'@ECHO OFF'
ARG EXTENSION
'DIR *.'EXTENSION
/*  or
'DIR *. ¦¦ 'EXTENSION
*/
```

4. Add the REXX verb EXIT to the end of your solution to the first problem in this chapter. What is the effect?

```
A:
/*CH05P04.cmd*/
ARG EXTENSION
'DIR *.'EXTENSION
/*  or
'DIR *. ¦¦ 'EXTENSION
*/
EXIT
```

No effect. The program would have ended even without the EXIT.

5. Add the OS/2 command EXIT to the end of your solution to the first problem in this chapter. What is the effect?

```
A:
/*CH05P05.cmd*/
ARG EXTENSION
'DIR *.'EXTENSION
/*  or
'DIR *. ¦¦ 'EXTENSION
*/
'EXIT'
```

It closes the OS/2 window, or OS/2 full screen.

CHAPTER 6

1. Is 43 = 4.3E1?

A: Yes — 4.3 X 10 to the first power equals 4.3 X 10.

2. Is 43 = = 4.3E1?

A: No — = = means equal in all respects, not just equivalent.

3. Complete this program segment:
```
/*CH06P03Q.CMD*/
NUMBER = +98765
IF NUMBER          +12345
THEN
    SAY "THE NUMBER IS 12345"
END
ELSE SAY "I DON'T KNOW WHAT IT IS EQUAL TO"
```

A:
```
/*CH06P03A.CMD */
NUMBER = +98765
IF NUMBER = +12345
THEN
   DO
     SAY "THE NUMBER IS 12345"
   END
ELSE
   SAY "I DON'T KNOW WHAT IT IS EQUAL TO"
```

4. Write a program that will store the number 12 as a constant and store the number 13 as a constant. Then write the instructions that will compare the numbers and find them equal.

A:
```
/*CH06P04.CMD */
NUMBERA = 12
NUMBERB = 13
Numeric digits 2
Numeric Fuzz 1
If NUMBERA = NUMBERB THEN SAY "THEY ARE EQUAL"
```

5. What does this program display?
```
A = 5
B = 4
SAY A = B
```

A: 0
A = B is false, so it becomes 0.

6. What does this program display? Try it to find out.
```
A = 2 + 2 = 2
SAY A
```

A: 3.
2 = 2 becomes a 1, so 2 + 1 = 3.

7. Write a program that will ask for a number (a temperature), then another number. Compare the two numbers. If the first is lower than the second, display 'rising'. If the second is lower than the first, display 'falling'. If the two numbers are equal, display 'steady'.

A:
```
/*CH06P07.CMD*/
say 'Please type in a temperature'
pull first_temp
say 'Please type in another temperature'
pull second_temp
if first_temp < second_temp then say 'rising'
if second_temp < first_temp then say 'falling'
if first_temp = second_temp then say 'steady'
```

CHAPTER 7

1. If you execute this program with the command shown, what are the results?
```
/*CH07P01.CMD */
ARG YOUR_NAME ADDRESS "/" JUNK
SAY "YOUR NAME IS " YOUR_NAME
SAY "YOU LIVE AT  " ADDRESS
/*
==> CH07P01 JOHN 22 1/2 MAY ST LIMA
*/
```

A: YOUR NAME IS JOHN
   YOU LIVE AT 22 1

The info to the right of the / goes into JUNK. The info to the left of the / goes into YOUR_NAME ADDRESS.

2. If you execute this program with the command shown what are the results?

```
/*CH07P02.CMD*/
ARG  2 YOUR_NAME 5 6 ADDRESS 9
SAY "YOUR NAME IS " YOUR_NAME
SAY "YOU LIVE AT  " ADDRESS
/*
==> CH07P02 JOHN 22 1/2 MAY ST LIMA PERU
*/
```

A: YOUR NAME IS OHN
  YOU LIVE AT   22
  YOUR_NAME contains columns 2 - 4   ohn
  ADDRESS   contains columns 5 - 8   22 1

3. Write a program that accepts two ARGS: day of week and weather. If the weather is sunny or cloudy and it is Friday, display "Head for golf course!" But if it's Friday and raining, display "Head for office!"

A:
```
/* CH07P03.CMD  */
Arg Day_of_week Weather
If (Weather = "SUNNY"  ¦ Weather = "CLOUDY"),
  & Day_of_week = "FRIDAY"
 Then say "Head for Golf Course"
If Weather = "SUNNY" ¦ Day_of_week = "FRIDAY"
Then say "Head for Office"
```

4. Write a program that breaks up the information contained in a variable into three variables. Place this information in the first variable VAR1:

ABCDEFGHIJKLMNOP

Use the proper PARSE instruction to break up the first variable this way:

VAR2 gets columns 3 and 4
VAR3 gets columns 6 through 9
VAR4 gets columns 9 through 14
Display VAR2
Display VAR3
Display VAR4

Expected Results:

CD
FGHI
IJKLMN

A:
```
/* CH07P04.CMD  */
VAR1 = "ABCDEFGHIJKLMNOP"
PARSE VAR VAR1 3 VAR2 5 6 VAR3 10 9 VAR4 14
SAY VAR2
SAY VAR3
SAY VAR4
```

5. What would this say
```
/*CH07P05.CMD */
ARG N1 N2 N3
SAY N2 N3 N1
```

if it is executed this way?
= = > CH07P05 MARYELLEN SUE KAREN

A: SUE KAREN MARYELLEN

6. This ARG, and this manner of execution, produces what display?

```
/*CH07P06.CMD*/
ARG NUM1 NUM2 NUM3 .
TOTAL = NUM1 + NUM2 + NUM3
SAY TOTAL
```

= = = > CH07P06 10 20 30 40 50 60

A: 60
   40, 50, and 60 are thrown away.

7. Write a program that accepts three pieces of information from the command line and displays them in reverse order. If more than three are entered, display an error message. Expected results:

= = > CH07P07 peter paul mary
MARY PAUL PETER
= = > CH07P07 peter paul mary ringo
I said enter only three items please!

A:
```
/*CH07P07.CMD     */
ARG A B C D
IF D <> ''
THEN SAY "I said enter only three items please!"
ELSE SAY C B A
```

8. You want the user to type in three and only three items (words) of information, separated by spaces. What does your PULL look like?

A: PULL V1 V2 V3 .

9. Write a program that asks you to type in three words (only) and displays them in reverse order. Expected results:

```
= = = > CH07P09
= = = > a b c
      C B A
= = = > CH07P09
= = = > a b c d
      C B A
```

A:
```
/*CH07P09.CMD */
SAY "PLEASE ENTER 3 WORDS (ONLY)"
PULL W1 W2 W3 .
SAY W3 W2 W1
```

10. Write a front-end program for the ERASE OS/2 command, named BYEBYE.CMD. Have it ask, "Are you sure?" before deleting. If the file specification is "junk.dat", don't ask. Expected results:

```
= = = > BYEBYE abc.dat
   ARE YOU SURE? Y/N
= = = > n
   NOT DELETED
= = = > BYEBYE junk.dat
   DELETED
```

A:
```
/* BYEBYE.CMD*/
ARG FILE_NAME
IF FILE_NAME = "JUNK.DAT"
THEN "ERASE " FILE_NAME
ELSE
  DO
    SAY "ARE YOU SURE? Y/N "
    PULL REPLY
    IF REPLY = "Y" THEN "ERASE " FILE_NAME
    ELSE SAY "NOT DELETED"
  END
```

11. Write a program that computes the percent of increase of one number over another. Ask for the two amounts from the keyboard. The formula is

% increase = 100 * ((new - old) / old)

Imagine your old salary was $21,203 and your new is $80,000. You would figure the % increase as

% increase = 100 * ((80000 - 21203) / 21203)

Expected results:

```
= = = > CH07P11
Please enter your old salary
= = = > 100
Please enter your new salary
= = = > 120
 % increase is  20
```

A:
```
/* CH07P11.CMD */
Say "Please enter your old salary "
Pull Old
Say "Please enter your new salary "
Pull New
Percent_increase = 100 * ((New - Old) / Old )
Say "% increase is "  Percent_increase
```

12. Ask for the weather from the keyboard and the day of the week. If it is raining, ask how many inches. If it is Friday and sunny or cloudy, display "Head for golf course." If it is Saturday and less than a half inch, display "Fishing pole, please." Expected results:

```
= = = > CH07P12
   WHAT IS THE WEATHER?
= = = > SUNNY
   WHAT DAY OF THE WEEK?
= = = > FRIDAY
   HEAD FOR GOLF COURSE
= = = > CH07P12
   WHAT IS THE WEATHER?
= = = > RAINING
   WHAT DAY OF THE WEEK?
= = = > SATURDAY
   HOW MANY INCHES OF RAIN?
   .4
   FISHING POLE PLEASE
```

A:
```
/* CH07P12.CMD */
Say "What is the weather?"
Pull Weather
Say "What day of the week?"
Pull Day_of_week
If Weather = "RAINING"
then
    do
      Say "How many inches of rain?"
      Pull Inches
    end


If Day_of_week = "FRIDAY" ,
 & (Weather = "SUNNY" | Weather = "CLOUDY")
then Say "Head for golf course"
If Day_of_week = "SATURDAY" & inches < .5
then Say "Fishing pole please"
```

CHAPTER 8

1. Your program is running in a Presentation Manager window, apparently not doing anything, and won't stop. How can you start up interactive debugging to see what it is doing?

A: Click on OPTIONS, then click on interactive trace. Then you can single-step through your program by hitting ENTER.

2. You are in interactive trace, single-stepping through the program. You have had enough. What do you type in to make the program run without any trace?

A: TRACE ?N
or
   TRACE OFF
Then hit ENTER once again.

3. What is the OS/2 command that will turn on interactive debugging for your REXX programs?

A: SET RXTRACE = ON.

4. Can you put "SET RXTRACE = ON" in your program to turn on interactive debug? Try it to find out.

A: Yes. It is an OS/2 command and can be used in a program.

5. Run your percent increase program with interactive trace on. During interactive trace turn on TRACE Intermediate. Watch how the variables are processed.

CHAPTER 9

1. ERRORTEXT(RC) is used in which type of trap?

A: The REXX SYNTAX trap. It is not used in environment command ERROR traps.

2. Complete this program.

```
/*CH09P02Q.CMD */
SIGNAL ON
"TURN DOWN VOLUME"
EXIT


SAY "COMMAND TO OS/2 FAILED"
```

A:

```
/*CH09P02A.CMD */
SIGNAL ON ERROR
"TURN DOWN VOLUME"
EXIT

ERROR:
SAY "COMMAND TO OS/2 FAILED"
EXIT
```

3. Write a program that asks for a file name and then issues the OS/2 command DIR on it. Set up an ERROR trap to intercept the command that is not working. In the ERROR trap, display the line of the program in error and the error code from OS/2. Ask for the file name again, reexecute the command, and exit. Expected results:

```
= = = >  CH09P03
    PLEASE ENTER FILE NAME
= = = >  junk.dat
    CANNOT EXECUTE  COMMAND
    OS/2 ERROR CODE IS 18
    LINE IN ERROR IS "DIR " file_name
    PLEASE REENTER
= = = >  okfile.dat
    OKFILE.DAT       100 9-9-94 9:33a
```

A:
```
/* CH09P03.CMD  *
SIGNAL ON ERROR
SAY "PLEASE ENTER FILE NAME"
PULL file_name
"DIR " file_name
EXIT

ERROR:

SAY "CANNOT EXECUTE COMMAND"
SAY "OS/2 ERROR CODE IS " RC
SAY "LINE IN ERROR IS " SOURCELINE(SIGL)
SAY "PLEASE REENTER"
PULL file_name
"DIR " file_name
EXIT
```

CHAPTER 10

1. Write a program that will multiply two numbers. Ask the user for the two numbers, and set up a trap to intercept any error, such as invalid numbers.

A:
```
/*CH10P01.CMD */
SAY "PLEASE ENTER TWO NUMBERS"
PULL NUMBER1 NUMBER2
SIGNAL ON SYNTAX
SAY NUMBER1 * NUMBER2
EXIT
SYNTAX: SAY "SOMETHING WRONG WITH YOUR NUMBERS"
EXIT
```

2. Run this program to determine the effect of parentheses on arithmetic operations.

```
/*CH10P02.CMD*/

SAY (1 + 2) * 3
SAY 1 + (2 * 3)
SAY 1 +  2 * 3
What is displayed?
```

A: 9
7
7

3. Create a simple program to calculate the effect of compound interest. Ask for the following items from the keyboard:
Principal
Percent of interest (yearly)
Number of years money kept in account
Compounding frequency (How many times per year is interest compounded? 1 = yearly; 12 = monthly; 52 = weekly; 365 = daily)
Perform the following calculations:
Compute the yearly rate of interest as yearly percent of interest / 100.
Compute r (the rate) as yearly rate of interest / compounding frequency.
Compute n (number of times compounded) as how many years X compounding frequency.
Compute final amount as principal X $((1 + r)^n)$.
Display final amount.
Keep this program, since you will be improving on it later.

A:

```
/*CH10P03.CMD*/
/* define variables
final amount = p *  ((1+r)**n)
p = principal
r = rate of interest (expressed as decimal fraction
    per compounding period)
n = number of interest periods
*/

/* get from terminal*/
say "Compound interest calculator"
say
say "$w invested at x% annual interest compounded y
times per year"
say "for a period of z years will grow to a total of
$??"

say "Please enter principal (amount of initial deposit)"
pull p
say "Please enter yearly percent of interest (e.g. 7 for
7%)"
pull yearly_percent_of_interest
say "Please enter number of years money is kept in
account"
pull how_many_years
say "How many times is interest compounded per year?"
say "for example, if yearly, enter 1"
say "                monthly, enter 12"
say "                weekly,  enter 52"
say "                daily,   enter 365"
pull compounding_frequency

/* compute*/
yearly_rate_of_interest = yearly_percent_of_interest /
100
r = yearly_rate_of_interest / compounding_frequency
n = how_many_years * compounding_frequency
final_amount = p * ((1 + r) ** n)

/* display */
say "$"p " invested at " yearly_percent_of_interest"%
annual interest"
say "compounded " compounding_frequency " times per
year"
say "for a period of " how_many_years " years"
say "will grow to a total of " final_amount
say
```

CHAPTER 11

1. Correct this segment of code:

```
/*CH11P01Q.CMD with errors */
NAME = "MIKE"
SAY "This won't work"
CASE
  WHEN "NAME" = "JOHN" THEN SAY "GRADE IS 78"
  WHEN  NAME  = "MARY" THEN SAY "GRADE IS 84"
  WHEN  NAME  = "MIKE" THEN SAY "GRADE IS 89"
  WHEN  NAME  = "MONA" THEN SAY "GRADE IS 91"
ELSE  THEN SAY "NOT ON ROSTER"
```

A:

```
/*CH11P01A.CMD*/
NAME = "MIKE"
SELECT
  WHEN  NAME  = "JOHN" THEN SAY "GRADE IS 78"
  WHEN  NAME  = "MARY" THEN SAY "GRADE IS 84"
  WHEN  NAME  = "MIKE" THEN SAY "GRADE IS 89"
  WHEN  NAME  = "MONA" THEN SAY "GRADE IS 91"
  OTHERWISE  SAY "NOT ON ROSTER"
END
```

2. Are these two segments of code equivalent?

```
SELECT
  WHEN  NAME  = "ERIC" THEN SAY "GRADE IS 83"
  OTHERWISE  SAY "NOT ON ROSTER"
END
```

```
IF NAME = "ERIC"
THEN SAY "GRADE IS 83"
ELSE SAY "NOT ON ROSTER"
```

A: Yes.

CHAPTER 12

1. Will this line of instruction be passed to the environment?

PULL var1 var2 var3

A: No. REXX understands the keyword PULL.

2. Will this line of instruction be passed to the environment?

BARK "PLEASE ENTER NAME"

A: Yes. REXX doesn't understand BARK.

3. If this command works, what will be in RC?

"ERASE ABC.DAT"

A: 0.

CHAPTER 13

1. True or false: There must be a space after the name of the function and before the parenthesis when you use a function.

A: No. There must be no space between the function name and the parenthesis.

2. When you call a built-in function with CALL, where is the answer given?

A: In the special variable RESULT.

3. Accept two numbers from the keyboard, and check to be sure they are valid numbers. Subtract one from the other. Drop the sign of the answer, and display the answer. Expected results:

```
= = = > CH13P03 100 20
    80
= = = > CH13P03 20 100
    80
```

A:
```
/*CH13P03.CMD */
ARG NUM1 NUM2 .
IF DATATYPE(NUM1) <> "NUM"
THEN
 DO
   SAY "FIRST NUMBER INVALID"
 END
IF DATATYPE(NUM2) <> "NUM"
THEN
 DO
   SAY "SECOND NUMBER INVALID"
 END

SAY ABS(NUM1 - NUM2)
```

4. Using a function, create a program that will convert one character string to another. Set it up so that if you type in:

GREAT
it will print out:
BUENO

A:
```
/*CH13P04.CMD */
String = "GREAT"
SAY TRANSLATE(STRING,"BUENO","GREAT'")
```

5. Write a program that will accept a hex number, a plus or minus sign, and another hex number; then add or subtract based on the sign. Display the answer in hex. Expected results:

```
= = = > CH13P05 e - 2
   C
= = = > CH13P05 e + 2
   10
```

A:
```
/* CH13P05.CMD */
Arg Hex1 Sign Hex2
Ans = 0
Dec1 = X2D(Hex1)
Dec2 = X2D(Hex2)
If Sign = "+"
Then Ans = Dec1 + Dec2
If Sign = "-"
Then Ans = Dec1 - Dec2
Say  D2X(Ans)
```

6. Here is a working example of a program that will convert all the letters in a string of characters to lower case. Modify it so that it converts from lower case to upper case. (Be aware that the REXX PARSE UPPER instruction will do the same thing.)

```
/*CH13P06Q.CMD converts upper to lower*/
instring = "THIS WAS IN UPPER CASE"
upper_alpha = "ABCDEFGHIJKLMNOPQRSTUVWXYZ"
lower_alpha = "abcdefghijklmnopqrstuvwxyz"
outstring = translate(instring,lower_alpha,upper_alpha)
Say "Here is the converted string"
Say outstring
```

A:
```
/*CH13P06A.CMD converts lower to upper */
instring = "this was in lower"
upper_alpha = "ABCDEFGHIJKLMNOPQRSTUVWXYZ"
lower_alpha = "abcdefghijklmnopqrstuvwxyz"
outstring = translate(instring,upper_alpha,lower_alpha)
Say "Here is the converted string"
Say outstring
```

CHAPTER 14

1. True or false: In REXX, user-written functions/subroutines may be used either as functions or subroutines.

A: True.

2. True or false: If you use the function as a function, you do it this way: function-name(data).

A: True.

3. True or false: If you use the function as a subroutine, you do it this way:
CALL function-name data
and the answer comes back in RESULT.

A: True.

4. Write an internal function/subroutine that will concatenate two items passed to it (without spaces). Invoke it as a function, then as a subroutine. Check automatically within the program that both ways produce the same result. Expected results:

```
= = = > CH14P04
   INVOKED AS FUNCTION: CATDOG
   INVOKED AS SUBROUTINE: CATDOG
   RESULTS ARE EQUAL
```

A:
```
/*CH14P04.CMD*/
CALL CONCAT "CAT","DOG"

SAVE_RESULT = RESULT
SAY "INVOKED AS FUNCTION:" CONCAT("CAT","DOG")
SAY "INVOKED AS SUBROUTINE:" RESULT
IF SAVE_RESULT == CONCAT("CAT","DOG")
THEN SAY "RESULTS ARE EQUAL"
ELSE SAY "RESULTS NOT EQUAL"
EXIT

CONCAT: PROCEDURE

ARG A,B

RETURN A ¦¦ B
```

5. Redo the percent increase problem as an external subroutine, naming it PERCENTI.CMD (see Problem 12 in Chapter 7). Have it accept two parameters (that is, arguments): first, old salary; second, new salary. Have it return the percent increase on the RETURN statement. Check both numbers for numeric. If either is not valid, display a message and return a zero.

Write another program to test this one by calling it as a function, then as a subroutine. Place both in the same directory.

A:

```
/* PERCENTI.CMD REXX Chapter 14 problem 5
   external subroutine/function that
 calculates percent of increase */
ARG Old_salary , New_salary
If datatype(Old_salary) = "NUM",
&  datatype(New_salary) = "NUM"
then nop
else
  do
   Say "Number is invalid"
   Return 0
  end


Return 100 *  ((New_salary  -  Old_salary)  /
old_salary)

/*  CH14P05M  REXX  Main  program  to  test
%increase subroutine */
Say "PERCENTI"(20000 , 22000 )
Call "PERCENTI" 20000 , 22000
Say Result
```

6. Using the solution to Problem 4, write your concatenate function/subroutine as an external function/subroutine (leave the internal function/subroutine where it is). Call the external function/subroutine in such a way that you are sure to invoke the external, not the internal function/subroutine. Prove that you invoked the external, not the internal.

A:

```
/*CH14P06M.CMD*/
CALL CONCAT "CAT","DOG"            /* internal */

SAVE_RESULT = RESULT
IF  SAVE_RESULT  ==  CONCAT("CAT","DOG")  /*
external */
THEN SAY "RESULTS ARE EQUAL"
ELSE SAY "RESULTS NOT EQUAL"
EXIT

CONCAT: PROCEDURE /*INTERNAL*/
ARG A,B
SAY "IM IN THE INTERNAL"
RETURN A ¦¦ B


/*CONCAT.CMD          EXTERNAL*/
ARG A,B
SAY "IM IN THE EXTERNAL"
RETURN A ¦¦ B
```

7. Create a metric conversion external function/subroutine named Metric. It will accept two arguments: UNIT and QUANTITY. UNIT has these possible values:
LITER QUART MILE KILOMETER
It returns a number equivalent to QUANTITY in the other measuring system, based on this table:

1 liter	= 1.057 quarts
1 quart	= .946 liters
1 mile	= 8/5 kilometers
1 kilometer	= .625 miles

Also write a main program that invokes this as a function. Expected results:

```
===> CH14P07M kilometer 1000
   625 MILES
```

A:
```
/* CH14P07E.CMD REXX external subr METRIC */

ARG UNIT , QUANTITY

IF UNIT = "LITER" THEN ANSWER = QUANTITY * 1.057
IF UNIT = "QUART" THEN ANSWER = QUANTITY * .946
IF UNIT = "MILE"  THEN ANSWER = QUANTITY * (8/5)
IF UNIT = "KILOMETER" THEN ANSWER = QUANTITY * .625
RETURN ANSWER


/*CH14P07M.CMD REXX MAIN PROGRAM */

SAY "10 MILES IS " "METRIC"("MILE",10) "KM"
/*ANOTHER WAY*/
CALL "METRIC" "MILE",10
SAY "10 MILES IS " RESULT "KM"
```

CHAPTER 15

1. What is the missing word?

```
DO FOREVER
   SAY "WHAT NUMBER AM I THINKING OF. 1-10"
   PULL NUMBER
   IF NUMBER = 7
   THEN
   SAY "STILL HAVEN'T GOT IT"
END
SAY "GOOD GUESS. GOING TO TRY THE LOTTERY NEXT?"
```

A:
```
/*CH15P01.CMD*/
DO FOREVER
   SAY "WHAT NUMBER AM I THINKING OF. 1-10"
   PULL NUMBER
   IF NUMBER = 7
   THEN   LEAVE
   SAY "STILL HAVEN'T GOT IT"
END
SAY "GOOD GUESS. GOING TO TRY THE LOTTERY NEXT?"
```

2. Write a program that asks the user to enter a series of numbers, but never the same one twice in a row. Limit it to 10 numbers.

A:
```
/*CH15P02.CMD*/
DO 10
   SAY "ENTER A NUMBER (DIFFERENT FROM LAST ONE)"
   PULL NUMBER
   IF NUMBER = PREVIOUS_NUMBER
   THEN   SAY "SAME AS LAST ONE!"
   PREVIOUS_NUMBER = NUMBER
END
```

3. Write an external subroutine to compute the square root of a number passed to it. Name it SQRT.CMD. It will accept one ARG: the number. Validate the number. If negative, or not numeric, display a message, and return a zero. Make your guess one-half of the number.
Repeat this loop 50 times
  Make new guess = (guess + (number / guess)) / 2
  Make guess = new guess
End-repeat
Return the new guess to the caller.   Write a main program that calls this function/subroutine. Execute the main program.

A:
```
/*   SQRT.CMD   REXX   function/subroutine    to
calculate  square  root  negative  numbers  not
allowed */
ARG Number
/* Validate Number */
If datatype(Number) <> "NUM"
then
  do
   Say "Argument passed not a number "
   Return 0
  end
If Number < 0
then
  do
   Say "Cannot process negative numbers"
   Return 0
  end
```

```
/* Initialize Variables */
Guess = Number / 2
/* Keep guessing till guess is close */
Do 50
   New_guess = (Guess + (Number / Guess)) / 2
   Guess = New_guess
  /* For debugging say New_guess */

/* For debugging, say New_guess * New_guess */
Return New_guess

/* CH15P03M REXX program to test square root
function/subroutine*/
Say "SQRT"(144)
Say "SQRT"(-144)
Call "SQRT" 144   1
Say RESULT
```

4. Set secret number equal to 13. Write a program to keep asking the user to enter a number from 1 to 20 until the secret number is guessed. Limit the loop to 10 guesses. Expected results:

= = > CH15P04
   PLEASE ENTER YOUR GUESS, FROM 1 TO 20
= = > 2
   WRONG
= = > 7
   WRONG
= = > 13
   RIGHT

A:

```
/* CH15P04.CMD  */
Secret_number = 13
Guess = ""
Do 10
   Say "Please enter your guess, from 1 to 20"
   Pull Guess
   If Guess = secret_number
   Then
     Do
       Say "RIGHT"
       LEAVE
     End
   Else
     Do
       Say "WRONG"
     End
End /* Do 10 */
```

5. Improve on your compound interest program written in Chapter 10, Question 3. The added requirements are listed below under "Enhancements." Create a simple program to calculate the effect of compound interest. Ask for the following items from the keyboard:

Principal
Percent of interest (yearly)
Number of years money kept in account
Compounding frequency (How many times per year is interest compounded? 1 = yearly; 12 = monthly; 52 = weekly; 365 = daily)
Perform the following calculations:
Compute the yearly rate of interest as yearly percent of interest / 100.
Compute r (the rate) as yearly rate of interest / compounding frequency.
Compute n (number of times compounded) as how many years X compounding frequency.
Compute final amount as principal X $((1 + r)^n)$.

Display final amount.

Enhancements. Put the dialogue with the person, calculations, and display into a loop that will repeat until you type in "NO." After getting the amounts from the keyboard, verify the following:
If principal is blank, end the loop.
If percent blank, or years blank, or years over 100, or principal not numeric, or percent not numeric, or years not numeric, then start the loop over again.

A:

```
/*CH15P05.CMD    REXX     compound     interest
calculator
   final amount = p *  ((1+r)**n)
   p = principal
   r = rate of interest (expressed as decimal
fraction
       per compounding period)
   n = number of interest periods
*/
reply_from_terminal = "unknown"
do until reply_from_terminal = "NO"

   /* get from terminal*/
   say "Compound interest calculator"
   say
   say   "$w   invested   at   x%   annual   int.
compounded y times per year"
   say "for a period of z years will grow to a
total of $??"

   say  "Please  enter  principal  (amount  of
initial deposit)"
   pull p
   say "Please enter yearly percent of interest
(e.g. 7 for 7%)"
   pull yearly_percent_of_interest
   say "Please enter number of years money is
kept in account"
   pull how_many_years
   say "How many times is interest compounded
per year?"
   say "for example, if yearly, enter 1"
   say "                monthly, enter 12"
   say "                weekly,  enter 52"
   say "                daily,   enter 365"
   pull compounding_frequency

   /* verify */
   if p = "" then leave
   if  yearly_percent_of_interest  =  ""  then
iterate
   if compounding_frequency = "" then iterate
```

```
   if how_many_years = "" then iterate
   if how_many_years > 100
   then
       do
         say "too many years "
         iterate
       end
   if datatype(p) <> "NUM" then iterate
   if  datatype(yearly_percent_of_interest)  <>
"NUM" then iterate
   if datatype(compounding_frequency) <> "NUM"
then iterate
   if  datatype(how_many_years)  <>  "NUM"  then
iterate

   /* compute*/
   yearly_rate_of_interest    =
yearly_percent_of_interest / 100
   r   =    yearly_rate_of_interest    /
compounding_frequency
   n = how_many_years * compounding_frequency
   final_amount = p * ((1 + r) ** n)

   /* display */
   say    "$"p    "   invested    at    "
yearly_percent_of_interest"% annual interest"
   say "compounded " compounding_frequency "
times per year"
   say "for a period of " how_many_years "
years"
   say "will grow to a total of " final_amount
   say
   say "Do you want to do another? YES/NO"
   pull reply_from_terminal
end /* do until */
```

CHAPTER 16

1. What will this line of a REXX program do?
SAY QUEUED()

A: It will display how many lines there are in the Data Queue.

2. There is nothing in the Data Queue, and your program says PULL. What happens?

A: The program stops and waits for you to type something at the keyboard.

3. Your program does 10 PUSHes, and 9 PULLs. What happens?

A: A line of data remains in the Data Queue until you close the window you are executing in.

4. Your program does 9 PUSHes, and 10 PULLs. What happens?

A: The program stops and waits for you to type something at the keyboard.

CHAPTER 17

1. Write a program with a loop that sets NUMBER.1 through NUMBER.10 to the numbers 101 thru 110; then loop through the array, displaying the contents of NUMBER.1 through NUMBER.11 — yes NUMBER.11, — to see what happens.
A:
```
/*CH17p01.CMD*/
DO I = 1 TO 10
   NUMBER.I = I + 100
END
DO I = 1 TO 11
   SAY NUMBER.I
END
```

CHAPTER 18

1. Create a program that reads the file SAMP1.DAT one line (record) at a time. Display each line.

A:

```
/*CH18P01.CMD  reads  a  file  one  line  at  a
time*/
Input_file = 'c:\rexxprgs\samp1.dat'
DO while lines(input_file) > 0
    call linein(input_file)
    say 'Read this:' result
end
```

2. Copy the file SAMP1.DAT to the file SAMP1.DEL using LINEIN and LINEOUT.

A:

```
/*CH18P02.CMD copy a file to another*/
Input_file = 'c:\rexxprgs\samp1.dat'
Output_file = 'c:\rexxprgs\samp1.del'
DO while lines(input_file) > 0
    call linein(input_file)
    say 'Read this:' result
    call lineout output_file,result
end
```

3. Improve on Problem 2. Check to see if the file SAMP1.DEL exists. If it exists, delete it before copying.

A:

```
/*CH18P03.CMD copy a file to another.   If the output
file exists, delete it first*/
Input_file = 'c:\rexxprgs\samp1.dat'
Output_file = 'c:\rexxprgs\samp1.del'
If STREAM(output_file,'C','QUERY EXISTS') = ""
then
  do
    say  output_file 'does not exist, creating'
  end
else
  do
    say  output_file 'exists, deleting'
    'erase ' output_file
  end
DO while lines(input_file) > 0
    call linein(input_file)
    say 'Read this:' result
    call lineout output_file,result
end
```

4. Using output redirection (see Section 3.10,) put the output of a DIR *.CMD OS/2 command into a datafile named DIRTEMP.TMP. Using file IO, read the file DIRTEMP.TMP. Examine each line of the file DIRTEMP.TMP. If any line contains the string 'SAYHI.CMD,' display the line.

A:

```
/*CH18P04.CMD*/
'DIR *.CMD  >  DIRTEMP.TMP'
DO WHILE LINES('DIRTEMP.TMP') > 0
    LINE_READ =  LINEIN('DIRTEMP.TMP')
    IF POS('SAYHI.CMD',LINE_READ) > 0
    THEN SAY LINE_READ
END
```

5. Modify the previous problem. Instead of displaying the line containing 'SAYHI.CMD', display the contents of the file SAYHI.CMD.

```
/*CH18P05.CMD*/
'DIR *.CMD  >  DIRTEMP.TMP'
DO WHILE LINES('DIRTEMP.TMP') > 0
    LINE_READ =  LINEIN('DIRTEMP.TMP')
    IF POS('SAYHI.CMD',LINE_READ) > 0
    THEN 'TYPE SAYHI.CMD'  END
```

CHAPTER 19

1. Create a quick calculator program. Use INTERPRET to execute an expression that is typed in, then display the result and name it CH19P01. It will be used this way:

= = > CH19P01 1 + 1

It will then display "2".

A:

```
/* CH19P01.CMD Quick calculator */

ARG Expression
Signal on syntax
Interpret "Say " Expression
Exit
Syntax:
Say "Syntax error in expression " Expression
Exit
```

Appendix B

OS/2 COMMANDS

Topics

B.1 Some Considerations
B.2 OS/2 Commands

B.1 SOME CONSIDERATIONS

I have listed and described some of the OS/2 commands you should know in order to take full advantage of the power of REXX. I have not included all the OS/2 commands that are available, nor have I shown all their options.

If you need one of these commands in your REXX exec, you'll need to enclose the command in apostrophes or quotation marks. The DIR command shown below would be found in a REXX program looking like this:

```
'DIR \REXXPRGS\*.CMD'
```

B.2 OS/2 COMMANDS

Command: ATTRIB

Purpose:
To display and possibly change certain attributes of a file: the read-only and archive attributes.

Examples:
To make the file A.DAT in the directory REXXPRGS a read-only file:
```
ATTRIB +R \REXXPRGS\A.DAT
```

To change a hidden file named HIDE.DAT in the directory REXXPRGS to visible:

```
ATTRIB -H \REXXPRGS\A.DAT
```

To view the attributes and names of all the files in the directory REXXPRGS:

```
ATTRIB \REXXPRGS\*.*
```

Command: CALL

Purpose:
When used in a REXX program or a batch file, executes another Batch File (.BAT or .CMD), written in Batch File language or REXX. Control goes to the other Batch File, and when it finishes, control goes back to the statement after the CALL. This is not used to execute a REXX function or subroutine. Use the REXX verb CALL (not in quotes) for that.

Example:
This example shows how, in a REXX program, to execute a Batch File named ABC.BAT or ABC.CMD:

```
"CALL ABC"
```

Executing the Batch File named CDE and passing it two parameters:

```
"CALL CDE     Marie Denise"
```

Command: CHDIR   **Abbreviation: CD**

Purpose:
To make a directory the current one.

Example:
To change to the REXXPRGS directory:
CD \REXXPRGS

To change to the parent directory of the current directory:
CD ..

To change to the root directory:
CD \

Command: CLS

Purpose:
To clear the screen in an OS/2 Window or Full Screen.

Example:
CLS

Note :
> *There is a REXX function, SYSCLS, which will do the same thing as CLS.*

Command: COPY

Purpose:
To create a duplicate of a file.

Example:
COPY A.DAT B.DAT

Command: DATE

Purpose:
To display the current date and optionally change it.

Example:
DATE

Command: DEL

Purpose:
To delete a file.

Example:
DEL ABC.DAT

Command: DIR

Purpose:
To list the names of the files in a directory.

Example to list names of files in the current directory:
DIR

Example to list names of programs in the directory REXXPRGS:
DIR \REXXPRGS*.CMD

Example to list names of files in the current directory, shown with file names only, in several columns across the screen:
DIR /W

Example to list names of files one screen full at a time, then stop and wait until you press a key to continue:
DIR /P

Command: **ERASE**

Purpose:
To delete a file.

Example:
ERASE ABC.DAT

Command: **EXIT**

Purpose:
To close the OS/2 Window or Full Screen. Terminates the current process.

Example:
EXIT

Command: **FIND**

Purpose:
To search for a character string in files, and to show the line containing the string and its sequential line number. Note that upper and lower case are significant in the character string.

Example of finding the word OTHERWISE in the file SELX01.CMD:

FIND /N "OTHERWISE" SELEX01.CMD

Example of using output redirection to place the output of FIND in a file. You can examine the file by TYPEing it, or reading it in your program.

FIND /N "OTHERWISE" SELEX01.CMD > OUT.DAT
TYPE OUT.DAT

Example of using FIND as an OS/2 pipe filter. This will find any file whose name contains the word "ROUND." You can substitute another program for DIR.

DIR C:\REXXPRGS ¦ FIND /N "ROUND"

Command: MKDIR   **Abbreviation: MD**

Purpose:
To create a directory.

Example:
MD \REXXPRGS

Command: MORE

Purpose:
This pipe filter holds its input and waits until there is a screen full, then displays --more-- and waits until you press ENTER.

Examples:
DIR ¦ MORE

TYPE README ¦ MORE

SHOW50 ¦ MORE

Command: PRINT

Purpose:
To print a file.

Example:
PRINT \REXXPRGS\MYPROG.CMD

Command: PROMPT

Purpose:
To change the characters displayed at the command line in an OS/2 Window or OS/2 Full Screen indicating that OS/2 is ready for your next command.

Example:
PROMPT $P

Command: RMDIR   **Abbreviation: RD**

Purpose:
To delete a directory.

Example:
RD \REXXPRGS

Command: SET

Purpose:
Creates or changes an environment variable. Environment variables affect only the OS/2 Window, OS/2 Full Screen, or DOS Window you are in. They remain in effect until you close the window. They are available to any OS/2 command, program, REXX program, or Batch File that you execute in the window. They are a way of communicating globally among processes in a window. You may choose any name for the environment variable, but be aware that if you use a name that is already in use, you may change it and adversely affect other programs and processes in the window.

Example to set the environment variable PGMDIR to the value C:\REXXPRGS::
SET PGMDIR=C:\REXXPRGS

Command: SORT

Purpose:
To arrange the records in a file in sequence.

Example of sorting the file JUMBLE.DAT and displaying the sorted results on the monitor:
```
SORT < JUMBLE.DAT
```

Example of sorting the file JUMBLE.DAT and creating a new sorted file named SORTED.DAT:
```
SORT < JUMBLE.DAT > SORTED.DAT
TYPE SORTED.DAT
```

Example of sorting based on the data starting in column or position 14:
```
SORT /+14 < JUMBLE.DAT > SORTED.DAT
TYPE SORTED.DAT
```

Example of using SORT as a pipe filter to sort the output of a command:

```
DIR ¦ SORT
```

Command: START

Purpose:
To run a program in a window and to display a title in the window.

Example:
```
START "My program is running" TESTPM2
```

Command: TIME

Purpose:
To display the current time and optionally change it.

Example:
```
TIME
```

Command: TREE

Purpose:
To display the current directory structure. Shows the directories and their subdirectories that are on the current drive.

Example:
TREE

Example to show the current directory structure and the names of the files as well:
TREE /F

Example to place the current directory structure into a file named TREE.DAT, which can be examined by a REXX program, or the TYPE command:
TREE > TREE.DAT

Command: TYPE

Purpose:
To display a file on the screen.

Example:
TYPE MYPROG.CMD

Appendix C

REXX INSTRUCTIONS

All the REXX verbs supported under OS/2 are listed.

A description of each instruction is given along with several examples of its use.

ADDRESS

Directs REXX to pass commands to a specific environment or command processor.

Environments:

Under OS/2:
CMD (OS/2)

Under TSO:
TSO (the default)
ISPEXEC (ISPF)
ISREDIT (ISPF editor)

Under CMS:
CMS (the default for programs whose file type is EXEC)
XEDIT (the default for programs whose file type is XEDIT: XEDIT macros)
COMMAND (the CMS command processor, bypasses synonyms, requires uppercase, requires EXEC for EXEC's, CP for CP commands)

ADDRESS *environment*

Changes default *environment*. Subsequent commands will be sent to that environment.

>TSO Example:
>
>ADDRESS ISPEXEC
>"DISPLAY PANEL(PANEL123)"

ADDRESS *environment "command"*

Sends *command* to *environment*. Only the command specified is sent to that environment.

>TSO Example:
>
>ADDRESS ISPEXEC "DISPLAY PANEL(PANEL123)"

ARG

ARG *variable-1 ... variable-n*

Short form of PARSE UPPER ARG. In a main program it receives information typed in on the command line next to the name of the program. In a function/subroutine it receives information passed to it on a function invocation or subroutine call.

The information is received in *variable-1* through *variable-n*.

>Example:
>
>ARG FILENAME

CALL

Invokes a subroutine, whether internal or external. The subroutine should terminate with a RETURN instruction that specifies a string to be passed back to the caller.

Turns on or off an error trap that continues executing.

CALL *subroutine* "*string*"
SAY RESULT

String is passed to *subroutine*, which picks it up on its ARG statement. The string that the subroutine specified on its RETURN statement can be picked up with the special variable RESULT.

Example:

```
CALL LENGTH "ABCD"
SAY RESULT /* 4 */
```

CALL *condition name*

CALL may also be used to initialize an error condition trap (see SIGNAL). If the error condition trap is entered, a RETURN at the end will send control back to the instruction after the one that failed.

Condition names:

```
ERROR
FAILURE
HALT
NOTREADY    /* OS/2 only */
```

Examples:

```
CALL ON ERROR      /* command to environment not correct */
CALL ON FAILURE    /* command to environment doesn't exist */
CALL ON HALT       /* attention interrupt */
CALL ON NOTREADY   /* OS/2 only. Error in input/output */
```

DO

Begins a group of instructions that are performed repeatedly, controlled by a variable or a REXX language element.

```
Examples:
/* incrementing a variable */
DO I = 1 to 10
 SAY I
END

/* subtracts 1 from the variable each time through the loop*/
DO I = 10 TO 1 BY -1
 SAY "COUNTDOWN " I
END

/* loops without limit; end loop with LEAVE instruction */
DO FOREVER
 IF TIME() > "16:00:00" THEN LEAVE
END

/* loops until a condition is true */
DO UNTIL TIME > "16:00:00"
 SAY "WORK"
END

/* loops as long as a condition is true */
DO WHILE TIME < "16:00:00"
 SAY "WORK"
END

/* loops a fixed number of times */
DO 10
 SAY "HELLO"
END
```

DROP

DROP *variable*

Undefines *variable*. Causes REXX to take the string (which previously was a variable) as a literal, equal to its name, but uppercased.

Examples:

```
GREETING = "HELLO"
SAY GREETING
---> HELLO
DROP GREETING
SAY GREETING
---> GREETING
```

END

Terminates a group of instructions controlled by a DO. Terminates a SELECT structure.

```
Example:
DO I = 1 TO 10
 SAY I
END
```

END *variable*

Terminates a group of instructions controlled by a DO that increments *variable*. *Variable* is optional, but is used to make it easier to check for matching DO's and END's.

Example:

```
DO I = 1 TO 10
 SAY I
END I
```

ENDLOCAL OS/2 only.

Restores the current drive and directory that were saved by a SETLOCAL instruction.

```
Example:
ENDLOCAL
```

EXIT

Ends the REXX program and returns control to the caller, whatever the caller may be. May pass back a return code (numeric only) to the caller. If caller is OS/2. the return code may be examined by the IF ERRORLEVEL command. If the caller is a REXX program, the return code may by examined by the RC special variable.

Examples:

EXIT
EXIT 8

EXPOSE

EXPOSE *variable-1 variable-n*

Used with the PROCEDURE instruction on an internal function/ subroutine to allow *variable-1* through *variable-n* to be shared with the main part of the program. Makes those variables global. Generally found right after the internal function/subroutine's label.

Example:

SUBR: PROCEDURE EXPOSE VAR1 /* VAR1 is shared with the main part of the program; all others are protected. */

IF

IF *expression*
THEN *instruction*
ELSE *instruction*

Controls conditional execution of one or more instructions. Checks to see if *expression* is true. If it is, then the *instruction* after the THEN is executed. If it is false, then the *instruction* after the ELSE is executed.

IF allows only one instruction after the THEN or the ELSE, but a DO END sequence will allow use of more than one instruction.

Expression may use one of these comparison operators:

=	**Equal**. If numeric, when compared algebraically. (1.0 is equal to 001.000.) If not numeric, when padded with leading or trailing spaces. ("Sue" is equal to " Sue "). Case is significant: "SUE" is not equal to "sue."
< >	**Not equal**, the negation of "=." Algebraic comparison and padding are performed.
> <	**Not equal**, the negation of "=." Algebraic comparison and padding are performed.
\ =	**Not equal**, the negation of "=." Algebraic comparison and padding are performed.
¬ =	**Not equal**, the negation of "=." (The symbol "¬" may not be found on all keyboards.) Algebraic comparison and padding are performed.
^=	**Not equal**, the negation of "=." (The symbol "^" may not be found on all keyboards.) Algebraic comparison and padding are performed.
>	**Greater than**. Algebraic comparison and padding are performed.
<	**Less than**. Algebraic comparison and padding are performed.
> =	**Greater than or equal to**. Algebraic comparison and padding are performed.
¬ <	**Not less than**. (The symbol "¬" may not be found on all keyboards.) Algebraic comparison and padding are performed.

\<   **Not less than.** Algebraic comparison and padding are performed.

< =   **Less than or equal to.** Algebraic comparison and padding are performed.

¬ >   **Not greater than.** (The symbol "¬" may not be found on all keyboards.) Algebraic comparison and padding are performed.

\>   **Not greater than.** Algebraic comparison and padding are performed.

= =   **Strictly equal on a character-by-character basis.** No algebraic comparison or padding is done.

¬ = =   **Strictly not equal,** the negation of "= =." (The symbol "¬" may not be found on all keyboards.) No algebraic comparison or padding is done.

\= =   **Strictly not equal,** the negation of "= =." No algebraic comparison or padding is done.

> >   **Strictly greater than.** No algebraic comparison or padding is done.

> > =   **Strictly greater than or equal to.** No algebraic comparison or padding is done.

< <   **Strictly less than.** No algebraic comparison or padding is done.

< < =   **Strictly less than or equal to.** No algebraic comparison or padding is done.

¬ > >   **Strictly not greater than.** (The symbol "¬" may not be found on all keyboards.) No algebraic comparison or padding is done.

¬ < <   **Strictly not less than.** (The symbol "¬" may not be found on all keyboards.) No algebraic comparison or padding is done.

Expression may use one of these comparison connectors:

&   **And**. The conditions on both sides of this must be true.

| **Or**. One or both of the conditions on either side of this must be true.

&&   **Exclusive Or**. Only one of the conditions on either side of this must be true.

Examples:

```
IF A = 1
THEN SAY "A IS EQUAL TO 1"
ELSE SAY "IT IS NOT"

IF A = 1
THEN
  DO
   SAY "A IS EQUAL TO 1"
   SAY "DO YOU AGREE?"
  END
ELSE
  DO
   SAY "IT IS NOT"
   SAY "WHAT DO YOU THINK?"
  END


IF REPLY = = "YES"
THEN
  DO
   SAY "YOUR REPLY REALLY IS A YES"
  END
ELSE
  DO
   SAY "IT REALLY IS NOT"
  END
```

```
IF DAY_OF_WEEK = "FRIDAY" & TEMP > 90
THEN SAY "HEAD FOR THE BEACH"
ELSE SAY "HEAD FOR THE SLOPES"
```

INTERPRET

INTERPRET *string* **or** *variable*

Causes REXX to look at data (a *string* or the contents of a *variable*) as if it were seeing it for the first time. The data may be a REXX instruction or a command intended for the operating system.

Examples:

```
INTERPRET "SAY 'HI' "

PART1 = "S"
PART2 = "ay 'Hello' "
INTERPRET PART1 ¦ ¦ PART2
```

ITERATE

ITERATE

Within a DO END sequence, sends control to the DO, skipping the instructions between the ITERATE and END. ITERATE goes to the DO of the loop it is in. If it is in the innermost loop, it goes only to the innermost loop's DO.

Examples:

```
DO I = 1 TO 20
  IF I = 13 THEN ITERATE /* to avoid scaring the superstitious
*/
  SAY I
END
```

```
DO 20
  DO I = 1 TO 20
    IF I = 13 THEN ITERATE /* goes to DO on preceding line*/
    SAY I
  END
END
```

ITERATE *variable*

If ITERATE is found in a loop that steps through a *variable*, ITERATE may reference that variable. This makes REXX check to be sure the ITERATE is in the correct loop, and control leaves that loop.

Examples:

```
DO I = 1 TO 20
  IF I = 13 THEN ITERATE I
  SAY I
END
```

LEAVE

LEAVE

Within a DO END sequence, sends control to the statement after the END, thus terminating the loop in an orderly fashion. LEAVE ends the loop it is in. If it is in the innermost loop, it leaves only the innermost loop.

Examples:

```
DO FOREVER
  IF TIME() > "16:00:00" THEN LEAVE
END
```

LEAVE *variable*

If LEAVE is found in a loop that steps through a *variable*, LEAVE may reference that variable. This makes REXX check to be sure the LEAVE is in the correct loop, and control leaves that loop.

Examples:

```
DO I = 1 TO 100000
  IF TIME() > "16:00:00" THEN LEAVE I
END
```

NOP

NOP

Null instruction that does nothing. Used in an **IF THEN ELSE** sequence when no action is desired in an outcome.

Examples:

```
IF A = B THEN NOP
ELSE SAY "SORRY A IS NOT EQUAL TO B"
```

NUMERIC

NUMERIC *option*

Sets the way numbers are handled in arithmetic operations and comparisons.

Options: (explained below)

```
DIGITS
FORM
FUZZ
```

NUMERIC DIGITS *number*

Sets the precision of arithmetic operations. Causes REXX to use *number* digits in arithmetic operations (but not in built-in functions). The system default is 9. Use this instruction if you need more or less. You may use from 1 to (perhaps) 20000. There is a high overhead with large precision.

Rounding is performed when an arithmetic operation produces more digits than *number*.

NUMERIC FORM SCIENTIFIC or ENGINEERING

Sets the way large numbers are shown in exponential notation.

Examples:

NUMERIC FORM SCIENTIFIC (the default)
SAY 1.0001 * 100000000000
--> 1.00010000E + 11

NUMERIC FORM ENGINEERING
SAY 1.0001 * 100000000000
--> 100.010000E + 9

NUMERIC FUZZ *number*

Controls the number of low order digits ignored in numeric comparisons. Allows approximations instead of strict equality.

Examples:

NUMERIC FUZZ 1
IF 987654321 = 987654322
THEN SAY "SURPRISE"
ELSE SAY "THIS WON'T HAPPEN"

OTHERWISE

Introduces the default alternative in the SELECT structure, the path that is taken if no other alternative is true.

OTHERWISE is not required after a SELECT.

An END is required at the very end of the structure, whether or not there is an OTHERWISE.

Examples:

```
SELECT
  WHEN DAY = 1 THEN SAY "MONDAY"
  WHEN DAY = 2 THEN SAY "TUESDAY"
  WHEN DAY = 3 THEN SAY "WEDNESDAY"
  WHEN DAY = 4 THEN SAY "THURSDAY"
  WHEN DAY = 5 THEN SAY "FRIDAY"
  WHEN DAY = 6 THEN SAY "SATURDAY"
  WHEN DAY = 7 THEN SAY "SUNDAY"
OTHERWISE
  DO /* recommended for OTHERWISE */
    SAY "ARE YOU ON MARS?"
  END /* recommended for OTHERWISE */
END /* required for the SELECT */
```

PARSE

PARSE [UPPER] *origin template*

Performs character string manipulation according to various rules that may be specified in the instruction. Data is taken from *origin* and processed by *template*, with the final result being that all the variables in the template are changed or set in some way.

If UPPER is specified, all letters are upper cased; otherwise, they are left in the case they were in.

Origins:

ARG   the command line

PULL   the Data Queue

LINEIN   (OS/2 only) the terminal without passing through the Data Queue

SOURCE   internal system settings about the environment and the program

VALUE   a literal, function, or possibly a variable

VAR   a variable

VERSION   internal system information about the version of REXX you are using

Templates:

Just variables   Data is distributed into the variables, delimited by spaces.

Example:

```
PARSE UPPER ARG VAR1 VAR2 VAR3
SAY VAR1
SAY VAR2
SAY VAR3

/* the following is entered at the command line */
JOHN RINGO PAUL
```

Results:

```
JOHN
RINGO
PAUL
```

Literal string and variables Data is first split at the position of the literal string and then examined in two parts: the part on the left of the literal string, then the part on the right of the literal string. Finally it is distributed into the variables, delimited by spaces.

Example:

```
PARSE UPPER ARG VAR1 VAR2 "!" VAR3
SAY VAR1
SAY VAR2
SAY VAR3
```

```
/* the following is entered at the command line */
John said "Yo! Where are you going?"
```

Results:

```
JOHN
SAID "YO
WHERE ARE YOU GOING?"
```

Column delimiters and variables Data is first split at the columns specified. Note that for each variable, the columns that are placed into it may be determined by examining the numbers on either side of it. The number on the left is its starting column, the number on the right, minus 1, is its ending column.

Examples:

```
PARSE UPPER ARG 1 VAR1 4  VAR2 8 VAR3 11
SAY VAR1
SAY VAR2
SAY VAR3
```

```
/* the following is entered at the command line */
ABCDEFGHIJKLMNOPQRSTUVWXYZ
```

Results:

```
ABC
DEFG
HIJ
```

```
PARSE UPPER ARG 1 VAR1 4 6 VAR2 8 5  VAR3 11
SAY VAR1
SAY VAR2
SAY VAR3

/* the following is entered at the command line */
ABCDEFGHIJKLMNOPQRSTUVWXYZ
```

Results:

```
ABC
FG
EFGHIJK
```

PROCEDURE

subroutine: PROCEDURE

Used in an internal function/subroutine named *subroutine* to protect the variables of the main part of the program from any possible change, and even from being examined, by the function/subroutine. Makes all variables in the function/subroutine local.

Example:

```
SUBR1: PROCEDURE
```

PULL

Short form of PARSE UPPER PULL. Takes a line from the Data Queue or, if it is empty, from the terminal input buffer. See PARSE UPPER PULL.

PUSH

PUSH *string* or *variable*

Puts a line consisting of *variable*, or *string*, into the Data Queue. Data is put into the Data Queue LIFO (Last In, First Out).

Example:

PUSH "HAS FLEAS"
PUSH "MY DOG"
PULL LINE
SAY LINE
PULL LINE
SAY LINE

QUEUE

QUEUE *string* or *variable*

Puts a line consisting of *variable* or *string* into the Data Queue. Data is put into the Data Queue FIFO (First In, First Out).

Examples:

QUEUE "MY DOG"
QUEUE "HAS FLEAS"
PULL LINE
SAY LINE
PULL LINE
SAY LINE

RETURN

RETURN *string* or *variable*

In a function/subroutine, sends control back to the instruction after the one that invoked the function/subroutine. Passes back *string* or *variable* to the caller, except in an error trap.

Example:

SUBR:
ARG NUM1,NUM2
TOTAL = NUM1 + NUM2
RETURN TOTAL

SAY

SAY *string* or *variable*

Displays a line on the monitor, consisting of *string* or *variable*.

Example:

SAY "AAAAAHHH"

A = 1
SAY A

SELECT

REXX's implementation of the CASE structure. Allows selection of just one of several possible alternatives.

An END is required at the very end of the structure, whether an OTHERWISE is used or not.

Examples:

```
SELECT
  WHEN DAY = 1 THEN SAY "MONDAY"
  WHEN DAY = 2 THEN SAY "TUESDAY"
  WHEN DAY = 3 THEN SAY "WEDNESDAY"
  WHEN DAY = 4 THEN SAY "THURSDAY"
  WHEN DAY = 5 THEN SAY "FRIDAY"
  WHEN DAY = 6 THEN SAY "SATURDAY"
  WHEN DAY = 7 THEN SAY "SUNDAY"
END /* required for SELECT */


SELECT
  WHEN DAY = 1 THEN SAY "MONDAY"
  WHEN DAY = 2 THEN SAY "TUESDAY"
  WHEN DAY = 3 THEN SAY "WEDNESDAY"
  WHEN DAY = 4 THEN SAY "THURSDAY"
  WHEN DAY = 5 THEN SAY "FRIDAY"
  WHEN DAY = 6 THEN SAY "SATURDAY"
  WHEN DAY = 7 THEN SAY "SUNDAY"
OTHERWISE
  DO /* recommended for OTHERWISE */
    SAY "ARE YOU ON MARS?"
    SAY "OR IS IT VENUS?"
  END /* recommended for OTHERWISE */
END /* required for SELECT */
```

SETLOCAL OS/2 only.

Saves the current working drive and directory. The ENDLOCAL instruction can restore them.

SIGNAL

SIGNAL ON or OFF *label*

Turns on or off a condition trap named by *label*. The condition trap can intercept an exceptional condition whenever it occurs after that. The condition trap is physically located at the end of the program.

Labels:

SYNTAX	REXX syntax error
ERROR	command to environment not correct
FAILURE	command to environment doesn't exist
NOVALUE	uninitialized variable
HALT	attention interrupt
NOTREADY	OS/2 only. Error in input/output

Examples:

```
SIGNAL ON SYNTAX
/*intervening instructions */
EXIT
SYNTAX:
SAY "ENTERED SYNTAX TRAP"
SAY "SYNTAX ERROR IS " ERRORTEXT(RC)
SAY "LINE NUMBER IN ERROR IS " SIGL
SAY "LINE IN ERROR IS " SOURCELINE(SIGL)
EXIT


SIGNAL ON ERROR
/*intervening instructions */
EXIT
ERROR:
SAY "ENTERED ERROR TRAP"
SAY "RETURN CODE FROM ENVIRONMENT IS " RC
SAY "LINE NUMBER IN ERROR IS " SIGL
SAY "LINE IN ERROR IS " SOURCELINE(SIGL)
EXIT
```

```
SIGNAL ON FAILURE
/*intervening instructions */
EXIT
FAILURE:
SAY "ENTERED FAILURE TRAP"
SAY "RETURN CODE FROM ENVIRONMENT IS " RC
SAY "LINE NUMBER IN ERROR IS " SIGL
SAY "LINE IN ERROR IS " SOURCELINE(SIGL)
EXIT


SIGNAL ON NOVALUE
/*intervening instructions */
EXIT
NOVALUE:
SAY "ENTERED NOVALUE TRAP"
SAY "STRING IN ERROR IS " CONDITION("D")
SAY "LINE NUMBER IN ERROR IS " SIGL
SAY "LINE IN ERROR IS " SOURCELINE(SIGL)
EXIT


SIGNAL ON HALT
/*intervening instructions */
EXIT
HALT:
SAY "ENTERED HALT TRAP"
SAY "ABOUT TO TERMINATE PROGRAM"
SAY "PRESS ENTER TO PROCEED"
PULL .
EXIT


SIGNAL ON NOTREADY /*OS/2 only*/
/*intervening instructions */
EXIT
NOTREADY:
SAY "ENTERED NOTREADY TRAP"
SAY "LINE NUMBER IN ERROR IS " SIGL
SAY "LINE IN ERROR IS " SOURCELINE(SIGL)
EXIT
```

SIGNAL *label*

SIGNAL followed by *label* is an unconditional "GO TO." This should be used with caution because its use will interfere with REXX's control structures such as DO . . . END.

TRACE

Controls tracing and interactive debugging.

Examples (starting with those that trace the least and ending with those that trace the most):

TRACE O (Off)	Nothing traced.
TRACE N (Normal) (the default)	Trace Environment commands that fail/error out; REXX verbs that fail.
TRACE F (Failure)	Trace Environment commands that abend, or don't exist.
TRACE E (Error)	Trace Environment commands that don't work.
TRACE L (Labels)	Trace labels.
TRACE A (All)	Trace labels, commands, REXX verbs.
TRACE S (Scan)	Trace labels, commands, and REXX verbs, but don't execute *anything*.
TRACE R (Results)	Trace labels, commands, REXX verbs, changed variables.

TRACE I (Intermediate)	Trace labels, commands, REXX verbs, changed variables; intermediate results ex: C = (4*3) + 2.
TRACE ?R (Results)	Trace labels, commands, REXX verbs, changed variables; *interactive debug.*
TRACE ?I (Intermediate)	Trace labels, commands, REXX verbs, changed variables, intermediate results ex: C = (4*3) + 2; *interactive debug.*

Appendix D:

REXX FUNCTIONS

All the REXX functions supported under OS/2 are listed.

Some of the functions shown will work only if you preregister them with OS/2. I recommend you do what is suggested under RXFUNCADD, below, before you try to use any REXX functions.

Functions may be used in two ways:

1. By letting REXX substitute the result of the function's processing for the function invocation, for example:

```
SAY LENGTH('ABCDEF') /*becomes SAY 6,
                which then displays a "6" at the terminal*/

SAVE_LENGTH = LENGTH(NAME)        /* assignment */

SAY 'NAME CONTAINS ',
    LENGTH(NAME) ' LETTERS'     /* substitution */

SAY "DOUBLING YOUR NAME'S LENGTH GIVES",
    LENGTH(NAME) * 2 'LETTERS'/* arith. expression */
```

Notes:
- *There must not be a space between the name of the function and the parenthesis.*
- *The result of the function is not available in the variable RESULT.*
- *Separate parameters with commas, not spaces, as in LEFT('ABCD',2).*

2. Using the reserved variable RESULT to obtain the result of the function's processing, for example:

```
CALL LENGTH 'ABCDEF'
SAY RESULT        /* result contains a 6, which is displayed */

CALL LENGTH 'ABCDEF'
SAVE_LENGTH = RESULT      /* assignment */

CALL LENGTH NAME
SAY 'NAME CONTAINS ',
    RESULT ' LETTERS'      /* substitution*/

CALL LENGTH NAME
SAY"DOUBLING YOUR NAME'S LENGTH GIVES",
    RESULT * 2 ' LETTERS ' /* arithmetic expression */
```

> *Notes:*
> - *You must do a CALL if you wish to receive the result of the function in the variable RESULT.*
> - *Separate parameters with commas, not spaces, as in CALL LEFT 'ABCD',2.*
> - *Parentheses are not used.*

ABBREV

SAY ABBREV(*word, abbrev, length*)

Asks if *abbrev* is a valid abbreviation of *word*, considering *length* characters, of *abbrev*. If *length* is omitted, all of *abbrev* is examined.
Returns:

```
If YES ---> 1
If NO  ---> 0
```

Example:

```
SAY ABBREV('ALLOCATE','AL',2)
---> 1
```

SAY ABBREV('ALLOCATE','AL')
---> 1

SAY ABBREV('ALLOCATE','ALK',2)
---> 0

SAY ABBREV('ALLOCATE','ALK')
---> 0

ABS

SAY ABS(*number*)

Drops the sign of *number*. Formats the result according to current NUMERIC settings.

Example:

SAY ABS(-123.45)
---> 123.45

ADDRESS

SAY ADDRESS()

Returns the current environment that commands are being sent to.

Returns:

---> CMD	{ under OS/2
---> PMREXX	{ under OS/2 Presentation Manager
---> TSO	{
---> MVS	{ under TSO
---> ISPEXEC	{
---> CMS	{
---> COMMAND	{ under CMS
---> XEDIT	{

Examples:

SAY ADDRESS()
---> CMD
---> TSO
---> COMMAND

ARG

SAY ARG()

Asks how many argument strings were passed. (Commas delimit argument strings.) You can pass several to a function/subroutine, but only one to a main program (executed from the command line in an OS/2 Window or Full Screen).

Returns:

---> 0
---> 1
---> etc

Examples:

CALL SUBR 'SALLY', 'KAREN' 'SUSAN'
EXIT
SUBR:
  SAY ARG()
  ---> 2
    RETURN

SAY ARG(*number*)

If *number* is a 1, returns the first argument string. If *number* is a 2, returns the second argument string, and so on.

Examples:

```
CALL SUBR 'SALLY', 'KAREN' 'SUSAN'
EXIT
SUBR:
 SAY ARG(2)
 ---> KAREN SUSAN
   RETURN
```

SAY ARG(*number,* 'EXISTS')

If the argument numbered *number* exists, it returns a 1; otherwise it returns a 0. EXISTS may be abbreviated 'E.' Only a function or subroutine executed by a REXX CALL may receive more than one argument.

Examples:

```
/* in calling program */
CALL MYEXEC 'SALLY', 'KAREN' 'SUSAN'

/* in called program */
SAY ARG(2,'EXISTS')
---> 1

/* in calling program */
CALL MYEXEC 'SALLY', 'KAREN' 'SUSAN'

/* in called program */
SAY ARG(5,'EXISTS')
---> 0
```

SAY ARG(*number,* 'OMITTED')

If the argument numbered *number* was not supplied, it returns a 1; otherwise returns a 0. OMITTED may be abbreviated 'O.'

Examples:

```
/* in calling program */
CALL MYEXEC 'SALLY', 'KAREN' 'SUSAN'

/* in called program */
SAY ARG(2,'OMITTED')
---> 0

/* in calling program */
CALL MYEXEC 'SALLY', 'KAREN' 'SUSAN'

/* in called program */
SAY ARG(5,'OMITTED')
---> 1
```

BEEP OS/2 only

CALL BEEP *frequency, duration*

Sounds the speaker at *frequency* for *duration* in milliseconds. The valid range for *frequency* is from 37 to 32767. The range for *duration* is from 1 to 60000.

Example:

CALL BEEP 1000, 1000

BITAND

SAY BITAND(*string1, string2, pad*)

String1 and *string2* are logically ANDed, with *pad* used to fill out the shorter string on the right. Each bit in the result depends on the corresponding bit in *string1* and *string2*. Each bit in the result is set to a 1 if the corresponding bit in both strings is a 1; otherwise, the result bit is set to 0.

Example:

SAY BITAND('01'X,'0F'X)
---> '01'X

BITOR

SAY BITOR(*string1, string2, pad*)

String1 and *string2* are logically ORed, with *pad* used to fill out the shorter string on the right. Each bit in the result depends on the corresponding bit in *string1* and *string2*. Each bit in the result is set to a 1 if the corresponding bit in either string is a 1; otherwise, the result bit is set to 0.

Example:

SAY BITOR('01'X,'0F'X)
---> '0F'X

SAY BITOR('01'X,'0E'X)
---> '0F'X

BITXOR

SAY BITXOR(*string1, string2, pad*)

String1 and *string2* are logically ORed, with *pad* used to fill out the shorter string on the right. Each bit in the result depends on the corresponding bit in *string1* and *string2*. Each bit in the result is set to a 1 if only one of the corresponding bits (but not both) in either string is a 1, otherwise the result bit is set to 0.

Example:

SAY BITXOR('01'X,'0F'X)
---> '0E'X

SAY BITXOR('01'X,'0E'X)
---> '0F'X

B2X OS/2 only

SAY B2X(*string*)

Converts *binary string* to a 'hexadecimal' representation.

Examples:

SAY B2X('1111 0000')
---> F0

CENTER

SAY CENTER(*string, length, pad*)

Centers *string* within a larger string of *length*. *Pad*, if present, is the pad character used instead of spaces.

Examples:

SAY CENTER('MIDDLE',14)
--->   MIDDLE

SAY CENTER('MIDDLE',14,'-')
---> ----MIDDLE---

CHARIN OS/2 only.

CALL CHARIN *'file name'*
SAY RESULT

Reads one character from the *file name* specified. Does not recognize end of line, or end of file. To tell if end of file has been reached, check CHARS('*file name*'). If it returns a 0, you are at the end of the file.

File name may be the name of a data file, or it may be:

  CON:
  KBD:
  COM1: (communications port)
  COM2:
  QUEUE:

  Example:

```
/*reads every character in file, one at a time*/
DO WHILE CHARS('C:MYFILE.DAT') > 0
  CALL CHARIN 'C:MYFILE.DAT'
  SAY RESULT
END
```

CALL CHARIN *'file name', start char, how many*
SAY RESULT

Reads *how many* characters from the *file name* specified, starting at *start char*. Does not recognize end of line or end of file. To tell if end of file has been reached, check CHARS(*'file name'*). If it returns a 0, you are at the end of the file.

```
Example:
/*reads every character in file, one at a time*/
/* starting with the 100'th */
DO WHILE CHARS('C:MYFILE.DAT') > 0
  CALL CHARIN 'C:MYFILE.DAT',100,1
  SAY RESULT
END
```

CHAROUT OS/2 only.

CALL CHAROUT *'file name', string*
SAY RESULT

Writes *string* to the *file name* specified. RESULT contains the number of characters that could not be written, so a 0 indicates a successful write. If the file already exists, it continues writing after the end of the file.

File name may be the name of a data file, or it may be:

> CON:
> PRN:
> LPT1:
> LPT2:
> COM1: (communications port)
> COM2:
> QUEUE:
> STDERR:

> Example:

> CALL CHAROUT 'C:MYFILE.DAT','This is being written'
> SAY RESULT (hopefully a 0)

CALL CHAROUT *'file name', string, start char*
SAY RESULT

Writes *string* to the *file name* specified. RESULT contains the number of characters that could not be written, so a 0 indicates a successful write. It starts writing at *start char* and overwrites whatever may be there. Use a starting character of 1 to start writing at the beginning of the file and overwrite the entire file.

> Example:

> CALL CHAROUT 'C:MYFILE.DAT','This is being written',100
> SAY RESULT (hopefully a 0)

CALL CHAROUT 'C:MYFILE.DAT'

This statement, which specifies only the file name, just closes the file.

CHARS OS/2 only.

SAY CHARS(*'file name'*)

Tells how many characters remain to be read in *file name*. If it returns a 0, there are no more characters remaining in the file, meaning that it is at the end of file.

Example:

```
/*reads every character in file, one at a time*/
DO WHILE CHARS('C:MYFILE.DAT') > 0
   CALL CHARIN 'C:MYFILE.DAT'
   SAY RESULT
END
```

COMPARE

SAY COMPARE(*string1, string2, pad*)

Compares *string1* to *string2*. *Pad*, if present, is the pad character used to fill out the shorter string. If *pad* is not present, spaces are used. If both strings are equal, it returns a 0; otherwise, it returns the character position of inequality.

Examples:

```
SAY COMPARE('APPLES','APPLES')
---> 0

SAY COMPARE('APPLES','APPLESAUCE')
---> 7
```

CONDITION

SAY CONDITION*(type)*

When used in a condition trap (ERROR, FAILURE, NOVALUE, HALT, SYNTAX), it gives information about the condition that occurred.

Types:

C — gives name of the condition that occurred
(ERROR, FAILURE, NOVALUE, HALT, SYNTAX).
D — when possible, gives the string that actually caused the error.

I — gives the instruction that sent to the trap: SIGNAL or CALL.

S — gives the current status of the condition that was trapped: ON, OFF, or DELAY (currently trapped, further trapping disabled to avoid recursive entry to the trap).

Examples:

SIGNAL ON ERROR
'LISTCAT DOG'
EXIT
ERROR:
SAY CONDITION('C')
---> ERROR
SAY CONDITION('D')
---> LISTCAT DOG
EXIT

COPIES

SAY COPIES*(string, how many)*

Returns *how many* copies of *string*, side by side.

Examples:

SAY COPIES('DO',2)
---> DODO

SAY COPIES('DO',0)
--->   (zero characters, or the null string)

C2D

SAY C2D(*string*)

Converts *string* to a binary representation, then to a decimal value.

Examples:

SAY C2D('B')
---> 66

SAY C2D('b')
---> 98

SAY C2D('10'X)
---> 160

C2X

SAY C2X(*string*)

Converts *string* to a 'hexadecimal' representation.

Example:

SAY C2X('A123')
---> 41313233

DATATYPE

SAY DATATYPE(*string*)

Returns NUM if *string* is a valid number; otherwise, CHAR.

Returns:

---> NUM
---> CHAR

Examples:

SAY DATATYPE(1234)
---> NUM
SAY DATATYPE(X234)
--> CHAR

SAY DATATYPE(*string, type*)

Returns 1 if *string* corresponds to *type*; otherwise, 0. *Note:* You may need
to strip extraneous spaces for this to work:
SAY DATATYPE(SPACE('ABCD',0),'U').

Types:

A — alphanumeric A-Z, a-z, 0-9
B — binary digits 1 and 0
D — double byte character set
L — lower-case letters
M — mixed case
N — valid number
S — symbol: valid REXX symbol
U — upper-case letters
W — whole number
X — hexadecimal number   0-9 or A-F

Returns:

---> 1
---> 0

Examples:

SAY DATATYPE('A234','N')
---> 0
SAY DATATYPE('A234','A')
---> 1
SAY DATATYPE('ABCDEF','U')
---> 1
SAY DATATYPE('aBCDEF','U')
---> 0

DATE

SAY DATE()

Returns current date in format 25 Dec 1993.

Example:

SAY DATE()
---> 25 Dec 1993

SAY DATE(*type*)

Returns date corrresponding to *type*.
Types:

B — basedate: number of complete days since
Jan 1, year 1. Example: 727024.
C — century: number of days in this century to now. Example: 33430.
D — days: number of days so far this year. Example: 193.
E — European date: format dd/mm/yy
J — Julian date: format yyddd
M — Name of current month
O — Ordered: date suitable for sorting: yy/mm/dd
S — Sorting: date suitable for sorting: yyyymmdd
U — USA format: mm/dd/yy
W — Name of current weekday

Examples:

SAY DATE('W')
---> Friday

SAY DATE('J')
---> 93359

SAY DATE('S')
---> 19931225

DELSTR

SAY DELSTR(*string, start char, length*)

Deletes characters from *string* beginning at *start char*, for a length of *length*.

Examples:

SAY DELSTR('ABCDEF',2,3)
---> AEF

```
/* a way to remove a string from within another string */
BIGSTR = 'ISSUES'
DELET = 'SUE'
NEWSTR =,
DELSTR(BIGSTR,POS(DELET,BIGSTR),LENGTH(DELET))
SAY NEWSTR /* iss */
```

DELWORD

SAY DELWORD(*string, start word, how many words*)

Deletes *how many words* words from *string*, beginning with *start word*.

Example:

SAY DELWORD('Mary had a little lamb',2,3)
---> Mary lamb

DIGITS

SAY DIGITS()

Returns the current setting of NUMERIC DIGITS.

Example:

NUMERIC DIGITS 7
SAY DIGITS()
---> 7

DIRECTORY OS/2 only

CALL DIRECTORY 'directory'
SAY RESULT

Captures the current directory in the special variable RESULT and then changes the current directory to *directory*.

Example:

DIRECTORY 'C:\REXXPRGS'
SAY RESULT 'WAS THE DIRECTORY BEFORE'

CALL DIRECTORY ""
SAY RESULT

Captures the current directory in the special variable RESULT.

Example:

DIRECTORY ""
SAY RESULT 'IS THE CURRENT DIRECTORY'

D2C

SAY D2C(*number*)

Converts a decimal *number* to a binary value. The inverse of C2D.

Examples:

SAY D2C(66)
---> B

SAY D2C(98)
---> b

D2X

SAY D2X(*number*)

Converts a decimal *number* to a hexadecimal value. The inverse of X2D.

Examples:

SAY D2X(130)
---> 82

SAY D2X(15)
---> F

ENDLOCAL OS/2 only.

CALL ENDLOCAL
SAY RESULT

Restores the drive directory and environment variables that were in effect before the last SETLOCAL function was done. A 1 is returned in RESULT if the command was successful; a 0 is returned if it was not successful.

Example:

CALL ENDLOCAL
SAY RESULT

ERRORTEXT

SAY ERRORTEXT(*number*)

Returns the REXX syntax error message corresponding to *number*.

Example:

SAY ERRORTEXT(16)
---> LABEL NOT FOUND

FILESPEC

Analyzes a file specification and tells whichever of the following is requested: Drive, Path, Name of the file.

>Examples:
>
>SAY FILESPEC('DRIVE','C:\REXXPRGS\TEST.DAT')
>---> C:
>SAY FILESPEC('PATH','C:\REXXPRGS\TEST.DAT')
>---> \REXXPRGS\
>SAY FILESPEC('NAME','C:\REXXPRGS\TEST.DAT')
>---> TEST.DAT

FIND

SAY FIND(*string, phrase*)

>Returns the word number of the first word of *phrase* in *string*.
>Example:
>
>SAY FIND('MARY HAD A LITTLE LAMB','A LITTLE LAMB')
>---> 3

FORM

SAY FORM()

>Returns the current setting of NUMERIC FORM.
>Example:
>
>SAY FORM()
>---> SCIENTIFIC (the default)
>---> ENGINEERING

FORMAT

SAY FORMAT(*number, before decimal, after decimal*)

Formats a *number*. *Before decimal* is the number of characters before the decimal point, padded with blanks. *After decimal* is the number of characters after the decimal point, zero filled.

Example:

SAY FORMAT(123.45,5,3)
--->   123.450

FUZZ

SAY FUZZ()

Returns the current setting of NUMERIC FUZZ.

Examples:

SAY FUZZ()
---> 0
NUMERIC FUZZ 5
SAY FUZZ()
---> 5

INDEX

SAY INDEX(*string, find string*)

Finds *find string* within *string*. If not found, returns a 0. If found, returns the character position of *find string* within *string*.
Example:

SAY INDEX('is there a needle in the haystack?','needle')
---> 12

INSERT

NEW_STRING = INSERT(*string1, string2, position*)

Inserts *string1* into *string2* after character *position*.

Example:

SAY INSERT('E','ABCDF',4)
---> ABCDEF

LASTPOS

SAY LASTPOS(*string1, string2*)

Finds the last occurrence of *string1* in *string2*. Returns the character position of the last occurrence. Returns a 0 if it is not found.

Examples:

SAY LASTPOS('left','left right left')
---> 12

SAY LASTPOS('center','left right left')
---> 0

LEFT

SAY LEFT(*string, length*)

Extracts *length* characters from *string* starting at the left.

Example:

SAY LEFT('ABCDEF',3)
---> ABC

/* a way to force a variable to a specific length, padding with blanks
or truncating as needed */
REQUIRED_LENGTH = 10 /* for example */
THEVAR = LEFT(THEVAR,REQUIRED_LENGTH)

SAY LEFT(*string, length, pad*)

Extracts *length* characters from *string* starting at the left. Uses *pad* as a fill
character if *length* is more than the number of characters in *string*.

Example:

SAY LEFT('ABCDEF',7,'!')
---> ABCDEF!

LENGTH

SAY LENGTH(*string*)

Counts the characters in *string*.

Example:

SAY LENGTH('ABCDEF')
---> 6

LINEIN OS/2 only.

CALL LINEIN *'file name'*
SAY RESULT

Reads one line from the *file name* specified. Recognizes end of line, unlike CHARIN. To tell if end of file has been reached, check LINES('file name'). If it returns a 0, you are at the end of the file.

> Examples:
>
> /*reads every line in file, one at a time*/
> DO WHILE LINES('C:MYFILE.DAT') > 0
>   CALL LINEIN 'C:MYFILE.DAT'
>   SAY RESULT
> END
>
> /*GETS A LINE FROM THE KEYBOARD
> AND BYPASSES THE DATA QUEUE*/
> CALL LINEIN
> SAY RESULT

CALL LINEIN *'file name'*, *start line, how many*
SAY RESULT

Reads *how many* lines from the *file name* specified, starting at *start line*. To tell if end of file has been reached, check LINES(*'file name'*). If it returns a 0, you are at the end of the file.

> *File name* may be the name of a data file, or it may be:
>   CON:
>   KBD:
>   COM1: (communications port)
>   COM2:
>   QUEUE:

LINEOUT OS/2 only.

CALL LINEOUT *'file name', string*
SAY RESULT

Writes *string* to the *file name* specified. If the file exists already, it will start at the end of the file and extend the file. RESULT contains the number of lines that could not be written; a 0 indicates a successful write.

    Example:

    CALL LINEOUT 'C:MYFILE.DAT','This is being written'
    SAY RESULT (hopefully a 0)

CALL LINEOUT *'file name', string, start line*
SAY RESULT

Writes *string* to the *file name* specified, starting at *start line*, overwriting any data that may already exist. RESULT contains the number of lines that could not be written; a 0 indicates a successful write.

    Example:

    CALL LINEOUT 'C:MYFILE.DAT','This is being written',1
    SAY RESULT (hopefully a 0)

CALL LINEOUT *'file name'*

Closes the file.

    File name may be the name of a data file, or it may be:
      CON:
      PRN:
      LPT1:
      LPT2:
      COM1: (communications port)
      COM2:
      QUEUE:
      STDERR:

LINES OS/2 only.

SAY LINES(*'file name'*)

Tells how many lines remain to be read in the *file name*. If it returns a 0, there are no more lines remaining in the file, so it is at the end of file.

Example:

```
/*reads every line in file, one at a time*/
DO WHILE LINES('C:MYFILE.DAT') > 0
  CALL LINEIN 'C:MYFILE.DAT'
  SAY RESULT /* contains the line just read */
END
```

MAX

SAY MAX(*number1, number2, number20*)
Returns the highest of *numbers 1 through 20*.

Example:

```
SAY MAX(5,4,3,2)
---> 5
```

MIN

SAY MIN(*number1, number2, number20*)

Returns the lowest of *numbers 1 through 20*.

Example:

```
SAY MIN(5,4,3,2)
---> 2
```

OVERLAY

New_string = OVERLAY(*string1, string2, position*)

Replaces characters in *string2* with characters in *string1*, starting in character *position* of *string2*.

Example:

SAY OVERLAY('D','ABCXEF',4)
---> ABCDEF

POS

SAY POS(*string1, string2, start pos*)

Returns the position of *string1* in *string2*. Returns 0 if *string1* is not in *string2*. Begins its search at *start pos*. If *start pos* is absent, the search begins at the first character.

Example:

SAY POS('DEF','ABCDEFGHIJKLMNOP')
---> 4

QUEUED

SAY QUEUED()

Returns the number of lines in the stack.

Example:

SAY QUEUED()
---> 0
PUSH 'CART'
SAY QUEUED()
---> 1

RANDOM

SAY RANDOM(*min, max*)

Returns a random number between *min* and *max*.

Example:

SAY RANDOM(1,100)
---> 55

SAY RANDOM(*min, max, seed*)

Returns a random number between *min* and *max*. Specifying the same *seed* produces the same series each time on all systems that REXX is found on.

Examples:

SAY RANDOM(1,100,12345)
---> 5
SAY RANDOM(1,100,12345)
---> 5
SAY RANDOM(1,100)
---> 75
SAY RANDOM(1,100)
---> 21
SAY RANDOM(1,100)
---> 57

REVERSE

SAY REVERSE(*string*)

Reverses the characters of the *string*.

Example:

SAY REVERSE('GO')
---> OG

RIGHT

SAY RIGHT(*string, length*)

Extracts *length* characters from *string* starting at the right.

Example:

SAY RIGHT('ABCDEF',3)
---> DEF

SAY RIGHT(*string, length, pad*)

Extracts *length* characters from *string* starting at the right. Uses *pad* as a fill character if *length* is more than the number of characters in *string*.

Examples:

SAY RIGHT('ABCDEF',7,'!')
---> !ABCDEF

RXFUNCADD (OS/2 only)

You are most likely to use this function for one purpose only: registering certain other functions with REXX. (This is conceptually like loading them into memory where they are available for use.) Those functions are not useable until you do this.

What you have to do is very simple: put program statements similar to those shown just below in each program that uses one of the REXX functions that require preregistering.

```
/* showload.cmd (Figure 13.10) */
/* shows how to register a function with OS/2
   so that you can use it in your program

   change "syscls" shown below to the function name
   that you are actually using
*/
```

```
function_to_load = "syscls"
call rxfuncadd function_to_load,'rexxutil',,
     function_to_load
/* now you can use the function in this program*/
CALL SYSCLS
Say "SYSCLS has been loaded"
```

Here is a list of the functions that won't work unless you register them with the program statements shown above.

RXMESSAGEBOX
SYSCLS
SYSCREATEOBJECT
SYSCURPOS
SYSCURSTATE
SYSDEREGISTEROBJECTCLASS
SYSDESTROYOBJECT
SYSDRIVEINFO
SYSDRIVEMAP
SYSDROPFUNCS
SYSFILEDELETE
SYSFILESEARCH
SYSFILETREE
SYSGETEA
SYSGETKEY
SYSGETMESSAGE
SYSINI (not covered here)
SYSMKDIR
SYSOS2VER
SYSPUTEA
SYSQUEUECLASSLIST
SYSREGISTEROBJECTCLASS
SYSRMDIR
SYSSEARCHPATH
SYSSETICON
SYSSETOBJECTDATA
SYSSLEEP
SYSTEMPFILENAME
SYSTEXTSCREENREAD
SYSTEXTSCREENSIZE
SYSWAITNAMEDPIPE

RXMESSAGEBOX OS/2 only

CALL RXMESSAGEBOX *'text', 'title', 'button', 'icon'*
       SAY 'CODE FOR KEY PRESSED WAS' RESULT

Displays a Presentation Manager message box where the message *text* figures prominently with *title* at the top. A *button* is included in the box as well as an *icon*. Requires preregistering, discussed under RXFUNCADD in this appendix. Can only be used under the Presentation Manager. This means you must execute your program by putting the word PMREXX in front of it, as for example: PMREXX MYPROG.

button may be:	
OK	An OK button (the default)
OKCANCEL	An OK button and a CANCEL button
CANCEL	A CANCEL button
ENTER	An ENTER button
ENTERCANCEL	An ENTER button and a CANCEL button
RETRYCANCEL	A RETRY button and a CANCEL button
ABORTRETRYCANCEL	An ABORT button, a RETRY button and a CANCEL button.
YESNO	A YES button and a NO button.
YESNOCANCEL	A YES button, a NO button, and a CANCEL button.

icon may be one of the following types

NONE	No icon is displayed.
HAND	
QUESTION	
EXCLAMATION	
ASTERISK	
INFORMATION	
QUERY	
WARNING	
ERROR	

RESULT contains a number corresponding to the key that was pressed.

    1 OK
    2 CANCEL
    3 ABORT
    4 RETRY
    5 IGNORE
    6 YES
    7 NO
    8 ENTER

Example:

```
CALL RXMESSAGEBOX 'OK to continue?', 'Sample message box',,
 'YESNO', 'QUESTION'
IF RESULT = 6
THEN SAY 'THANK YOU FOR PRESSING YES'
```

RXQUEUE OS/2 only

CALL RXQUEUE *'action','queue name'*
SAY RESULT

Creates and deletes data queues, makes them available for use, and queries their names.

action	
GET	gives the name of the queue currently in use
SET	sets a queue (makes it the current one)
DELETE	deletes the queue (you must explicitely deleted it)
CREATE	creates a queue (if it already exists, one is created with a different name that is available in RESULT)

CALL RXQUEUE 'GET'
SAY RESULT

The name of the current queue is given in RESULT. SESSION is the name of the default queue created automatically by REXX.

Example:

CALL RXQUEUE 'GET'
SAY 'THE CURRENT QUEUE IS' RESULT

CALL RXQUEUE 'CREATE', 'queue name'
SAY RESULT

Creates a queue named *queue name*. If *queue name* already exists one is created with a name chosen by REXX and available in RESULT. In order to use the queue you have created you need to do a set (see below).

Example:

CALL RXQUEUE CREATE', 'MYQUEUE'
SAY 'CREATED QUEUE' RESULT

CALL RXQUEUE SET', *'queue name'*
SAY RESULT

Makes the queue named *queue name* the current one. The name of the old queue is available in RESULT. You must have already created the queue in order to use it.

Example:

CALL RXQUEUE 'SET', 'MYQUEUE'
SAY 'THE PREVIOUS QUEUE WAS' RESULT

CALL RXQUEUE 'DELETE', *'queue name'*
SAY RESULT

Deletes the queue named *queue name*. If you don't delete it, it will continue to exist until you do, outlasting sessions, windows, and bootings. If the delete is successful, RESULT will contain a zero (0).

Example:

```
CALL RXQUEUE 'DELETE', 'MYQUEUE'
IF RESULT = 0
THEN SAY 'DELETED THE QUEUE'
```

SETLOCAL OS/2 only.

CALL SETLOCAL
SAY RESULT

Saves the drive directory and environment variables that are in effect. A 1 is returned in RESULT if the function was successful; a 0 is returned if it was not successful.

Example:

```
CALL SETLOCAL
SAY RESULT
```

SIGN

SAY SIGN(*number*)

Returns the sign of *number*.

Returns:

```
1  <--- if number is positive
0  <--- if number is zero
-1 <--- if  number is negative
```

Example:

```
SAY SIGN(-9)
---> -1
```

SOURCELINE

SAY SOURCELINE(*number*)

Returns original program statement with line number *number*.

Example:

```
/*REXX PROGRAM TO SHOW SOURCELINE*/
SAY SOURCELINE(1)
 ---> /*REXX PROGRAM TO SHOW SOURCELINE*/
```

SAY SOURCELINE()

Returns number of lines in the program.

Examples:

```
/*REXX PROGRAM TO SHOW SOURCELINE*/
SAY SOURCELINE()
 ---> 2
```

```
DO I = 1 TO SOURCELINE() /* displays entire program */
  SAY SOURCELINE(I)
END
```

SPACE

SAY SPACE(*string, how many blanks*)

Puts *how many blanks* blanks between words in *string*. If *how many blanks* is 0, strips blanks in *string*.

Examples:

SAY SPACE('THE FINAL FRONTIER',3)
---> THE   FINAL   FRONTIER

SAY SPACE('DONT SPACE OUT ON ME',0)
---> DONTSPACEOUTONME

SAY SPACE(*string, how many pad char, pad*)

Moves apart the words in *string* and puts *how many pad char* copies of *pad* between the words. If *how many pad char* is 0, strips blanks in *string*.

Examples:

SAY SPACE('THE FINAL FRONTIER',3,'!')
---> THE!!!FINAL!!!FRONTIER

SAY SPACE('DONT SPACE OUT ON ME',0,'!')
---> DONTSPACEOUTONME

STREAM OS/2 only.

CALL STREAM '*file name*', 'C', '*command*'
SAY RESULT

Performs the action indicated by *command* on *file name*. RESULT indicates the success or failure. If the command succeeded, RESULT will contain the name of the command. If the command failed, RESULT will contain an error message.

Commands:

QUERY EXISTS — Returns file name if OK; otherwise null.
QUERY SIZE — Returns the size in bytes.
QUERY DATETIME — Returns date and time stamps.
OPEN READ — Returns READY: if OK. Note the colon.

OPEN WRITE — Returns READY: if OK. Note the colon.
CLOSE — Returns READY: if OK. Note the colon.
SEEK *offset* — Sets the READ or WRITE position *offset* bytes away.

CALL STREAM 'C:MYFILE.DAT', 'C', 'CLOSE'

Closes the file.

IF STREAM('TMP.DAT','C','QUERY EXISTS') = ""
THEN SAY 'THE FILE EXISTS'
ELSE SAY 'THE FILE DOES NOT EXIST'

An excellent way to determine if a file exists or not.

CALL STREAM *'file name'*, 'S'
SAY RESULT

Finds out the status of *file name*. RESULT contains the current status.

Values of RESULT:

ERROR
NOTREADY
READY (ready for reading/writing; READY is without a colon)
UNKNOWN (indicates closed status or no such file)

STRIP

NEW_STRING = STRIP(*string, option*)

Strips blanks from *string* based on *option*:

Options:

> B — remove both leading and trailing blanks (default)
> T — remove trailing blanks
> L — remove leading blanks

> Example:

> NEW_STRING = STRIP(' MUCH BLANK SPACE ')
> SAY NEW_STRING
> ---> MUCH BLANK SPACE

NEW_STRING = STRIP(*string, option, character*)

Strips *character* from *string* based on *option*:

> *Options:*
> B — remove both leading and trailing *character* (default)
> T — remove trailing *character*
> L — remove leading *character*

> Example:

> NEW_STRING = STRIP('CAFE AU LAIT!!!!','T','!')
> SAY NEW_STRING
> ---> CAFE AU LAIT

SUBSTR

NEW_STRING = SUBSTR(*string, start position, length*)

Returns a portion of *string* beginning at *start position* for a length of *length*. Blanks are used if filler characters are needed.

> Example:

> SAY SUBSTR('PACE',2,3)
> ---> ACE

NEW_STRING = SUBSTR(*string, start position, length,pad*)

Returns a portion of *string* beginning at *start position* for a length of *length*. *Pad* is used if filler characters are needed.

Example:

SAY SUBSTR('PACE',2,5,'!')
---> ACE!!

SUBWORD

NEW_STRING = SUBWORD(*string, starting word, how many words*)

Returns a portion of *string* beginning at *starting word*, containing *how many words* words.

Examples:

NEW_STRING = SUBWORD('ET PHONE HOME COLLECT',2,2)

SAY NEW_STRING
---> PHONE HOME

SYMBOL

SAY SYMBOL(*name*)

Tells if *name* is a variable, literal, or if not a legal symbol.

Returns:

VAR   <--- if name is an assigned variable
LIT   <--- if name is a literal
BAD   <--- if name is not a legal symbol

Examples:

```
SAY SYMBOL('*-=:*')
---> BAD

TEAM = 'YANKEES'
SAY SYMBOL('YANKEES')
---> LIT
SAY SYMBOL('TEAM')
---> VAR
```

SYSCLS OS/2 only

CALL SYSCLS

Clears the screen. Does not work properly under Presentation Manager. Requires preregistering, discussed under RXFUNCADD in this appendix.

Example:

CALL SYSCLS

SYSCREATEOBJECT OS/2 only

CALL SYSCREATEOBJECT *classname, title, location, icon*
SAY RESULT

Creates a new instance of an object class. The name assigned is *classname,* *title* is assigned as the object's title, *location* is the path to the object's location, *icon* is the name of an icon file (extension .ICO). RESULT will contain a 1 if the creation was successful, a 0 if it was not. Requires preregistering, discussed under RXFUNCADD in this appendix.

Example:

```
CALL SYSCREATEOBJECT 'NEWOBJECT',,
'NEWDLL','C:\TOOLS\BIN'
```

SYSCURPOS OS/2 only

CALL SYSCURPOS
SAY RESULT

Will not work under the Presentation Manager. Tells the current cursor position. The cursor position is returned in RESULT. It consists of two numbers, row and column. Requires preregistering, discussed under RXFUNCADD in this appendix.

Example:

CALL SYSCURPOS
PARSE VAR RESULT ROW COLUMN
SAY 'CURSOR IS AT ROW' ROW 'COLUMN' COLUMN

CALL SYSCURPOS *row, column*
SAY RESULT

Will not work under the Presentation Manager. Moves the cursor to *row* and *column*. Tells the current cursor position. The cursor position is returned in RESULT. It consists of two numbers, row and column. Requires preregistering, discussed under RXFUNCADD in this appendix.

Example:

CALL SYSCURPOS 5, 10
SAY 'CURSOR WAS CURRENTLY AT' RESULT
PARSE VAR RESULT ROW COLUMN
SAY 'CURSOR IS AT ROW' ROW 'COLUMN' COLUMN

SYSCURSTATE OS/2 only

CALL SYSCURSTATE *on or off*

Will not work under the Presentation Manager. Displays or hides the cursor depending on *on or off*. ON displays the cursor. OFF hides the cursor. Requires preregistering, discussed under RXFUNCADD in this appendix.

Example:

CALL SYSCURSTATE OFF

SYSDEREGISTEROBJECTCLASS OS/2 only

CALL SYSDEREGISTEROBJECTCLASS *classname*
SAY RESULT

Removes an object class definition. The opposite of SYSREGISTEROBJECTCLASS. If it was successful a 1 is placed in RESULT. If it was not, a 0 is placed in RESULT. Requires preregistering, discussed under RXFUNCADD in this appendix.

Example:

CALL SYSDEREGISTEROBJECTCLASS 'OLDOBJECTCLASS'
IF RESULT = 1
THEN SAY 'SUCCESSFUL'

SYSDESTROYOBJECT

CALL SYSDESTROYOBJECT *objectname*
SAY RESULT

Destroys an existing Workplace Shell object. If it was successful a 1 is placed in RESULT. If it was not, a 0 is placed in RESULT. Requires preregistering, discussed under RXFUNCADD in this appendix.

Example:

CALL SYSDESTROYOBJECT 'MYOBJECT'
IF RESULT = 1
THEN SAY 'SUCCESSFUL'

SYSDRIVEINFO OS/2 only

SAY SYSDRIVEINFO(*drive*)

Gives information about the disk *drive* specified. Four words are returned: the disk drive letter, the number of bytes of free space, the total capacity of the drive, and the disk label. Requires preregistering, discussed under RXFUNCADD in this appendix.

Example:

SAY SYSDRIVEINFO('C:')
/* may return C: 12345678 83687424 MYDRIVE */

SYSDRIVEMAP OS/2 only

SAY SYSDRIVEMAP()

Gives the letters of the disk drives that are accessible. Requires preregistering, discussed under RXFUNCADD in this appendix.

Example:

SAY SYSDRIVEMAP
/* may return   C: D: */

SYSDROPFUNCS OS/2 only

CALL SYSDROPFUNCS

Drops all the special functions that require preregistering, making them unavailable until once again preregistered. Requires preregistering, discussed under RXFUNCADD in this appendix.

Example:

CALL SYSDROPFUNCS

SYSFILEDELETE OS/2 only

CALL SYSFILEDELETE *'file name'*
SAY RESULT

Deletes the file specified with file name. Does not display an error message if the file doesn't exist. It does, however, return a code number in RESULT that tells you what happened. Requires preregistering, discussed under RXFUNCADD in this appendix.

> Codes returned in RESULT:
> 1   successful
> 2   file not found
> 3   path not found
> 5   access denied
> 26   not a DOS disk
> 32   sharing violation
> 36   sharing buffer exceeded
> 87   invalid parameter
> 206   file name exceeds range error

> Example:

> CALL SYSFILEDELETE 'TEMP.DAT'
> IF RESULT = 0
> THEN SAY 'DELETE SUCCESSFUL'

SYSFILESEARCH OS/2 only

CALL SYSFILESEARCH *'string'*, *'file'*, *'REXX variable stem'*, 'N'

Finds all lines in *file* that contain *string*. The lines and their line numbers are returned in REXX variables built upon *REXX variable stem* (see Chapter 17). If the stem specified is LINE., then the first line found is returned in LINE.1. The number of items returned is placed in the '0' element based upon the stem, LINE.0 in this case. Requires preregistering, discussed under RXFUNCADD in this appendix.

Example:

```
CALL SYSFILESEARCH 'IF','MYPROG.CMD','LINE.','N'
SAY 'THE LINES THAT CONTAIN IF ARE:'
DO I = 1 TO LINE.0
  SAY LINE.I
  /* how to separate line numbers from the line contents*/
  PARSE VAR LINE.I NUMBER CONTENTS
  SAY 'LINE NUMBER IS' NUMBER
  SAY 'CONTENTS ARE' CONTENTS
END
```

SYSFILETREE OS/2 only

CALL SYSFILETREE *'file specification'*, *'REXX variable stem'*

Finds all files that match a *file specification*. The file information is returned in REXX variables built upon *REXX variable stem* (see Chapter 17). If the stem specified is LINE., then information on the first file found is returned in LINE.1. The number of items returned is placed in the '0' element based on the stem, LINE.0 in this case. Requires preregistering, discussed under RXFUNCADD in this appendix.

Example:

```
CALL SYSFILETREE '*.CMD', 'LINE.'
SAY 'THE FILES THAT MATCH ARE:'
DO I = 1 TO LINE.0
  SAY LINE.I
END
```

SYSGETEA OS/2 only

CALL SYSGETEA *'file'*, *'extended attribute'*, 1*'REXX variable'*
IF RESULT = 0 THEN SAY *REXX variable*

Gives details on the *extended attribute* of *file* in *REXX variable*. Note that *REXX variable* is in quotation marks or apostrophes. Requires preregistering, discussed under RXFUNCADD in this appendix.

Example:

CALL SYSGETEA 'CONFIG.SYS', 'TYPE','MYVARIABLE'
IF RESULT = 0 THEN SAY MYVARIABLE

SYSGETKEY OS/2 only

CALL SYSGETKEY 'ECHO' or 'NOECHO'
SAY RESULT

Gets the next key pressed from the keyboard buffer. The key pressed is returned in RESULT. If the keyboard buffer is empty, it waits until a key is pressed. The ENTER key does not have to be pressed. Requires preregistering, discussed under RXFUNCADD in this appendix. Does not work properly under the Presentation Manager.

Example:

CALL SYSGETKEY 'ECHO'
SAY RESULT 'WAS KEY PRESSED'

SYSGETMESSAGE OS/2 only

CALL SYSGETMESSAGE *'number'*
SAY RESULT

Gets the text of the OS/2 message corresponding to *number*. Requires preregistering, discussed under RXFUNCADD in this appendix.

Example:

CALL SYSGETMESSAGE '1'
SAY RESULT

SYSMKDIR OS/2 only

CALL SYSMKDIR '*directory*'
SAY RESULT

Creates a directory named *directory*. No message is displayed in case of error. Returns a code number in RESULT that tells if it was successful. Requires preregistering, discussed under RXFUNCADD in this appendix.

Example:

CALL SYSMKDIR 'C:\REXXPRGS'
SAY RESULT

Codes returned in RESULT:

0	successful
2	file not found
3	path not found
5	access denied
26	not a DOS disk
87	invalid parameter
108	drive locked
206	file name exceeds range error

SYSOS2VER OS/2 only

SAY SYSOS2VER()

Tells the current version of OS/2 you are running. Requires preregistering, discussed under RXFUNCADD in this appendix.

Example:

SAY SYSOS2VER()

SYSPUTEA OS/2 only

CALL SYSPUTEA *'file'*, 'extended attribute', 'value'
SAY RESULT

Writes the *value* of *extended attribute* to *file*. RESULT contains a 0 if the action was successful, otherwise it contains an error code. Requires preregistering, discussed under RXFUNCADD in this appendix.

Example:

CALL SYSPUTEA 'ABC.DAT', 'SECURITY','Unclassified'
IF RESULT = 0
THEN SAY 'SUCCESSFUL'

SYSQUERYCLASSLIST OS/2 only

CALL SYSQUERYCLASSLIST *'REXX variable stem'*

Gives a complete list of registered object classes. The classes are returned in REXX variables built upon *REXX variable stem* (see Chapter 17). If the stem specified is LINE., then the first class found is returned in LINE.1. The number of items returned is placed in the '0' element based on the stem, LINE.0 in this case. Requires preregistering, discussed under RXFUNCADD in this appendix.

Example:

CALL SYSQUERYCLASSLIST 'LINE.'
SAY 'THE CLASSES REGISTERED ARE:'
DO I = 1 TO LINE.0
  SAY LINE.I
END

SYSREGISTEROBJECTCLASS OS/2 only

CALL SYSREGISTEROBJECTCLASS *'class name', 'module name'*
SAY RESULT

Registers a new object class definition, using *class name* as a name and *module name* as the module containing the object definition. RESULT contains a 1 if the action was successful, otherwise it contains a 0. Requires preregistering, discussed under RXFUNCADD in this appendix.

Example:

CALL SYSREGISTEROBJECTCLASS ,'NEWOBJECT', 'NEWDLL'
IF RESULT = 1
THEN SAY 'SUCCESSFUL'

SYSRMDIR OS/2 only

CALL SYSRMDIR *'directory'*
SAY RESULT

Deletes a directory named *directory*. Does not display an error message in case of failure. Returns a code number in RESULT that tells if it was successful. Requires preregistering, discussed under RXFUNCADD in this appendix.

Example:

CALL SYSRMDIR 'REXXPRGS'
SAY RESULT

Codes returned in RESULT:

0	successful
2	file not found
3	path not found
5	access denied
16	current directory
26	not a DOS disk
87	invalid parameter
108	drive locked
206	file name exceeds range error

SYSSEARCHPATH OS/2 only

CALL SYSSEARCHPATH *environment variable, file name*
SAY RESULT

Searches a path specified in *environment variable* looking for a *file*. Environment variables are set in OS/2 in CONFIG.SYS, or in a SET OS/2 command. The normal environment variable to use here is PATH. Returns the full file specification in RESULT, if successful, otherwise returns a null string. Requires preregistering, discussed under RXFUNCADD in this appendix.

Example:

CALL SYSSEARCHPATH 'PATH', 'MYPROG01.CMD'
IF RESULT = ""
THEN SAY 'COULD NOT FIND FILE'
ELSE SAY RESULT

SYSSETICON OS/2 only

CALL SYSSETICON *file name, icon file name*
SAY RESULT

Associates an icon found in *icon file name* with a file named *file name*. Returns a 1 if successful, a 0 if not. Requires preregistering, discussed under RXFUNCADD in this appendix.

Example:

CALL SYSSETICON 'ABC.DAT', 'ABC.ICO'
IF RESULT = 1
THEN SAY 'SUCCESSFUL'
ELSE SAY 'COULD NOT ASSOCIATE '

SYSSLEEP OS/2 only

CALL SYSSLEEP *seconds*

Puts the program into a suspended state for the specified number of seconds. You may interrupt the program with CTRL and C or CTRL and Break. Requires preregistering, discussed under RXFUNCADD in this appendix.

Example:

CALL SYSSLEEP 1

SYSTEMPFILENAME OS/2 only

FILE_NAME = SYSTEMPFILENAME('*partial file specification*')
SAY FILE_NAME

Gives a file name that does not currently exist and that can be safely used as a temporary file name. *Partial file specification* consists of a drive, a directory, and a file name containing one or more question marks (?). This function replaces the question marks with numbers that it chooses. Requires preregistering, discussed under RXFUNCADD in this appendix.

Example:

```
TEMP_FILE = ,
SYSTEMPFILENAME('C:\REXXPRGS\TEMPFILE.???')
RESULT = TEMP_FILE
IF TEMP_FILE =""
THEN SAY 'COULD NOT PRODUCE TEMP NAME'
ELSE SAY TEMP_FILE 'IS THE TEMP FILE NAME'
   /*will give something like C:\REXXPRGS\TEMPFILE.123*/
```

SYSTEXTSCREENREAD OS/2 only

```
SCREEN_CH = SYSTEXTSCREENREAD(row, column, length)
SAY 'READ THESE CHARACTERS' SCREEN_CH
```

Reads characters off the screen. Starts reading at *row* and *column*, and reads *length* characters. Will not work under the Presentation Manager. Requires preregistering, discussed under RXFUNCADD in this appendix.

Example:

```
SCREEN_CH = SYSTEXTSCREENREAD(10, 20, 40)
SAY 'READ THESE CHARACTERS' SCREEN_CH
```

SYSTEXTSCREENSIZE OS/2 only

```
SCREEN_SIZE = SYSTEXTSCREENSIZE()
SAY 'SCREEN SIZE IS' SCREEN_SIZE
```

Tells the screen size with two numbers: rows and columns. Will not work under the Presentation Manager. Requires preregistering, discussed under RXFUNCADD in this appendix.

Example:

```
SCREEN_SIZE = SYSTEXTSCREENSIZE()
SAY 'SCREEN SIZE IS' SCREEN_SIZE
PARSE VAR SCREENSIZE ROWS COLUMNS
SAY ROWS 'ROWS'
SAY COLUMNS 'COLUMNS'
```

SYSWAITNAMEDPIPE OS/2 only

SAY RESULT

Waits for a named pipe. The success or failure is reported in RESULT. A 0 indicates that the action is complete, a 2 that the pipe could not be found, and 231 that there was a timeout. Requires preregistering, discussed under RXFUNCADD in this appendix.

Example:

```
CALL SYSWAITNAMEDPIPE 'ABC'
SAY RESULT
```

TIME

SAY TIME()

Returns the time of day formatted as 14:22:55.

SAY TIME(*type*)

Returns the time of day formatted according to *type*

Types:

(omitted)	---> 14:22:55
H	---> Hours since midnight: 14
M	---> Minutes since midnight: 22
S	---> Seconds since midnight: 55
E (first time)	---> Starts elapsed time counter
E (second time)	---> Gives elapsed time in seconds, since first E
R	---> Resets elapsed time counter to zero

Example:

SAY TIME('H')
---> 14 (or other hour)

TRACE

CALL TRACE *'trace option'*

Changes the trace option to the one specified. Same as using the command TRACE trace option.

Trace options:

N — Normal, the default: trace Syntax errors
E — Error: trace environment commands that don't work properly
F — Failure: trace environment commands that abend or don't exist
A — All: trace all clauses
R — Results: display results of REXX verbs
I — Intermediate: display intermediate results of REXX verbs
L — Labels: display labels that are entered
S — Scan: do not execute anything; just do a partial check for syntax
O — Off: turn off tracing

SAY TRACE()

Returns the current trace setting

Example:

CALL TRACE 'I'
SAY TRACE()
--> I

TRANSLATE

NEW_STRING = TRANSLATE(*string, output table, input table*)

Translates *string*, converting any occurrence of character 1 in *input table* to character 1 of *output table*; character 2 to character 2, and so on.

Examples:

/* note there is a space after NOYEM*/
SAY TRANSLATE('DINERO','NOYEM ','NIREDO')
---> MONEY

SAY TRANSLATE('Hi','abcdefghij','ABCDEFGHIJ')
---> hi

NEW_STRING = TRANSLATE(*string*)

Converts *string* to upper case.

Example:

SAY TRANSLATE('abcdefGHI')
---> ABCDEFGHI

TRUNC

SAY TRUNC(*number, decimal places*)

Returns the *number* with *decimal places* decimal places. Truncates or zero fills as needed.

Examples:

SAY TRUNC(1234.5,4)
---> 1234.5000
SAY TRUNC(1234.5,0)
---> 1234

VALUE

SAY VALUE(*symbol*)

Returns the contents of *symbol* after resolving it as a variable.

Examples:

PROG_NAME = 'COBOL'
COBOL = 'ENGLISH-LIKE'
SAY VALUE('PROG_NAME')
---> COBOL
SAY VALUE(PROG_NAME)
---> ENGLISH-LIKE

VERIFY

SAY VERIFY(*string1, string2*)

Are all the characters of *string1* made up of characters found in *string2*?

Returns:

if yes, ---> 0
if no, returns the position of first character in *string1*
      that is not in *string2*.

Examples:

SAY VERIFY('SUSAN','ABNTUSV')
---> 0
SAY VERIFY('SUSAN','ABCDEFG')
---> 1

WORD

SAY WORD(*string, n*)

Returns the *n*'th word in *string*.

Example:

SAY WORD('ET PHONE HOME COLLECT',2)
---> PHONE

WORDINDEX

SAY WORDINDEX(*string, n*)

Returns the character position of the *n*'th word in *string*.

Example:

SAY WORDINDEX('ET PHONE HOME COLLECT',2)
---> 4

WORDLENGTH

SAY WORDLENGTH(*string, n*)

Returns the length of the *n*'th word in *string*.

Example:
SAY WORDLENGTH('ET PHONE HOME COLLECT',2)
---> 5

WORDPOS

SAY WORDPOS(*phrase, string*)

Searches for *phrase* in *string*. Counts the words in *string* until there is a match. Returns the word count.

Example:

SAY WORDPOS('PHONE HOME','ET PHONE HOME COLLECT')
---> 2

SAY WORDPOS(*phrase, string, starting word*)

Searches for *phrase* in *string*, starting with *starting word*. Counts the words in *string* until there is a match. Returns the word count.

Example:

```
SAY WORDPOS('HI','HI HO HI HO OFF TO WORK WE GO',2)
---> 3
```

WORDS

SAY WORDS(*string*)

Counts the words in *string*. Returns the word count.

Example:

```
SAY WORDS('ET PHONE HOME COLLECT')
---> 4
```

XRANGE

SAY XRANGE(*starting character, ending character*)

You specify a starting character and an ending character. The function returns all the characters that lie between the two.

Example:

```
SAY XRANGE('A','D')
---> ABCD
```

Unprintable and nondisplay characters may be specified as Hexadecimal constants.

Examples:

SAY XRANGE('F1'X,'F5'X)
---> 12345

SAY XRANGE('00'X,'09'X)
---> 000102030405060708090 (This is the Hex value of what returned but is of course unprintable. The following example will clarify.)
IF XRANGE('00'X,'09'X) = '000102030405060708090X
THEN SAY 'IT IS EQUAL' /* true */

Also, note this:
SAY(C2X(XRANGE('00'X,'09'X))
---> 000102030405060708090

X2B OS/2 only.

SAY X2B(*hexstring*)

Converts *hexstring* to binary but displayed in character format.

Example:

SAY X2B('F0')
---> 11110000

X2C

SAY X2C(*hexstring*)

Converts *hexstring* to character.

Example:

SAY X2C('313233')
---> 123
/* Note: same as SAY '313233'X */

X2D

SAY X2D(*hexstring*)

Converts *hexstring* to decimal.

Examples:

SAY X2D(81)
---> 129
SAY X2D('F')
---> 15
SAY X2D('F1F2F3')
---> 15856371
SAY X2D(313233)
---> 3224115

Appendix E

REXX RESERVED VARIABLES

REXX has three variables that it uses in certain situations. You may display these variables or assign them to other variables, but should not change their value.

RC

Contains the return code that was set by an environment command. If the command functions properly, this normally contains a 0.

It also contains the number assigned to REXX syntax errors.

It is not set by REXX verbs or instructions such as IF, CALL, and so on.

Example:

```
SIGNAL ON SYNTAX
SAY "A" - "B"
EXIT
SYNTAX:
SAY RC "IS THE REXX ERROR NUMBER"
SAY ERRORTEXT(RC) "IS THE TEXT OF THE ERROR MESSAGE"
EXIT
```

RESULT

Contains the result or answer passed back by a function or subroutine that was invoked with a REXX CALL. It will contain whatever string or variable that was found on the function's or subroutine's RETURN statement. The function or subroutine may be built in, user-written internal, or user-written external.

Examples:

```
SAY RESULT     /* gives RESULT, since RESULT not yet set */
CALL LENGTH "ABCD"
SAY RESULT     /* gives 4 */
EXIT
```

```
CALL ADDEMUP 1, 2
SAY RESULT     /* gives 3 */
EXIT
ADDEMUP:
ARG NUMBER1, NUMBER2
RETURN  NUMBER1 + NUMBER2
```

SIGL

Contains the line number of the REXX program statement that caused a transfer of control into a subroutine or condition trap. This is very useful in debugging a program.

Examples:

```
SIGNAL ON SYNTAX
SAY "A" - "B"
EXIT
SYNTAX:
SAY SIGL "IS THE LINE NUMBER WITH THE ERROR"
EXIT
```

INDEX